The Fattening of America

How the Economy Makes Us Fat, If It Matters, and What to Do About It

Eric A. Finkelstein
Laurie Zuckerman

John Wiley & Sons, Inc.

Published by John Wiley & Sons, Inc., Hoboken, New Jersey.
Published simultaneously in Canada.

Wiley Bicentennial Logo: Richard J. Pacifico

For general information on our other products and services or for technical support, please contact our Customer Care Department within the United States at (800) 762-2974, outside the United States at (317) 572-3993 or fax (317) 572-4002.

Wiley also publishes its books in a variety of electronic formats. Some content that appears in print may not be available in electronic formats. For more information about Wiley products, visit our Web site at www.wiley.com.

Library of Congress Cataloging-in-Publication Data:

Finkelstein, Eric.
  The fattening of America : how the economy makes us fat, if it matters, and what to do about it / Eric A. Finkelstein and Laurie Zuckerman.
      p. cm.
  Includes bibliographical references and index.
  ISBN 978-0-470-12466-6 (cloth)
  1. Obesity—Economic aspects—United States. I. Zuckerman, Laurie, 1972- II. Title.
  RA645.O23F56 2008
  362.196'39800973—dc22
                                                                  2007029932

Printed in the United States of America.

10 9 8 7 6 5 4 3 2 1

To my family, Thoa, Max, Kyra, and Leah, whose utility was greatly reduced during the writing of this book. And to the somewhat fictionalized Uncle Al and other friends and family referenced throughout. Your sense of humor is greatly appreciated.

—Eric A. Finkelstein

To my husband, Josh, my daughter, Yana, and my son, Aleksander. Here's to getting through this one. . . .

—Laurie Zuckerman

Contents

CONTENTS

Introduction

Answering the Age-Old Question:
Why Is Uncle Al So Fat?

Ever notice that as your parents get older, you tend to have the same conversation with them over and over? For me, the conversation typically begins at baggage claim when I pick them up for a weekend visit. Mom will whisper, much louder than I would like: "There are a lot of people here who could participate in your study."

She is referring to a paper I published a few years back that quantified the increase in medical expenditures resulting from obesity in the United States. Translation: "There are a lot of fat people here."

At this point in the conversation, my dad proclaims, with no effort to keep his voice down: "You know who's fat? Uncle Al. Uncle Al is fat and getting fatter!" And we're off and running.

On the one hand, I should be flattered that my parents have taken an interest in my work. As a health economist, I have spent the past seven years studying economic issues related to obesity. On the other hand, the rift between my dad and Uncle Al (my dad's half brother) is well known in the family circle, and Dad rarely misses an opportunity to take a jab at Uncle Al regardless of the conversation topic.

But I have to admit, Dad has some interesting points. First, he notes, with some reluctance, that Uncle Al is no dummy. Clearly, he must know that his excess weight increases the risk of a host of medical problems, some of which Uncle Al has already developed. Second, he points out that Uncle Al is a partner in a successful law firm and is in the top income bracket in the country. Surely, he can afford to buy the healthiest foods, join the best gym, and pay whatever price is required to maintain a healthy weight. Why then, is he still fat and, according to Dad, getting fatter?

Usually, we are in the car and heading to my house when I ask the same question I pose every other time we've had this conversation: "Why do you care whether or not Uncle Al is fat?"

"I don't care," he answers immediately. "As far as I'm concerned, Uncle Al can do whatever the hell he wants."

But as it turns out, maybe we should care. For Uncle Al is not the only one who's fat. As Dad often points out, Mom could stand to lose a few pounds herself, as could one of my sisters. Uncle Al's son, my cousin Carl, is at least 20 pounds heavier than he was in his early 20s, although as we discuss in Chapter 2, the father and son have gained weight for very different reasons. In fact, if you were to weigh in the entire Finkelstein family, you would find that my family is pretty typical of the U.S. population. About one third of us are fat and another third are on the brink.

The government, by the way, refers to fat adults as *obese* and fat kids as *overweight*. We'll stick with their terminology, although I'm not convinced these terms truly lessen the blow. In total, including Uncle Al, Cousin Carl, my mom, and my sister, there are over 62 million adults in the United States who are obese. An additional 12.5 million kids are overweight.

So maybe you should care. For the rise in obesity rates is having a profound impact on the U.S. economy—and on our wallets. There is a nearly endless barrage of news stories describing how obesity is making our businesses less competitive, pushing good jobs overseas, hurting our military readiness, increasing our taxes, and helping to bankrupt the Medicare and Medicaid programs. And, by the way, it also turns out to be pretty bad for your health.

Usually, by the time we reach our house, either Mom has forbidden us to continue talking about Uncle Al or Dad and I are no longer on speaking terms. Since we never get to finish the conversation, and because your family has an Uncle Al too, it seems appropriate to put my thoughts into writing and finally explain to Dad why Uncle Al is fat, just why we might care about that, and what should (or shouldn't) be done to address rising rates of obesity.

America's Growing Waistline

- Two thirds of Americans are overweight or obese.
- Over the past three decades, the number of obese individuals has more than doubled.
- The increase occurred for all population subsets, including children, the elderly, and all racial/ethnic groups up and down the socioeconomic spectrum.

How This Book Is Organized

Chapter 1 gives you the lay of the obesity landscape. It describes how America—and the world, for that matter—has seen a significant growth spurt in obesity rates over the past several decades. The chapter then briefly discusses the adverse health consequences of obesity.

Chapter 2 begins to hone in on the causes behind the obesity epidemic, concentrating on "calories in." Chapter 3, which focuses on "calories out," continues the argument that economic forces, which have simultaneously lowered the cost of food consumption and increased the cost of physical activity, have largely driven the sudden obesity rise. In Chapter 4 we take the discussion beyond the calories in/calories out equation to evaluate other factors that may (or may not) be contributing to an obesity-inducing environment. We continue this discussion in Chapter 5, and look at the role that health insurance and medical technology play in reducing the costs associated with obesity. **When considering costs, we focus not only on the monetary costs, but also on the time and other opportunity costs associated with undertaking certain activities.**

Chapter 6 switches gears from causes to consequences. We ask and answer the key question: So we're fat—who cares? The chapter explores the implications of obesity for taxpayers, for the U.S. government, and for employers whose business model does not involve selling products and services to obese consumers.

In Chapter 7 we look at the government's role in response to the obesity epidemic from an economic standpoint, and actually question whether they should have any role at all. Chapter 8 specifically addresses the pros and cons of proposed government strategies aimed at reducing obesity rates in adults, and Chapter 9 presents a similar analysis for strategies that target youth.

Chapter 10 then lays out some groundwork for how businesses can respond to problems related to obesity. It presents private-sector strategies for reducing rates of obesity and gauges their likelihood of success. Chapter 11 goes on to examine the flip side, what we call the ObesEconomy, the multibillion-dollar market that America's ballooning waistline has created for obesity-related products and services.

Finally, even though this is decidedly not a "how to lose weight book" (God knows, there are enough of those out there already), we couldn't resist the temptation to offer some advice on how to lose weight like an economist. That's served up to you with a portion-controlled grain of salt in Chapter 12.

Is Obesity a Problem Worth Fighting?

Before you begin reading this book in earnest, it's important to get one thing straight. Contrary to what "Mary" (I prefer not to disclose her real name) recently implied after I gave a presentation on the economics of obesity at the National Institutes of Health, I am not a "fattist." That is to say, I have nothing against obese people. Mary, a member of the Medical Advocacy Project of the Council on Size & Weight Discrimination, a self-proclaimed "size acceptance" group, told an audience of several dozen obesity researchers that my presentation sounded like "fat people are bad for business, fat people are bad for government, fat people are just plain bad. . . ." She then began to cry.

Needless to say, it was not a good scene. I never got a chance to mount a rebuttal. If I had, I would have told her that while not everyone can be skinny, I believe the vast majority of overweight people could weigh less than they currently do if the environment were more conducive to weight loss.

What do I mean by that? America's obesity epidemic has been shaped by economics. A basic tenet of economics is that people respond to their environment in predictable ways. If the cost of a particular product or activity decreases, or the benefits of that product or activity increase, then people will consume more of that product and spend more time doing that activity, and vice versa. As we discuss throughout this book, obesity is a product of our economic and technological success. Thanks to declining food costs and the ever-increasing usage of technology, we're eating more calories and burning off fewer. As a result, we are gaining weight—lots of it—a consequence that any economist worth his weight would predict.

However—and this may come as a shock to many of you—to economists, it is not entirely clear that obesity is a problem worth fighting (certainly not the way we've been attacking it). Sure, obesity is bad for your health, but the fact remains that good diet and exercise are extremely difficult to sustain, especially in today's environment. In fact, as the world now stands, many, including my Uncle Al, may prefer to be "fat and happy" (as my dad puts it) rather than make the sacrifices necessary to be thin. And isn't it their choice?

Moreover, even if we are convinced that obesity is worth fighting, we are not going to significantly reduce rates of obesity solely through public health or media campaigns. These programs often do a good job of raising awareness, but they fail to address the core issue. If we are to reverse the rising tide of obesity, it is going to happen because economic incentives are instituted that encourage individuals to make sustained changes in behavior in spite of, or perhaps even as a result of, a changing environment.

But who would provide these incentives? Businesses? The government? Do rising obesity rates even justify private or government intervention? There are no easy answers. Moreover, which specific policies government or the private sector chooses to adopt or reject—that is, which policies we as a society choose to adopt or reject—will depend on our making a series of difficult choices with enormous fiscal, political, public health, and even moral consequences.

Yet underneath these issues lies one simple truth: There are few of us who could not take actions to improve our health through better diet and more exercise, regardless of our weight. I believe that my research, which looks at obesity as more of an economic phenomenon than a health issue, may help contribute to creating that "right" environment.

Hopefully, Mary will read a copy of the book and let me know if she finds this response persuasive. I hope you do as well. I also hope that this book will allow for a more informed discussion of why Uncle Al is fat the next time my folks come to town.

Chapter 1

Craze or Crisis?

What does Uncle Al, a rich American attorney, have in common with the women of Mauritania, a barren West African country?

The answer is this: Mauritanian women are getting thin for the very same reason that Uncle Al is getting fat—as a result of a changing economy.

You see, in Mauritania, a girl can possess no greater currency than rolls upon rolls of fat. In this vast nomadic nation, thin women are a sign of poverty. In contrast, voluptuous wives and daughters are visible displays of a man's wealth and power. So in a society where obesity is seen as a conduit to a rich husband, it became traditional for well-intentioned mothers and grandmothers to force-feed their daughters and granddaughters.

In recent years, however, force-feeding is fast disappearing. Why? Well, it's not because of the government's efforts to warn women of the dangers of obesity. These radio blasts were largely ignored in a society where fat is revered.[1] No, it's because years of drought have put the country in crisis. With food increasingly scarce and food prices

1

escalating rapidly, Mauritanians can barely afford to feed themselves—let alone overfeed their daughters.

So what about Uncle Al? He's certainly not in a famine. In fact, his weight has been changing for the opposite reason—he's in a land of feast. In America, for reasons we'll detail in the next two chapters, food prices are falling, not rising, especially for high-fat and high-calorie foods, and the costs, in terms of what Uncle Al would be missing out on, of being physically active continue to increase. As a result, so does Uncle Al's waistline.

So even though Uncle Al and Mauritanian women are on a divergent path, their changing weight is still a by-product of a changing economy. But that's where the comparison ends. Because while big might be beautiful in Mauritania, in America, "thin" is the revered cultural norm for most, especially Caucasians. So while the Mauritanians struggle to feed their families, here, for at least the past 20 years, books on how to lose weight—whether by dieting, exercising, or by using some magical machine or dietary supplement—have often topped best-seller lists. In fact, the *New York Times* began separating them (along with other self-help books) into a separate category from other nonfiction (though for many of these books, the fiction aisle may be a more appropriate location).

So Why Now?

Why, after decades of obsession with dieting and weight loss, has the obesity "crisis" become the subject of countless news articles, TV reports, and magazine covers? And, more to the point, why has what was once assumed to be a personal problem—whether of medical, genetic, or behavioral origin—suddenly become an issue for private foundations; school boards; lawmakers; and federal, state, and local government agencies (including child protective services in the case of at least one extremely overweight child)?

Is it simply the latest media craze? Is it griping from the many thousands of businesses who are upset about rising health care costs or their inability to compete in the global economy? Or is it hype from the many purveyors of weight-loss products and services whose profits escalate with each additional news story? We know Uncle Al has been gaining weight at a steady pace for decades, but is obesity really on the rise for the rest of the population?

Moreover, why should Dad care even if obesity is on the rise? Why should you? Are there broader implications for the economy, for policy makers, and for all Americans? If so, what should be done about it? Before we begin taking a hard look at these issues, let's take a step back and take a brief look at obesity trends across the nation—and the world.

My Soccer Team Eats Oranges

I have to admit that few things bother me more than seeing overweight kids. So when it comes to my own kids, as my wife repeatedly tells me, I'm a pain in the ass. I'm obsessed with what my five-year-old daughter and seven-year-old son eat. (My infant daughter is still strictly under her mother's domain, but she won't be for long.) The occasional treat is fine, but you will almost never find soda in our fridge, and there are strict limits on the few sugary snacks in our pantry. I can probably count our trips to fast-food venues (that I know of) on one hand. And if this isn't enough, I also make sure that my children get plenty of exercise. As most parents will tell you, this is no easy task these days. It's also a constant source of friction between my wife and me, as she is the one left to implement these draconian policies while I am at work or off writing this book.

And it's not just my own family who finds me so irritating. I coach my son's soccer team (largely because he wouldn't play if I did not). Although many teams drink Gatorade and eat Popsicles after practice and games, I limit our team's consumption to water and oranges. This, too, is a real challenge, as I have to constantly remind parents not to bring "rewards" for the team after practice and games. I once had to tell a mom to put the powdered donuts and Juicy Juice® back into her car. I told her what I tell the rest of the parents over and over—water turns out to be a pretty good way to hydrate your kids. Looking at what transpires on some of the other fields, I would not be surprised if many kids actually gain weight as a result of being in the league. By the way, although we are not supposed to keep score, it did not go unnoticed (by me) that our team of six year olds went undefeated; the lack of Gatorade was not an obstacle to the team's on-field success. Of course, maybe it was my great coaching. . . .

I make no excuses for my sometimes off-putting behavior—I'm a killjoy for a reason. As an obesity researcher, I see statistics on a daily basis that paint an increasingly depressing picture for our children's future—a picture that, as a father and as a coach, I would like to change.

So what kind of picture are we talking about? Currently, about 17 percent of U.S. children are overweight, and many more are at-risk of becoming overweight based on the government's definition of excess weight among youth.[2] *Overweight* is the government's polite term for obese kids, and *at-risk* is their terminology for overweight kids.

As an aside, if you find these terms misleading, you are not alone. Recently, an expert panel made up of members of the American Medical Association and the Centers for Disease Control and Prevention (CDC) met to discuss a change in terminology. They claimed that these terms did not adequately represent the weight problem facing America's youth.[3] I'm sure my dad would agree.

Regardless of terminology, even more alarming than the high prevalence is the rate at which excess weight is rising among America's youth. Government data reveals that the rate of overweight 6 to 11 year olds tripled from 4 percent to almost 19 percent during the past 30 years. The rate for 12 to 19 year olds mirrored that jump, with an increase in prevalence from 6 percent to over 17 percent.[4] Even preschoolers are putting on the pounds. Since 1990, twice as many children between the ages of 2 and 5 are overweight (13.9 percent compared to 7.2 percent).[5]

Though children of all ethnic groups have gained weight, certain racial, ethnic, and socioeconomic groups have put on the most. As was the case 30 years ago, excess weight remains more common among African-American and Hispanic children than among whites. Whereas the gap between ethnic groups is shrinking for adults, it is growing for kids. According to a national study, from 1986 to 1998, overweight prevalence rose by more than 120 percent among African-American and Hispanic children compared with 50 percent among Caucasians.[6]

So what are the consequences for these kids? Sadly, given societal norms that reward thinness, these kids are likely to face significant discrimination throughout their lives. Moreover, discrimination and prejudice can begin at a very young age. Studies on children as young as five years old show that they have already absorbed our cultural bias against fat.[7]

Being the target of prejudice can be devastating for overweight children. They are more likely to be sad, lonely, and nervous. One study shocked even a jaded obesity researcher like me: The study found that children who were overweight rated their quality of life as being similar to children who were being treated for cancer.[8] Talk about a sobering comparison!

And the effects can stick around. Being overweight during childhood can have lasting effects on self-esteem, body image, and economic mobility.[9] Overweight children sometimes perceive themselves as unattractive, which may lead to depression, disordered eating, and risky behaviors such as tobacco and alcohol abuse.[10]

Even parents have been known to discriminate against their own overweight children. One study showed that parents of overweight daughters will not spend as much money on their daughters' college education as parents of normal-weight daughters.[11]

If the social impact is heartbreaking, the health prognosis for these children is equally disturbing.

I'll bet if we asked Uncle Al, he would say that, due to advancements in medical technology, my Cousin Carl (his son) will have a longer life span than he will have, and that his new grandbaby will live even longer.

Well, researchers at the University of Illinois at Chicago have made a surprising new prediction: Due to increases in the prevalence of childhood obesity, today's children may not live as long as their parents.[12] The study suggests that weight problems could cancel out life-extending benefits of medical advances in the coming decades. As a direct result, the United States could be facing its first sustained drop in life expectancy in the modern era.

"It's one thing for an adult of 45 or 55 to develop type 2 diabetes and then experience the life-threatening complications of that—kidney failure, heart attack, stroke—in their late 50s or 60s," said Dr. David Ludwig. "But for a 4-year-old or 6-year-old who's obese to develop type 2 diabetes at 14 or 16 raises the possibility of devastating complications before reaching age 30. It's really a staggering prospect."[13]

Indeed, children are increasingly showing up in pediatricians' offices with type 2 diabetes and other conditions once known only to adults (type 2 diabetes was once synonymous with adult-onset diabetes, but thanks to the rise in childhood obesity and the prevalence of this condition in overweight kids, that is no longer the case). The American Diabetes Association now estimates that as many as 45 percent of new cases of pediatric diabetes may be type 2 (not the more common type 1, or juvenile diabetes).[14] In fact, one study found that the number of type 2 diabetes prescriptions among children doubled from 2002 to 2005.[15]

Excess weight during childhood can also significantly increase the risk of disease and obesity in adulthood. Cardiovascular risk factors, for example, can be carried from childhood into adulthood, which predispose adults to severe chronic conditions such as heart failure.[16]

A recent study reported that increasing rates of childhood obesity also appear to be causing girls to reach puberty at an earlier age.[17] Results showed that the mean age of onset of breast development, which had been close to 11 years in earlier studies, is now approximately 10 years in Caucasian girls and just under nine years in African-American girls. The study's author reported: "Earlier onset of puberty in girls has been associated with a number of adverse outcomes, including psychiatric disorders and deficits in psychosocial functioning, earlier initiation of alcohol use, sexual intercourse and teenage pregnancy and increased rates of adult obesity and reproductive cancers."

So this is the kind of bleak information I encounter every day. And, yes, it bothers me. As we'll discuss in subsequent chapters, while adults have the ability to make informed choices related to diet, exercise, and weight, children do not. Most of their food consumption and physical activity decisions are made for them by parents or school administrators. So when I see a kid who is overweight, knowing that his or her excess weight will be very difficult to reverse later in life and could lead to life-long health problems and a shorter life expectancy, I feel that parents and society are not doing their job.

As a result, I am willing to be the unpopular father and coach who deprives kids of their "reward" at the end of a hard practice. And if I think our friends are not feeding their kids a healthy diet, I let them know that, too. As I said, I'm obsessed. But, hopefully, the soccer moms will read this book and understand why Coach Eric is so annoying. If not, they can always switch their kids to a different team (although they may no longer go undefeated if they do).

So How about Adults? Are We Gaining, Too?

The story of obesity is not limited to kids. When it comes to adults, about two thirds of Americans are now considered to be out of the "normal" weight range (making the term *normal* a bit of a misnomer), and an increasing number of those are at least 100 or more pounds overweight. I highly doubt that these numbers surprise you. A trip to the food court at your local mall likely provides enough evidence to convince you that the obesity epidemic is for real.

Just how is adult obesity measured? The CDC defines adult obesity using body mass index (BMI), which is calculated as weight in kilograms divided by height in meters squared. A BMI between 18.5 and 25 is considered normal. At 5 feet 10 inches tall and 180 pounds, I'm now a 26, which puts me at the low end of the overweight range (25–29.9). That's down, by the way, from a high of 29 (194 pounds) just after my son was born in 2000 (my wife and I had just moved to North Carolina and were frequent visitors to Golden Corral's tasty and affordable all-you-can-eat buffet and other purveyors of fine southern cuisine. We also developed a penchant for sweet tea, which, although very high in calories, is delicious). Adults with a BMI over 30 are considered obese. At 5 feet 10 inches, I would have to weigh 210 pounds, about 35 pounds over my "ideal" weight, to get this honor. I would guess Uncle Al is about a 34, and that's being a bit generous.

Prior to the 1960s, little data existed to quantify obesity rates for the general U.S. population. However, data that did exist, largely from U.S. Army soldiers, suggests that obesity rates began creeping up in the early to mid-twentieth century.[18] This slight increase was hardly problematic and likely represented a rising mean weight that resulted from increased food availability, reductions in the prevalence of infectious diseases, and a higher standard of living that resulted from a growing economy. Then we hit the 1980s, and suddenly the rate of obesity began to skyrocket. As you can see in Figure 1.1, the percentage of the population that is obese (meaning a BMI of 30 or higher) was only 13 percent of the total U.S. population between 1960 and 1962.[19] By 2004, a whopping 32 percent of American adults were obese.

Let's dig a little deeper into obesity statistics in America. Though obesity's reach stretches broadly across the socioeconomic spectrum, it

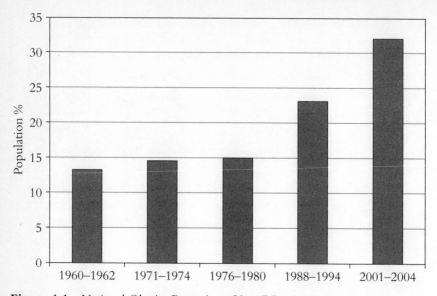

Figure 1.1   National Obesity Rates (ages 20 to 74)
Source: "Health, United States, 2006." Centers for Disease Control and Prevention, http://www.cdc
.gov/nchs/data/hus/hus06.pdf#073.

hits low-income Americans the hardest (see Figure 1.2). This trend,
however, seems to be shifting. The gap in obesity rates between the richest and poorest Americans has narrowed sharply in recent years.

And, just like we saw when we looked at trends in children's obesity,
although all ethnic groups have seen an increase in their BMI, certain
ethnic groups have gained more weight. Interestingly, as you can see in
Figure 1.3, the differential pace of weight gain across racial/ethnic
groups during the past few decades has served to almost equalize the
weights of male white Americans, male African-Americans, and male
Mexican-Americans.

This picture, however, is radically different for women. The prevalence of obesity among white women today is roughly 30 percent,
whereas this figure increases to 40 percent for Mexican women and to
over 50 percent for African-American women (see Figure 1.4).

But no matter how we dissect the data, you get the point: Americans,
like Uncle Al, are indeed fat and getting fatter. In fact, the average adult
male is roughly 10 pounds heavier today than he was just 10 years ago,

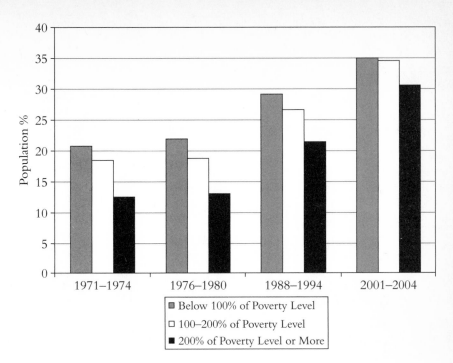

Figure 1.2 National Obesity Rates, by Poverty Status (ages 20 to 74)
SOURCE: "Health, United States, 2006." Centers for Disease Control and Prevention, www.cdc.gov/nchs/data/hus/hus06.pdf#073.

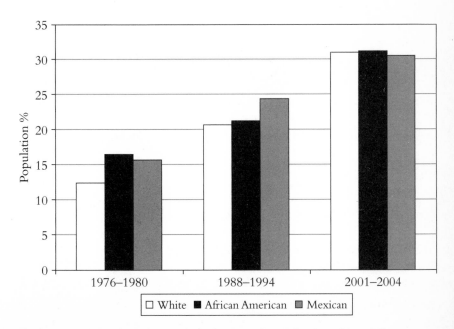

Figure 1.3 National Obesity Rates by Race for Males (ages 20 to 74)
SOURCE: "Health, United States, 2006." Centers for Disease Control and Prevention, www.cdc.gov/nchs/data/hus/hus06.pdf#073.

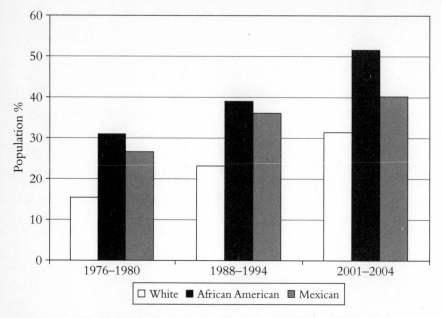

Figure 1.4   National Obesity Rates by Race for Females (ages 20 to 74)
SOURCE: "Health, United States, 2006." Centers for Disease Control and Prevention, www.cdc.gov/nchs/data/hus/hus06.pdf#073.

and the average adult female is about 11 pounds heavier. If we go back as far as the mid- to late 1970s, men are roughly 17 pounds heavier and women are roughly 20 pounds heavier.[20]

A Growing Waistline Can Be Bad for Your Health

If carrying some extra pounds just affected how you looked in a bikini, then the rising tide of obesity wouldn't be so worrisome, especially to the one third of the population who is not overweight. However, as you are probably aware, obesity increases the risk for a host of serious medical problems. In fact, according to one recent study, poor diet and physical inactivity may soon overtake tobacco as the leading cause of death in America.[21] The study reported that the three leading causes of death were tobacco (435,000 deaths; 18.1 percent of total U.S. deaths), poor diet and physical inactivity (365,000 deaths; 15.2 percent), and alcohol consumption (85,000 deaths; 3.5 percent).

And though evidence suggests significant racial and ethnic differences in the susceptibility to obesity-related illnesses, obesity-related health consequences are widely found across all racial groups, and the likelihood of developing these conditions increases with increasing weight.

Uncle Al, for example, recently developed diabetes. That puts him in good company with the other 21 million adults in the United States who have this condition.[22] But not all diabetes is caused by obesity. My dad, who is skinny, also has diabetes. The data suggest that about 70 percent of diabetes cases in the United States are caused by excess weight.[23] Obese adults have about 10 times the risk of developing diabetes compared with normal-weight adults. Those who have severe obesity—100 pounds or more overweight—have about 20 times the risk.[24] Diabetes, in turn, increases the risk for a host of other health problems, including blindness, gout, amputations, kidney disease, infections, and cardiovascular disease.[25]

Obesity also greatly increases the risks of developing hypertension (high blood pressure) and high cholesterol. Sadly, Uncle Al now has both of these. Together, the effects of excess fat, high cholesterol, and high blood pressure damage the cardiovascular system and may lead to any number of complications.

In addition to complications of diabetes and hypertension, obesity adversely affects nearly every system of the human body (see Figure 1.5). Lower back pain, for example, has limited Uncle Al's ability to play golf, his favorite leisure activity.

Obesity among pregnant women also increases the risks for both mother and child. Examples of complications may include:

- Delayed identification of pregnancy (due both to excess weight, which masks the signs of pregnancy, and often to endocrine disorders more common in obese women that cause irregular menses).[26]
- Increased risk of developing pregnancy-induced hypertension, preeclampsia, and eclampsia.[27,28]
- A greater occurrence of labor-induced deliveries, instrument births, and higher cesarean delivery rates as well as a greater likelihood for blood loss during surgery.[29-33]
- Postpartum hemorrhage and postoperative infections, such as endometritis, phlebitis, urinary tract infections (UTIs), and wound infections.[34]

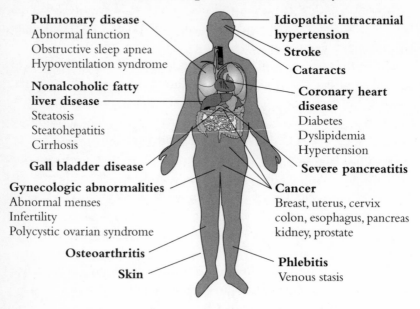

Figure 1.5 Medical Complications of Obesity
SOURCE: NAASO, The Obesity Society.

- For women undergoing a vaginal delivery (which, by the way, is increasingly less common), obesity is also associated with higher incidence of developing a thromboembolism (blood clot).[35,36]

In addition to adverse health effects of obesity on the mother, obesity in pregnancy negatively affects the fetus through an increased incidence of various birth defects.[37–41] One study reported that hospital readmissions are three times higher for children born to obese mothers.[42] These children are also more likely to grow up and become obese adults and develop the complications described above.

Those who are obese know that the impact extends far beyond the medical consequences. In fact, for many obese adults, these factors may be of secondary importance. Even as more Americans become overweight, the standard for attractiveness has largely stayed the same: thin and fit. If you don't fit the mold, you are likely to face substantial discrimination, no matter what your age.

Overweight adults are often cast as lacking in self-discipline, lazy, and mentally slow. As a result, they can face discrimination in employment, housing, and credit markets, and suffer from social stigma, social isolation, and low self-esteem.[43]

For all of the reasons discussed above, obesity results in reduced life expectancy. Although there remains some debate about the perfect weight to maximize longevity, evidence suggests that those who are 30 pounds overweight have a shorter life expectancy, and beyond this level, life expectancy decreases with increasing weight.[44,45] For example, one study published in the *Journal of the American Medical Association* (JAMA) found that those who are 30 pounds overweight lose between one and six years of life, while those who are about 100 pounds overweight[46] lose up to 13 years of life.[47]

But there is a flip side to this story. The good news is that even as obesity levels rise, at least in the United States, obesity has become a more manageable health problem than it once was, thanks to improving medical care (which we discuss in Chapter 5).

But Are We the Only Ones Gaining Weight?

If it's any comfort, Americans are not alone in their struggle with their growing waistlines. The world population has now reached the point where more people are overweight than undernourished—a trend found even in the world's poorest countries, especially in their urban areas. Whereas during the past century most nutrition research and policy concerning the developing world focused on poverty, undernutrition, and how to feed the world's burgeoning population, now policy has shifted toward how to control increasing rates of obesity, even among relatively poor societies.

The pandemic is growing at such a pace that prevalence statistics become rapidly outdated. Altogether, an astounding 1.6 billion people,[48] or roughly 25 percent of the planet's population, are higher than the normal weight range, and 400 million of these are considered obese, according to a fall 2005 report by the United Nations' World Health Organization (WHO). WHO predicts that if current trends continue, the number of overweight or obese people will increase to 2.3 billion and the number of obese will almost double to 700 million by 2015.

WHO estimates also show that more than 75 percent of women over the age of 30 are now overweight in countries as diverse as Barbados, Egypt, Malta, Mexico, South Africa, Turkey, and, of course, the United States. Estimates are similar for men, with more than 75 percent now overweight or obese in, for example, Argentina, Germany, Greece, Kuwait, New Zealand, Samoa, and the United Kingdom.

In fact, it may come as a surprise that America is not the fattest country—not by a long shot. Interestingly, the small western Pacific islands of Nauru and Tonga have the highest global prevalence of obesity, with 9 out of every 10 adults being overweight or obese. Largely due to genetics, however, the prevalence of obesity has always been high among these populations, whereas much of the rest of the world is quickly catching up.

Because even recent historical data on obesity rates are often missing outside of the United States and western Europe, it is difficult to quantify the super-size shift for much of the world. That said, where data are available, results show that many countries have seen larger increases in rates of obesity during the past decade than the United States. The United States has seen a 38 percent increase in obesity prevalence since the early 1990s. That puts us fairly low on the list. Countries as diverse as Iceland, Spain, New Zealand, the Czech Republic, and Saudi Arabia have all experienced larger increases. With the exception of Saudi Arabia, however, the prevalence of obesity remains larger in the United States than in these countries. However, it may just be a matter of time before they catch up. Figure 1.6 shows obesity prevalence rates for countries that have reliable data. As you can see, the United States is hardly alone when it comes to rising obesity rates.

The health consequences of obesity-related diseases are continuing to escalate worldwide. More people globally now die from chronic diseases like diabetes than from communicable diseases, including AIDS. And WHO expects that of the more than 366 million (4.4 percent of the world's population) that are predicted to have diabetes by the year 2030, three fourths will inhabit the third world (shocking considering that the third world only makes up two thirds of the world's population).[49]

Both India and China are already home to more people with diabetes than any other country. In China, for example, it is estimated that

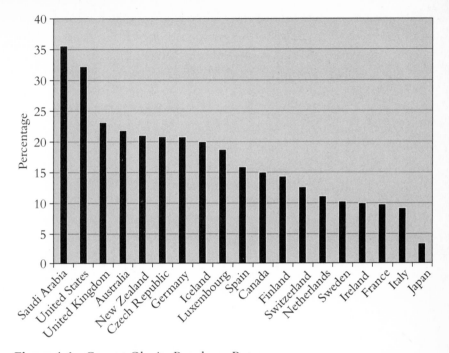

Figure 1.6 Current Obesity Prevalence Rates
SOURCE: "WHO: Global Database on Body Mass Index" and "OECD Factbook 2006: Quality of Life—Obesity."

about 6 percent of all adults have diabetes. While that is lower than the prevalence of diabetes in the United States—9.6 percent—new cases are emerging rapidly, particularly in China's larger cities. India is predicted to experience a much larger increase in the number of cases: from 31.7 million in 2000 to 79.4 million in 2030 (a 150 percent increase). Compare that to the projections for the United States: from 17.7 million in 2000 to 30.3 million in 2030, a 71 percent increase—alarming, but at least better than India.[50]

In India, diabetes is a disease of the affluent. "Jokingly in talks, I say you haven't made it in society until you get a touch of diabetes," said hospital executive Dr. V. Mohan, in a *New York Times* interview.[51]

He went on to say that people who once balanced water jugs and construction material on their heads now carry nothing heavier than a cell phone. At a four-star restaurant, he said, it is not unusual to see a patron yank out his kit and give himself an insulin injection. "In a changing India, it seems to go this way: Make good money and get cars, get houses, get servants, get meals out, get diabetes."

The Longer You Stay, the Bigger You Get

Although obesity is a growing problem all over the world, the evidence suggests that if you come to the United States, you are likely to gain weight at a faster pace than if you stay home. Studies have shown that the longer immigrants live in the United States, the more rapid their weight gain.[52] The typical 5-foot 4-inch immigrant woman gains an extra 9 pounds compared to an average woman who stayed in her home country. The typical 5-foot 9-inch immigrant man gains an extra 11 pounds.

So just why is it that Americans—and much of the world, for that matter—are gaining so much weight so quickly? We explore this question in the next few chapters.

Chapter 2

I'll Take a Deep-Fried Coca-Cola

J ust like Uncle Al has something in common with the women of Mauritania, it turns out he also shares some traits with alleged Al Qaeda terrorists. How so? Well, just imagine yourself cooped up in a 4-by-6-foot room for most of your waking hours. High-calorie meals are brought directly to you and you have little opportunity to exercise. What do you think would happen?

Odds are you'd get fat—real fat. For evidence, we need to look no further than the 432 alleged Al Qaeda and Taliban detainees now serving time in the Guantanamo Bay (Gitmo) detention facility in Cuba. Believe it or not, the average weight gain of these inmates has been 18 pounds since the camp opened in 2002.

One might question whether these individuals were underweight prior to arrival and, in fact, needed to be fattened up. Perhaps. But take, for example, one inmate who entered the camp at 215 pounds and who now weighs over 400.[1]

The fattening of Gitmo detainees may not be so different from the fattening of Uncle Al. The demands of Uncle Al's law firm require him to spend most of his waking hours in a 4-by-6 cell—I mean office (also with no window)—and most of his meals are also delivered. And judging from the meals we've shared together, they are unlikely to be of the low-cal variety. Because Uncle Al is not a terrorist, he is allowed to leave the compound—I mean law firm—on nights and weekends. This gives him the opportunity to play golf and burn off some of the excess calories he accrued during the workweek. As a result, Uncle Al's weight gain, although far greater than the 18-pound increase of Gitmo inmates, was accrued over a much longer period of time.

But what about the rest of us who are neither lawyers nor terrorists? Why are we gaining so much weight? The answer, it turns out, is in large part because the world around us is changing to the point where our food consumption and physical activity patterns are looking similar to those of a Gitmo detainee, or at best, a lawyer. This chapter explores how the reductions in the cost of food, and, as a direct consequence, the "super-sizing" of our meals (and snacks), have encouraged us to consume more than ever before. Chapter 3 then goes on to describe the flip side: how we are burning off fewer calories thanks to technological advancements that are causing us to become increasingly sedentary at work and at home.

First Things First

As you read the next few chapters, it is important to keep in mind that the rise in obesity rates experienced during the past two decades could be explained by a net caloric imbalance of about 100 calories per day.[2] In fact, a caloric imbalance of this amount could generate an average weight gain of about 10 pounds per year (where 3,500 excess calories translates into about one pound of weight gain). This point is significant because it highlights how small changes in diet and exercise patterns can, over time, lead to large increases in weight. It also points out the difficulty of trying

Table 2.1   Foods Equivalent to about 100 Calories

Foods	Calories
8 fluid ounces of Coca-Cola	162
10 teaspoons of sugar	150
2 slices of white bread	130
1 ounce of Cheerios	110
12 to 15 almonds	110
10 French fries	110
2 Oreo cookies	106
1 banana	105
4 Hershey's Kisses	100
3 ounces of fat-free vanilla ice cream	100
1 slice of French bread	100
1 tablespoon of peanut butter	95
1 tablespoon of ranch dressing	90
1 cup of skim milk	90
1 cup of blueberries	80

to identify the cause, or causes, of the obesity epidemic, as any one factor may contribute only a fraction of the total imbalance.

To put these numbers into perspective, Table 2.1 presents quantities of some common foods that range in the neighborhood of 100 calories. As you can see, all it takes to offset the fragile balance between maintaining a steady weight and following the path of a Gitmo detainee (or Uncle Al) are just a few extra luscious Hershey's Kisses a day.

Cheap Food Gets Cheaper

Between the late 1970s and today, men have increased their daily food intake by about 180 calories (the equivalent of a pint of imported beer), and women have increased their daily food intake by about 360 calories (less than a four-ounce slice of chocolate cake). On average, according to the Centers for Disease Control and Prevention (CDC), men now consume 2,600 calories per day and women now consume 1,900 calories per day.[3] These increases are more than enough to create the rise in obesity rates shown above and, consistent with these findings, women have experienced greater weight gain than men. In fact, it is likely that the number of calories consumed is even higher than the CDC data show. These numbers are based on food diaries by a random sample of adults. It's human nature to "fudge" calorie diaries because: (1) individuals eat less than usual when they know that others will see their data, and (2) due to laziness, embarrassment, or other reasons, individuals tend not to report all that they consume.

However you slice it, the plain fact is that Americans are consuming more calories than ever. So what is behind our increasing calorie consumption? The answer, in a word, is economics. During the past four decades, food costs, in terms of both money and preparation (time) costs, have been steadily dropping. Since 1960, the relative price of food compared with other goods has decreased by about 16 percent. Since 1978,

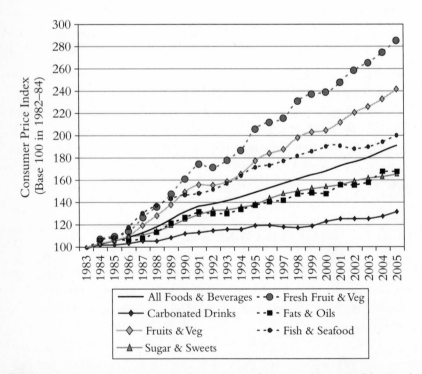

Figure 2.1   Price Comparison: Relative Price of More and Less Healthy Foods, 1983–2005

SOURCE: Author calculations based on the Consumer Price Index—All Urban Consumers (U.S. City Averages, 1983–2005).

food prices have dropped 38 percent relative to the prices of other goods and services.[4] But what is even more relevant is the fact that high-calorie foods have become much cheaper compared with healthier alternatives such as fish, fruits, and vegetables.

Since 1983, prices of fresh fruits and vegetables, fish, and dairy products have increased by 190 percent, 144 percent, 100 percent, and 82 percent, respectively, whereas fats and oils, sugars and sweets, and carbonated beverages, for example, increased at much lower rates—by 70 percent, 66 percent, and 32 percent, respectively.[5] As shown in Figure 2.1, when compared to the general price for all foods and beverages, the prices of healthier foods have become relatively more expensive and the prices of unhealthy foods, those with lots of added sugars and added fats, have become cheaper.

So just what is the relationship between food consumption and food prices? Economics 101 teaches us that as the price of food becomes cheaper, people will eat more. So does that play out in the real world? Let's take a look at an example. Figure 2.2 compares trends in the

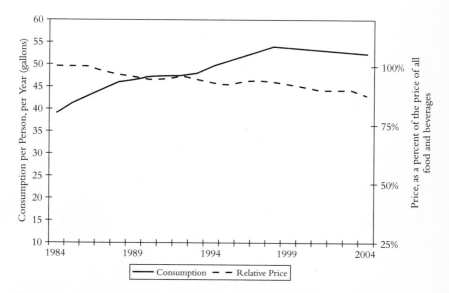

Figure 2.2   Changes in Per-Capita Consumption and Relative Price of Carbonated Beverages, 1978–2003
Source: Economic Research Service, USDA; Bureau of Labor Statistics. www.ers.usda.gov/data/foodconsumption/FoodAvailQueriable.aspx#midForm. http://data.bls.gov/PDQ/outside .jsp?survey=cu.

relative price (compared to the consumer price index for food) and quantity of carbonated beverages. It reveals that the large reduction in the relative price of carbonated beverages since 1978 has translated into a large increase in its consumption. For most people, an ice cold Coca-Cola used to be a treat reserved for special occasions. Now it's become part of our daily fare. I've even seen parents filling baby bottles with Coke at the free refill machines at our local Taco Bell (it's not just Britney Spears).

These low prices also translate into larger portions. Whereas the average-size Coke used to be 8 ounces, a 20-ounce bottle is now the norm. As a result, in 2004, the average American consumed 52 gallons of soft drinks, or an average of 16 ounces per day. This is 50 percent more than the amount consumed in 1980.[6,7] Today, soft drinks comprise about 7 percent of all calories consumed, making them the number one food consumed in the American diet.[8] We did some additional analysis and found that if the average American drank water instead of sugar-sweetened beverages, he would weigh about 15 pounds less than he does now.

A similar trend can be seen looking at fats and oils, common additives in high-calorie foods. Their prices dropped by about 16 percent during the past few decades. This price drop was accompanied by a 50 percent increase in consumption.

These findings illustrate, as we might reasonably expect, that price plays a major role in determining what and how much we eat. And for food producers, price is also a key component of decisions concerning which ingredients to use. So it logically follows that falling food prices, especially for fattening foods, are at least partly responsible for the rise in obesity rates.

This leads us to another question: Why have relative prices for high-calorie and high-fat foods decreased when compared to prices for healthy options?

The Rise of French-Fried Potatoes

The answer lies largely in advances in food processing, preservation, and cooking technologies that have allowed more foods to be produced in a central location and then consumed quickly and cheaply. Innovations such as vacuum packing, improved preservatives, deep freezing, stretch-wrap films, irradiation, hydrogen peroxide sterilization, and microwaves, to name a few, have significantly lowered the monetary and nonmonetary cost of food, including the time cost of acquiring, preparing, cooking, and cleaning up after food, as well as the financial cost of purchasing food.[9] Foods more dependent on technology are often those with the greatest amounts of added sugars and fats and therefore the highest in calories. It is exactly these foods that have seen the greatest drop in prices and preparation time, and as a result, the greatest increases in consumption.

Potatoes provide a great example. Prior to World War II, potatoes were primarily prepared by baking, boiling, or mashing. Potato chips were rarely found in the pantry, and French fries were seldom put on the table simply because it took too much time to prepare.[10] Following the war, the 1950s were a period of technological innovation dubbed "The Golden Age of Food Processing." Because more and more households boasted a refrigerator with an accompanying freezer, the door was opened to pre-prepared food.

Then came the advance of the centralized factory, where workers would peel, chop, and cook French fry precursors, deep freeze them at −40 degrees, and ship them to their requisite fast-food chain or grocery store location. At this point, the fries were subsequently defrosted and deep fried (at the fast-food restaurant) or baked (and later microwaved) at home.[11]

As a consequence of this new technology, the price of French fries dropped considerably, as did the time required to get them onto the table. Recipes for homemade French fries suggest they take about 40 minutes to prepare—a messy, laborious, oil-splattering prospect. Ore-Ida French fries, however, should be ready to eat straight out of the package in less than 14 minutes if baked.

It should not be surprising, then, that both frozen potatoes and chips and shoestrings (fries), foods that require food technology for production or consumption, have experienced the greatest increase in consumption. In fact, the average American now consumes almost 60 pounds of frozen potato products per year, more than triple the amount in 1965. About 80 percent of frozen products were French fries, with the balance consumed in other forms such as hash browns, tater tots, and home fries. Conversely, only fresh potatoes, unaffected by technology, have experienced a decrease in consumption since 1960.[12] And French fries are just one example that illustrates that as food prices and preparation time decrease, an increase in consumption is bound to follow.

The introduction of the microwave oven further reshaped the face of the traditional family dinner. While only 8 percent of American homes had microwaves in 1978, 83 percent had them by 1999, and 95 percent currently have them.[13,14] The widespread availability and convenience of the microwave made it even easier for prepackaged food, subjected to various rounds of deep freezing, artificial flavoring, and preservatives, to play a more prominent role at meal times. These foods, too, tend to be higher in calories than those cooked from scratch. Yet the convenience and low costs of prepackaged foods have increasingly made them a preferred option at meal time.

But it's not just meal time that has been affected. Because technology has driven down food costs while decreasing the amount of time (and energy) it takes to prepare food, it has become much easier to snack between meals—a new national pastime. A group of researchers who compared food diaries kept by approximately 60,000 Americans between the late 1970s and the mid-1990s found that food consumption between meals significantly increased.[15] Snacking is also supported by the sheer volume of restaurants, cafeterias, snack bars, vending machines, and other locations where we can purchase ready-to-eat foods at low prices. In fact, this market sector doubled in size between the 1970s and the mid-1990s.[16] Given these changes, it's a wonder we're not even fatter!

Please Pass the High-Fructose Corn Syrup

Here is another interesting theory, or at least an interesting history lesson, to explain why we're gaining weight. When the Great Depression hit the United States in 1929, the federal Farm Board was established as a sign of the government's commitment to provide stability to the agricultural industry. President Roosevelt introduced agricultural assistance programs in 1933 as part of the New Deal. These programs proposed to raise farm prices by limiting production, buying excess crops in years of overproduction, and guaranteeing prices even in times of economic hardship. In reality, these programs have resulted in enormous subsidies to farmers who produce certain crops.

Why is this relevant? The reason is this: Two of the most highly subsidized crops today are corn and soybeans. As a result, many farmers opt to raise these crops rather than fruits and vegetables.[17] This increased supply not only *lowers* the market price of these crops, but it conversely *increases* the price of fruits and vegetables due to their reduced availability. (Back to Economics 101, the basic theory of supply and demand tells us that a decrease in supply tends to raise prices.)

So are these subsidies making us fat? As noted at the beginning of this chapter, given the relatively small changes in calories that are necessary to generate the rise in obesity rates seen over the past 30 years, it's tough to determine what role these subsidies play. Would Uncle Al have gotten fatter in the absence of these subsidies? You bet he would have. Would he be as fat? It's hard to say.

We do know that the relatively high cost of fresh fruit and vegetables reduces consumption (more on this later in the section). At the same time, food manufacturers have an incentive to add inexpensive corn-based and soybean-based products to their foods, and the low price is clearly part of the motivation.

Consider high-fructose corn syrup, which was originally developed in the 1970s. Its price is now about 20 percent cheaper than table sugar, so it is no wonder that it is the sweetener of choice for food suppliers. But besides its low price tag, high-fructose corn syrup also has other advantages for suppliers. It's easy to transport. It helps keep foods from drying out. It isn't as vulnerable to freezer burn as sugar. It has a long shelf life without changes in sweetness or flavor quality. And it gives baked goods like breads and cookies that nice golden color. As a result, high-fructose corn syrup now makes up 40 percent of non-calorie-free sweeteners in all foods. In fact, Americans now consume more high-fructose corn syrup than they do old-fashioned sugar.

Because high-fructose corn syrup is relatively inexpensive, so too are the products that contain it. That's why food purveyors can afford to tempt us with bargains like five bags of candy for $5, a six-pack of muffins for $1.99, or a two-liter bottle of Coke for 89 cents. For Uncle Al and many others, these bargains are often too good to pass up.

In addition to greater consumption of products made with high-fructose corn syrup because of its increasingly low cost, there is now some debate (and some counterdebate by the Corn Refiners

Association and others) about whether high-fructose corn syrup actually *causes* us to eat more. The argument is that unlike the type of sugar found in real "sugar" from sugar cane or sugar beet, that is, sucrose, the primary sugar in high-fructose corn syrup, called fructose, is processed differently by the body.

The difference is important, because while glucose, a by-product of sucrose, triggers an appetite-suppressing signal in the body, fructose, the theory goes, does not. If correct, this suggests that we are not nearly as sated by fructose as we are by glucose, and may be more likely to eat more of high-fructose corn syrup–containing products than we would had they contained old-fashioned sugar.[18]

Whether or not this theory holds true, the reality is that, according to Department of Agriculture data, the average American consumes roughly 60 pounds worth of high-fructose corn syrup per year.[19] For someone like Uncle Al, that number is probably even higher.

Hydrogenated fats provide another example of how derivatives from highly subsidized crops make their way into the food supply chain. Hydrogenated fats, which are made from soybeans, are a common ingredient in prepackaged and ready-to-eat snacks and meals, and fast food. When you order deep-fried foods (French fries, donuts, chicken nuggets), the odds are quite good that they were fried in hydrogenated fat (vegetable shortening). These fats are also commonly found in processed foods in the supermarket including pastries, box mixes, chips, frozen pizzas and dinners, crackers, cookies, and soups. In fact, hydrogenated fats are used in almost every piece of sliced bread found in American grocery stores.

Moreover, foods containing these products are far more likely to be energy dense—that is, they have a high caloric value per pound of food. For example, potato chips made with hydrogenated fats have an energy density of approximately 2,500 calories/pound and chocolate made with corn syrup has an energy density of approximately 2,400 calories/pound. On the other hand, fruits and vegetables have energy densities that range between 40 and 200 calories/pound.[20] These differences make the costs per calorie much more attractive for energy-dense foods (i.e., those made with added sugars and added fats), so it's no surprise that these foods are consumed in much greater quantities.[21] It will cost you roughly 80 cents to eat 1,000 calories worth of potato chips.

In comparison, to eat 1,000 calories worth of fresh carrots, you would have to plunk down about $4.[22] Although some of this difference may well be driven by the subsidy, large differences in the cost per calorie would remain even in the absence of subsidies due to the energy density of these foods.

Researcher Adam Drewnowski points out that these high-energy foods not only cost less per calorie, they also taste better. So it is not surprising that more than 50 percent of the typical American diet consists of products that contain added fats and sugars.[23]

But whereas Uncle Al likely eats more energy-dense foods because of their great taste, Cousin Carl, who is always short on cash, probably chooses the energy-dense diet because of its low cost—well, that and the great taste. Even if Cousin Carl were a health nut (which he definitely is not), for a person living on a shoestring budget, the energy-dense diet with its cheap and satisfying added sugars and added fats is the more economical approach—especially as compared to consuming more expensive, less satisfying alternatives like vegetables and fruits.

As Drewnowski explains it, not everyone has equal access to healthier foods. Foods composed of refined grains, added sugars, or fats likely represent the lowest-cost option for Cousin Carl and other low-income individuals. Data from the Bureau of Labor Statistics indicates that income disparities do affect diet quality. Food purchases made by high-income households differ markedly from those made by low-income households.[24] In 1992, households in the top 20 percent of wage earners spent roughly 2.6 percent of their total expenditures on food. The poorest 20 percent of households spent roughly 19 percent of their money on food. Wealthier households bought higher-quality meats, more fish and seafood, more fruits and vegetables, and more convenience foods.

As Americans have moved toward a diet composed increasingly of prepackaged and prepared foods with lots of added sugars and added fats, the world has gradually followed suit. The so-called "Western diet" originated in the United States, caught on in Europe and the world's other rich nations, and then finally cascaded to the rest of the world. It's ironic that the New Deal, which was designed in large part to help put food in the mouths of the one third of the population that was hardest hit by the Depression, may have helped reduce food costs and spur innovations in food technology that contribute, at least in some part, to helping put potato chips, Coca-Cola, and candy bars in the hands of the world's most impoverished populations over half a century later.

Is this last statement a stretch? Well, maybe, but it's a line of questioning that does open our minds to some interesting questions about how government policy can bear consequences that cascade around the globe in totally unexpected ways (more about this conundrum in the chapters of the book related to government).

A Full Pound of Sausage, Bacon, and Ham: Have a Meaty Morning

One of the most important labor market trends over the past several decades is this: Mommy is helping to bring home the bacon. Since 1968, the rate of mothers with children under six years old who work has jumped by 60 percent, and the rate of mothers with children under age three who work has climbed by 72 percent. In fact, more than half of mothers with toddlers are employed.[25]

This trend is important for a number of different reasons (and we'll hit on these in more detail in Chapter 4). But in the context of "calories in," it has often been questioned whether, in the absence of a parent at home, there may be less careful monitoring of children's snacks after school.

In addition, two-income families have more money to spend on food and less time to spend preparing home-cooked meals. The result? An increasingly large percentage of America's food budget is going toward restaurant or prepackaged food that requires little to no preparation. In 1970, Americans spent only one third of their food budget on food away from home. By 2001, 47 percent of the total food budget was spent on food away from home.[26]

Lack of time to prepare meals is just one piece of the equation. Today's low prices, large portion sizes, and convenience make meals out a cheap and easy alternative—and for some, an alternative that becomes a way of life. I still remember the laughter that erupted when I asked a lawyer friend who lives in New York City if she ever cooked.

"Why would I cook?" she said. "I can walk outside and eat whatever I want without lifting a finger."

Increasingly, so can the rest of us. Why is this obesity promoting? For one simple reason: Food eaten away from home increases our caloric intake. By consuming restaurant food or prepackaged food, it is more difficult to control portion size and nutritional value, even for those who might want to.[27]

This difficulty is just getting worse due to the ever-increasing portion sizes of restaurant and prepackaged food, which once again, is a direct result of economics. Food typically accounts for only about a third of the total cost of running a restaurant. Elements such as rent, labor, equipment, advertising, and utilities make up the rest. As food prices have decreased, a low-cost strategy for restaurants and food suppliers to attract and retain consumers is to offer larger portions, which an increasingly obese clientele clearly values.

One large restaurant chain found out the hard way that reducing portion sizes is bad for business. In 2004, the restaurant chain Ruby Tuesday cut back on the sizes of pasta dishes, French fries, and some entrees. But this experiment was short lived. Why? Customers hated it. It took only five months for Ruby Tuesday to plump its portions back up.

Officials of the company conceded a "painful error," saying customers had protested the cuts via messages on Ruby Tuesday's web site, in phone calls, and to restaurant managers.[28] Ruby Tuesday, in fact, blamed its 5 percent drop in sales for that time period, in large part, on the portion downsizing. To win back customers, the company told analysts that it was launching a new ad campaign and 18 new menu items— including thick-cut onion rings and half-pound burgers.

"Even if they don't eat everything on the plate," Richard Johnson, Ruby Tuesday's senior vice president told a *New York Times* reporter, "they like that it's a generous portion."[29]

A "generous portion" is one thing. Then there is Ruby Tuesday's Ultimate Colossal Burger (2½ pounds of meat on a triple-decker bun with American and Monterey Jack cheeses, 1,677 calories—that's without the fries).

Other restaurant chains have also gone in the direction of flaunting the sheer enormity of their portions in efforts to attract customers. Just to name a few, there's the Denny's Grand Slam Slugger (1,128 calories before you add fruit topping, syrup, or margarine), Hardee's 2/3 pound

Monster Thickburger (1,410 calories), and Chipotle's 1¼-pound burrito advertised this way: "The first half is fun. The second half is masochism."

Burger King, too, makes no pretenses of moderation. In the last few years, it introduced a Triple Whopper, the BK Stacker with four beef patties, and an Enormous Omelet sandwich—a sausage, bacon, and cheese omelet on a bun. But these are small fries in comparison with its Meat 'Normous, a breakfast sandwich that Burger King pitched with the slogan: "A full pound of sausage, bacon, and ham. Have a meaty morning."

The super-sizing phenomenon may be good for business, but it can't be good for your health. Take the 2004 documentary, *Super Size Me,* in which filmmaker Morgan Spurlock ate only from McDonald's for a month, including breakfast, lunch, and dinner. Spurlock gained almost 30 pounds (over 10 in the first week), saw his cholesterol skyrocket, and experienced frequent nausea, chest pains, mood swings, liver problems, and a loss of sex drive.

But it was worth it, right? Not only did Spurlock make a hit documentary, but the wave of negative publicity following the documentary may well be at least part of the reason McDonald's and Wendy's dropped their "Supersize" and "Biggie" menus. Or did they? Marion Nestle, a professor of nutrition at New York University, and Lisa R. Young, a dietitian and NYU adjunct professor, tracked the history of the super-size phenomenon. They found that Wendy's "Biggie" brand was gone in name only. Wendy's simply renamed its "Biggie" drink, at 32 ounces, a "medium." A large drink now contains a whopping 42 ounces.

In its defense, Wendy's spokesman, Bob Bertini, said in a National Public Radio (NPR) report that the new 42-ounce soda, with up to 100 more calories than the old "biggie," is not really intended to be drunk in a single sitting, but rather consumed throughout the day.[30] Yeah, right.

Increased portions are not just a trick of the fast-food restaurants. Even most table-service restaurants have swapped 10-inch plates (once the industry standard) for 12-inch sizes to accommodate bigger portions.

So, clearly, it pays for restaurants to offer larger portions. It's just plain good business sense to give customers what they want (especially when it doesn't cost them very much to do). In fact, looking at the case of Ruby Tuesday, it's giving customers what they vehemently *demand* (again, we're back to good old-fashioned Economics 101—the law of supply and demand). In restaurants' efforts to attract customers and maximize profits, they cannot only promise more food, they can promise more value (i.e., more food at a lower cost). And who doesn't love that? Certainly, it appeals to Uncle Al and Cousin Carl (and to me).

And it's not just restaurants that are increasing portion sizes to increase sales. Researchers Young and Nestle compared serving sizes of foods from fast-food, take-out, and family-style restaurants as well as grocery stores from the 1970s to the present to examine the change in portion sizes over time.[31] They found that portion sizes began to increase rapidly in the early 1980s. Young and Nestle also examined how current portion sizing compares to U.S. Department of Agriculture (USDA) and Food and Drug Administration (FDA) recommendations. With the single exception of sliced white bread, all of the commonly available food portions that they measured far exceeded USDA and FDA standard portions. Cookies, cooked pasta, muffins, steaks, and bagels exceeded USDA standards by 700 percent, 480 percent, 333 percent, 224 percent, and 195 percent, respectively (see Table 2.2).

Too Much of a Good Thing

Truly, we live in a country that is rife with abundance. But here's the dilemma: Given the "value" of cheap, tasty, super-size-portioned, calorie-dense foods, it's becoming increasingly difficult to maintain a healthy weight. For example, a man of Uncle Al's size and stature should probably shoot for a 2,000-calorie-per-day diet. But let's see what he might consume on a typical day.

Suppose after a Starbucks Cafe Latte prepared with whole milk (260 calories), he skips breakfast. He chooses McDonald's for lunch because he is prepping for an important case and has to eat quickly. Let's say he decides on a Big Mac meal with French fries and a Coke, super-sized (what the heck, it's only $0.79 more). That puts him up to 1,880 calories (a Diet Coke would have saved him 410 calories). For dinner, suppose he decides to go out for Italian. To be health conscious, let's say he skips the calamari appetizer (1,000 calories) and starts with a house salad (260 calories) and red wine (83 calories per glass, but it is good for the heart). For a main course, let's go with one of Uncle Al's favorites, chicken

Table 2.2 Changes in Caloric Content of Popular Foods over the Past 20 Years

Food Item	Average Serving Size 20 Years Ago	Average Calories 20 Years Ago	Average Serving Size Today	Average Calories Today	Average Calorie Difference
Bagel	3-inch diameter	140	6-inch diameter	350	210
Muffin	1.5 ounces	210	4 ounces	500	290
Chicken Caesar salad	1.5 cups	390	3.5 cups	790	400
Turkey sandwich	White bread sandwich	320	Submarine sandwich	820	500
Cheeseburger	5.8 ounces	333	7.3 ounces	590	257
French fries	2.4 ounces	210	6.9 ounces	610	400
Pepperoni pizza	2 slices	500	2 large slices	850	350
Spaghetti and meatballs	1 cup pasta, sauce, 3 meatballs	500	2 cups pasta, sauce, 3 large meatballs	1,025	525
Chicken stir fry	2 cups	435	4.5 cups	865	430
Soda	6.5 ounces	85	20 ounces	250	165
Coffee	8 ounces, with whole milk and sugar	45	16 ounces, with whole milk and mocha syrup	350	305
Popcorn	5 cups	270	11 cups	630	360
Cheesecake	3 ounces	260	7 ounces	640	380
Chocolate chip cookie	1.5-inch diameter	55	3.5-inch diameter	275	220

SOURCE: National Health, Lung, and Blood Institute.

parmesan (1,500 calories). Even without the strawberry cheesecake for dessert (1,150 calories), he's up to over 3,660 calories for the day, even with skipping breakfast and not snacking.

At this rate, and given that he has no time to exercise during the workweek, it is no wonder Uncle Al has been gaining weight. Had he eaten a turkey sandwich and some fruit for lunch, and then had grilled chicken and veggies at home for dinner, his consumption for the day would have been only about 1200 calories, leaving plenty of room for a good breakfast and a small dessert. But c'mon, who has time to cook?

Kids Are Also Drinking the Kool-Aid

Since the late 1970s, children have increased their caloric consumption as well. Adolescent boys now average about 2,800 calories a day, an increase of 250 calories. Similarly, adolescent girls now average approximately 1,900 calories, an increase of 120 calories. (In comparison, adult men have increased their daily food intake by about 180 calories, and women have increased their daily food intake by about 360 calories.)

Children between the ages of 6 and 11 consume 21 to 23 teaspoons of added sugars per day, far surpassing the government recommendations of 6 to 12. They also eat three times as many chips/crackers/popcorn/pretzels as they did in the mid-1970s.[32] Adolescent boys now consume 22 ounces of soft drinks a day, up from 7 ounces in the 1970s. If none of these additional 15 ounces are diet soft drinks, this increase represents approximately 250 additional calories.[33]

So what's behind the increased caloric intake for kids? All of the obesity-inducing factors we have discussed already—the cheap super-sized meals, the diet becoming richer in fats and sugars, the snacking, the meals out—are still relevant, but there is one other often-cited culprit in the picture: our public schools.

Although the picture is beginning to change, schools have traditionally not been a beacon of healthy eating. A recent study has shown that children who eat school lunches consume 40 to 120 more calories as a result of this meal compared to children who bring their lunch from home.[34]

Then there are vending machines and snack foods—a hard-to-resist revenue stream for schools struggling to get by with significant state budget shortfalls. Some have even entered exclusive and highly controversial "pouring rights" agreements with soda manufacturers in order to create more discretionary funds.[35] Typically, these contracts require the schools to promise to sell a certain number of sodas a year, a relationship that opponents say transforms the school's role from being a provider of vending machines to being an active soda peddler.

And the picture just gets worse as kids get older. Availability of junk food increases with grade level—in 2000, 43 percent of elementary schools, 89 percent of middle schools, and 98 percent of high schools had student-accessible vending machines or stores where junk foods could be purchased.[36] We talk about school food policies—and what could be done to improve them—in detail in Chapter 11.

When Is Enough Enough?

Brian Wansink, the author of *Mindless Eating: Why We Eat More Than We Think* (Bantam, 2006), believes that the two-thirds of Americans who are overweight or obese got that way, at least in part, because they didn't realize how much they were eating.[37]

"We don't have any idea what the normal amount to eat is, so we look around for clues or signals," he said. "When all you see is that big portions of food cost less than small ones, it can be confusing."

Wansink's studies on university campuses and in test kitchens for institutions like the United States Army have produced some interesting results. Here's one example: Moviegoers in a Chicago suburb were given free stale popcorn in a variety of sized buckets. What was left in the buckets was weighed at the end of the movie. The people with larger buckets ate 53 percent more than people with smaller buckets. And people didn't eat the popcorn because they liked it, he said. They were driven by hidden persuaders: the distraction of the movie, the sound of other people eating popcorn, and the Pavlovian popcorn trigger that is activated when we step into a movie theater.

Wansink focuses on the psychological aspects of food choices, of which clearly there are many. However, many of the results that people ascribe to food addiction or food psychology may simply be applications of basic economic principles. For example, it is well known that Uncle Al, like the rest of us, eats more when he orders the Shoney's buffet than when he orders off the menu. Some might chalk this up to Uncle Al's inability to control his appetite. However, this is not the case. Once Uncle Al pays for the buffet, economic theory says he should continue eating if he gains any benefit at all from the food. This is because, unless he considers the long-term consequences of these additional bites of food on his weight and subsequent health, there is literally no cost to him for increased consumption. Although each additional bite may bring him less joy as he gets fuller and fuller, if the food tastes good, he might as well keep eating. Only when he is really stuffed, and an additional bite makes him worse off, should he stop eating.

This is not true when he orders off the menu. Once his plate is cleaned, for him to eat more food (barring stealing it off of my aunt's plate) requires him to purchase another meal. This cost, although perhaps only a few dollars, is enough for him to forgo additional consumption because by this time the value to him of additional food consumption has substantially decreased. Of course, he might be back for more (or dessert) when he has had some time to digest and the value of those additional bites begins to increase again.

This is economics, not psychology. Would Uncle Al eat free stale popcorn at a movie theatre? If it were better than nothing, you bet he would. And so would I. It *is* free, after all.

Of course, since today's environment provides a vast array of low-cost, tasty, and affordable snack foods, stale popcorn is a tough sell. For example, a recent visit to my county fair revealed options that included deep-fried candy bars, fried turkey legs the size of my thigh, and the latest concoction to hit the fair circuit—deep-fried Coke. A vendor by the name of Abel Gonzales Jr. took home the Big Tex Choice Awards Contest for that invention. His recipe: start with deep-fry Coca-Cola-flavored batter, drizzle Coke fountain syrup on top, and then top it off with whipped cream, cinnamon sugar, and a cherry. Sound excessive? Maybe, but hey, the fair comes around but once a year, right? I'm guessing this one stop at the concession stand was at least 600 calories, and probably a whole lot more.

In the next chapter, we take a closer look at how many trips around the midway it would take to work that little snack off.

Chapter 3

Why We're Moving Less

(Hint: It's Not Just the La-Z-Boy)

A t the end of Chapter 2, we posed a question: How many miles would you have to stroll around the fair to burn off the calories in a deep-fried Coca-Cola? The answer: about six miles, which is assuming you don't stop for the giant turkey drumstick (my personal favorite) along the way.[1] Of course, this assumes you are actually walking. I was amazed to see many kids of all ages and sizes being pushed by their parents in "baby" strollers. Then there were the many adults using motorized assistance devices to navigate the fairgrounds. Even for the ambulatory, I would be willing to wager that few fairgoers had a net calorie burn during their trip to the fair. But, as we noted in the preceding chapter, the fair comes around but once a year, so why not enjoy it?

The problem is that the rest of the year is not much better. Most of us do not consume as many calories in a typical day as we do at the fair, but, on the flip side, we probably don't burn off as many calories either. (After all, it's a long walk from the midway to the world's largest pig exhibit.)

As we discussed in the previous chapter, we are consuming substantially more calories today then we did in years past. To offset this increase, we would have to be increasing our levels of physical activity proportionally in order to maintain our current weight. Clearly, this is not happening.

Even though we are actually exercising more in our free time, well, very slightly more, these increases fall far short of what is required to offset the increases in food consumption—an imbalance that is certainly no surprise to any economist considering the environment producing these results. While it is getting easier and cheaper to take on a few hundred extra calories a day, as we discuss in detail below, burning them off is becoming increasingly more difficult.

But I Don't Have Time!

Because we typically think about physical activity as something we do in our free time, let's first examine our leisure-time physical activity. Here, we actually have some good news: Americans now have more free time than ever. It may seem hard to believe, but research tells us that since 1965, leisure time has increased by more than four hours per week, with the greatest jump occurring between 1965 and 1975.[2]

Second, Americans are actually using this time, at least to some very small degree, to work off some extra calories. Between 1985 and 1999, physical activity increased by 20 minutes per week. Of course, even if this time were spent jogging, that only translates into about an extra 200 calories burned per week, far less than what is necessary to compensate for the 1,000+ increase in weekly calories consumed.

Moreover, although the trend shows a slight improvement over time, roughly one fourth of U.S. adults get no leisure-time physical activity at all.[3] These results reveal that while Americans are, on average, slightly increasing their levels of leisure-time physical activity, there remains a large fraction of the population who maintain their "couch potato" status.

Although it may seem like a paradox on the surface, it is hardly surprising that leisure-time physical activity levels and obesity rates would be rising at the same time. In fact, economic theory would have predicted exactly this result.

To understand this, let's get back to Uncle Al. As a result of the changes we discussed in Chapter 2—the reductions in food prices, the increased food availability, and the shift toward consumption of foods heavily fortified with added sugars and added fats—Uncle Al has been steadily consuming more calories over the years. Consequently, he has been gaining weight. Uncle Al, like most of us, would prefer not to be fat, all else being equal. So an obvious strategy for him is to increase his levels of physical activity. The problem is that, even with a bit more free time available, he is unable, or better stated, unwilling, to increase his physical activity levels enough to compensate for the net increase in calories.

As you probably know all too well, it's far easier to consume a few hundred extra calories than it is to burn them off. Uncle Al could have used all of his additional free time to exercise, and perhaps even cut back on his hours at the firm. However, these are costly decisions for someone trying to climb the corporate ladder, and Uncle Al, like many of us, found that the amount of time and effort required to burn off all the additional calories was more than he was willing to take on.

For Uncle Al to burn off an extra 1,000 calories per week, he would have had to play roughly an additional 18 holes of golf every weekend. And while that might be fine with him, I don't think Mrs. Uncle Al would have allowed it. There are, of course, any number of other ways he could have burned off the weight in a manner that would be more amenable to my aunt (see Table 3.1). For example, he could have burned off the calories in just over an hour if he went out for a long jog, but I doubt that Uncle Al has moved that fast or that far in a single outing in the past 40 years. I do know that he, like many of us, has at various times joined a health club and made other fitness-related efforts to control his weight. The reality, however, is that most of us—and especially Uncle Al—have been unable (or perhaps better stated, unwilling) to increase our physical activity enough to offset the increase in food consumption. As a result, we got fat at the same time that the fitness craze kicked into high gear.

Table 3.1   Selected Activities and Corresponding Calories Burned per Hour, for Three Different Body Weights[4]

Activity	Cal/hr Burned, for 125–Pound Person	Cal/hr Burned, for 155–Pound Person	Cal/hr Burned, for 185–Pound Person
Bicycling, for leisure	228	281	336
Bicycling, moderate effort	456	562	672
Running, 12 min/mile	456	562	672
Running, 8 min/mile	713	879	1050
Basketball, nongame	342	422	504
Golf	257	316	378
Tennis	399	492	588
Walking, for leisure	143	176	210
Walking, brisk pace	228	281	336
Dancing	257	316	378
Vacuuming home	200	246	294
Shopping	131	162	193
Ironing	131	162	193
Cleaning house	171	211	252
Sitting quietly, watching TV, reading	57	70	84
Office work	86	105	126
Driving	114	141	168
Child care	171	211	252
Eating	85.5	105	126
Sleeping	51	63	76
Talking on phone	86	105	126
Mowing lawn (no riding mower)	314	387	462
Weeding garden	257	316	378

SOURCE: METs Compendium.

Not Quite the Jetsons, But . . .

In fact, Uncle Al has something else working against his efforts to lose weight (although I seriously doubt he would complain about it). Remember the days when people had to get out of their cars to open their garage doors, or even manually roll down their car windows (that's where the term *roll* came from)? Technology has radically lowered our energy expenditures at work, at home, and everywhere in between. Devices such as vacuum cleaners, washing machines, clothes dryers, dishwashers, microwaves, television remote controls, food processors, keyless car entry, lawn mowers, automatic sprinkler systems, and even electric can openers have reduced the amount of energy (i.e., calories burned) and time it takes to complete household and daily tasks.

I recently returned home from an obesity conference to find that my wife had purchased a new trash can with an electronic eye that triggers the lid to open whenever someone walks by. Now we can throw away our trash without even having to expend the energy required to manually lift the lid (or step on a foot lever). Talk about progress!

Although hard data on the cumulative amount of calories "saved" by these new technologies is unavailable, it is not a stretch to say we are burning far fewer "accidental" calories at home than we did in decades past. Let's look at an example. Throwing your clothes in the washing machine versus washing them by hand is estimated to result in 45 fewer calories being expended (which actually sounds pretty conservative to me thinking years back to the last time I hand-washed anything). The washer alone saves countless hours per year that can be spent doing other activities.[5]

So what are we doing with the time we used to spend washing dishes, peeling potatoes, and scrubbing clothes? Well, as we talked about earlier, we spend about 20 minutes of that extra four-plus hours per week exercising. As for the rest of our leisure time, there has been an explosion in the choices available for how to use it. When Uncle Al was a kid, there were far fewer options for home entertainment. He was largely limited to watching a few shows on a small black-and-white television, playing board or card games, reading, or playing outside. From all accounts, Uncle Al was an active, skinny kid growing up, who spent lots of time outdoors. This is largely because there weren't too many other options. Also, perhaps, he wanted to escape the aunts, uncles, and other family members who shared their small house at the time he was growing up.

His son, my cousin Carl, was born about 30 years later, in 1970, into a very different environment. He had all the same leisure-time options available as Uncle Al, but he was also an early recipient of Atari, an Apple computer, and cable television (boy, was I jealous). Cousin Carl was one of the first gamers I ever met. He spent far more time in front of a screen than he did playing outside.

Today, people laugh at the "games" that were available to Cousin Carl back in the day. Now, my kids could potentially access Nintendos, Xboxes, PlayStations, high-definition televisions with hundred of channels, the Internet, and a host of other new technologies that are competing against physical activity in our scarce leisure time. My wife and I have instituted some strategies aimed at limiting our kids' screen time. However, this task is becoming increasingly difficult as the kids grow older and get more clued in to the available entertainment options. Adults aren't much better. As you can see in Figure 3.1, much of our free time is dedicated to sedentary activities, including watching television, playing on the computer, hanging out, and reading.

Not surprisingly, TV viewing accounts for the majority of our leisure time. In fact, we are watching more TV than ever. The greatest

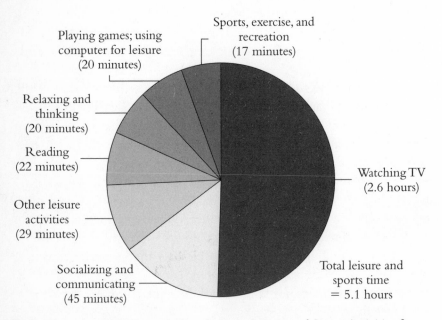

Figure 3.1 Average Hours per Day Spent in Leisure and Sports Activities for the Total Population by Selected Characteristics (2003 Annual Averages)
SOURCE: Bureau of Labor Statistics, Department of Labor, U.S. Government American Time Use Survey (ATUS) 2003, released September 2004.

change in TV watching occurred between 1965 and 1975, when it increased by 40 minutes per day. Since 1975, TV viewing has increased another 22 minutes.[6]

And, let's face it, this is not your father's television. Even if it's not a plasma or liquid crystal display (LCD), or even high-definition, today's televisions are far superior to those of decades past. The pictures are crisper, and the shows are better—well, this point may be debatable, but there are definitely lots more of them. And thanks to digital video recorders (e.g., TIVO), you never have to miss your favorite show. In fact, just thinking about it, I'm tempted to take a break from writing since I'm sure there is something great on the TV right now. Of course, I'd have to wrestle the remote away from my wife, who loves her reality television.

Moreover, fast-falling TV prices have made them increasingly more affordable. Plasma TVs with 50-inch screens that sold for $20,000 in 2000 were selling around the $1,500 to $2,000 mark as of spring 2007. As a result, it is no surprise that between 1970 and 2000, the number of homes with more than one TV went from 35 percent to 75 percent. During this same time period, the number of homes with cable TV has gone from 7 percent to 76 percent.[7,8] Obviously, these sedentary leisure-time activities burn off fewer calories than active ones.

And, thanks to technology, even some leisure-time physical activities have become mechanized. For example, when golf carts were first introduced, the idea was to enable elderly and physically limited players to participate in the game. Then, because golf carts were seen to speed up play, while providing golf courses with another source of income, carts became practically ubiquitous—radically reducing the calorie-burning power of Uncle Al's favorite pastime.

As a more recent example, consider shopping, which happens to be one of my wife's favorite pastimes. Whereas she used to shop by walking around the mall, she now shops from the kitchen table while surfing the Internet. Why make a trip to the mall when you can get what you need—from books to underwear—after a short browse online? And my wife is not alone. Total U.S. e-commerce sales for 2006 were estimated at $108.7 billion, according to the Census Bureau of the Department of Commerce, an increase of 23.5 percent from 2005.[9]

So, although we may have a few extra minutes of leisure, for many of us, engaging in physical activity during this time is not how we are choosing to spend it. In today's economy, physical activity has a hard time competing with the many other options available to us. Given this reality, an extra three minutes per day of leisure-time physical activity is actually fairly impressive.

Just Be a Marathon Runner

So just how much physical activity does it take to be healthy? Shape Up America[10] and many other organizations have adopted the 10,000 steps recommendation. The goal is to get off our couches, buy a pedometer and walk an average of 10,000 steps per day. Walking 10,000 steps, by the way, is equivalent to about five miles of walking (slightly less than what it takes to burn off that deep-fried Coca Cola). So the question is this: Is 10,000 steps a day a realistic goal for the typical American?

Not in my experience, it isn't. Several years ago my wife told me that I had better lose weight if I wanted to have credibility as an obesity researcher. As always, I did what I was told. Not only did I go out and buy a pedometer, but wanting to fulfill a lifelong ambition, I entered and ran my first marathon (in four hours and nine minutes). I ran at least 20 miles per week over the course of my four months of training. Every day, I logged my daily step activity on a spreadsheet (I know, I'm a geek).

My spreadsheet included all of my steps taken from the moment I got dressed in the morning until the moment I got undressed at night (admittedly, I might have taken a few more after that). Want to know what my average step count was during those four months of fairly rigorous training? About 10,700 steps per day—not much more than Shape Up America's recommendation.

How can that be? Are the recommendations so unrealistic? Do you have to be a marathon runner to "be healthy"?

Perhaps you do if you consider what I do when I'm not out for a run. Similar to Uncle Al and the alleged Al Qaeda terrorists locked up in Camp Gitmo, for at least 10 hours per day, I can be found sitting either in my cubicle or somewhere else (car, couch, bar . . .). Eventually I threw away the pedometer because I learned that I took about 5,000 steps on the days that I did not work out, and I took about 10,000 steps on the days that I did my three-mile run. For me to hit the step target I would need to run three miles per day seven days per week!

Is this a realistic goal for Uncle Al? Well, anything is possible, but the reality is that I doubt he has hit 10,000 steps more than a few times since entering law school over 30 years ago. He's not alone either. Few of the rest of us are hitting the target either.

The problem that Uncle Al and the rest of us are facing is that we are increasingly sedentary in our daily lives. Whereas, historically, much of our physical activity has been "accidental," that is, we have gotten it in on the job or by doing chores around the house, today that is increasingly no longer the case. Most Americans now have to make a *conscious* decision to strap on a pair of gym shoes and decide to go out and burn off some calories—a choice Americans a century ago would have found laughable.

We're Not Farmers Anymore

Americans used to work up a good sweat at their jobs. As an example, in the early 1900s, 41 percent of the workforce was found in agriculture, and most of these individuals were in manual jobs. By 1945, 16 percent of the workforce was employed in agriculture. By 1970, that number had dwindled to 4 percent. Today, less than 2 percent of the U.S. workforce is in agriculture.[11]

So why have so many farmers (or farmers' offspring) transitioned into other occupations? The answer is technology. The farming technology developed over the last century relies far less on human (and animal) power and more on machinery. For example, the 22 million work animals on the farms at the beginning of the twentieth century have been replaced with 5 million tractors.[12] These tractors not only require far less care than the 22 million work animals did, they offer a less energy-expending way to get work done around the farm (thus burning far fewer calories).

But the trend away from manual labor is not unique to farming. As a result of technology, a large proportion of goods-producing jobs (i.e., those generally existing in a labor-intensive environment) are disappearing, and those that remain have experienced significant automation.

As a result, it takes much less physical energy to perform these job functions than it did in decades past. For example, the work of car factory laborers is, in large part, replaced by robots on assembly lines. The work of long-shoremen has been mechanized by cranes and highly automated ports.

As a further example, I recently moved into a brand new house. On weekends, my kids and I would go and watch the house being built. I am not sure that I ever witnessed anyone swing a hammer or use a manual saw. They used pneumatic hammers and electric saws. They also had a small crane that lifted all the heavy lumber and drywall onto the second floor and lots of other labor-saving technologies. More than a few of these guys were overweight. But so what? My house was built quickly, probably better, and the best part was that it cost less than had the workers had to rely on old manual technology. And it was the (relatively) low cost that drove me to purchase this house and what suppliers are striving to supply. What they have found is that mechanization and reliance on technology, as opposed to manpower, is the way to remain competitive.

Goods-producing occupations are not the only ones that have become more sedentary over time. Service-oriented jobs have also seen technology lower the necessary energy expenditure.[13] For example, many workers in service industries from retail to mail delivery can radio messages to the stockroom using a short-wave radio rather than physically convey the message.

Even white-collar occupations that are not traditionally labor inten-sive have been affected. For example, to reward me for the positive press I received for a paper that we'll discuss in a subsequent chapter, my boss gave me my own printer. Now, instead of having to walk the 100 steps to the community printer a few times a day, I can merely turn 90 degrees to the right and pick up my output without leaving my chair. Lucky me! I'd better break out the pedometer to see how this reduces my step count. Of course, I've also had conference calls and countless e-mail exchanges with the guy in the office a few doors down because it is eas-ier than getting up and walking down the hall, so who am I to complain. And from my company's perspective, I am arguably more productive as a result of these technologies.

And so it goes. Mechanization has lowered the cost of production while simultaneously raising the costs of getting physical activity. Whereas we can buy goods and services more cheaply than ever before, we are now forced to pay to exercise. There is, in fact, compelling evidence to support the theory that working in a more sedentary occupation increases your chances of gaining weight. The National Longitudinal Survey of Youth followed individuals from 1979 to 2000, collecting information about occupational choices and job characteristics, as well as height and weight. Using this data, researchers Lakdawalla and Philipson showed that a male worker spending 18 years in the least fitness-demanding occupations (like mine) is expected to have a body mass index (BMI) roughly 3.5 points higher than a worker in the most demanding jobs.[14] For a man of average height, this equates to a 25-pound (or 14 percent) difference in weight.

Given that even the most fitness-demanding jobs are becoming less demanding and the fact that these jobs are growing scarcer every year, it is hardly surprising that Americans are gaining weight.

Sprawling Out

For those of us who work outside the home, here's yet another trend that is adding bulk to our waistlines: We are spending more and more time sitting in our cars. In 1960, 64 percent of people drove to work, 10 percent walked, and 12 percent used public transportation. In 2000, 88 percent drove to work, 3 percent walked, and 5 percent used public transportation.[15] The increase in commute time in the past few decades is again largely the result of economics.

As housing prices have increased in urban centers, individuals have flocked to the suburbs to buy affordable housing. In some cities like Washington, D.C., and San Francisco, it is not uncommon for individuals to commute 60 miles each way to and from work. Compared to other countries, relatively low gas prices have also allowed us to commute more cheaply. In total, today's adults spend more than 10 hours a week in transportation, split between transportation to leisure-time activities, home activities, and commuting to and from work.[16]

Although it is difficult to determine precisely how changes in the time we spend in sedentary transportation have affected obesity, it is likely to have made a significant impact. Hypothetically, if an individual were to walk five days a week for 20 minutes to and from work (or school) rather than drive, their weight could easily be six pounds less.[17]

Moreover, the added time we spend in transportation may be driving out time for more leisure-time physical activity. In one study, it was shown that individuals with longer commute times also had greater levels of obesity.[18] Based on a survey of Atlanta residents, the authors found that each half-hour a day spent in the car is associated with a 3 percent greater likelihood of being obese, and those who commuted by foot were far less likely to be obese.

Our Kids Are Also Slowing Down

Just like with adults, the upswing in kid's calorie consumption could have been offset if it coincided with an upswing in physical activity. But, again, just like with adults, the opposite effect is taking place. The U.S. surgeon general reports that roughly 25 percent of U.S. young people (ages 12 to 21 years) report no vigorous physical activity, and about 14 percent of young people report no recent vigorous or light to moderate physical activity.[19]

The picture is little better for young children, due at least in part because today's kids are spending more time than ever in school, in day care, and in after-school programs. As a result, free time for children 3 to 12 years of age has decreased by approximately 7 to 8 hours a week, or about 12 percent, between 1981 and 1997. Time in school has increased by approximately 2 hours a week, and time in day care has increased from 14 minutes to 3 hours a week, both because more children are in day care and because children who are in day care spend more time there than in years past. Interestingly, the amount of time children spend eating has decreased, reflecting the decrease in frequency with which families sit down together for meals, a change that is believed to promote poor eating habits and thus obesity.[20]

So guess what most busy kids are choosing to do in their reduced free time? *Hint:* It's not kicking a ball around at the park. Television and, to perhaps a lesser degree, video games, have long been the smoking gun in the childhood obesity discussion. And with some good reason: The average child's home has three TV sets.[21] Research studies tell us that

17 percent of children watch more than five hours of TV a day; 16 percent watch three to five hours of TV a day; 31 percent watch TV for one to three hours; while only 36 percent watch less than an hour of TV a day. Children who engage in the least vigorous physical activity or the most television viewing tend to be the most overweight.[22]

Increased use of the Internet is also a likely contributing factor. And kids are not just playing video games. Sites like MySpace, Facebook, and YouTube are becoming focal points for kids' virtual social lives.

The other factor often cited to contribute to decreased physical activity is the physical education (PE) program in schools. In 2001, a national survey of high schoolers showed that 45 percent do not engage in team sports, and 48 percent are not even enrolled in a PE class. Whereas 74 percent of freshmen take physical education, only 31 percent of seniors do.[23] Daily enrollment in high school PE has dropped from 42 percent in 1991 to 28 percent in 2003, and a third of high schoolers do not meet recommended levels of physical activity. In fact, 10 percent of high school students are completely sedentary.[24]

Given the increased pressures on schools to perform academically lest they face punitive consequences, PE requirements have decreased to accommodate additional academic instruction. Such a move may have raised the amount of homework and out-of-class study time, which would contribute to the high percentage of children who do not pursue physical activities, whether organized or not, outside of school.[25] We discuss this concern in detail in Chapter 9.

Wrapping It Up

So what's the take-home message of the last two chapters? Largely due to technology, the costs of food consumption have gone down while the costs of physical activity (including time and opportunity costs of not being able to engage in other activities) have gone up. The end result is that we are consuming more calories than ever before and burning off less.

If we were not so out of shape, we would be jumping for joy about these innovations. Highly affordable and tasty food has allowed Cousin Carl and other low-wage earners to feed their families for less money than ever before. New technologies have helped the economy expand at a rapid rate, a boon that has given all of us access to a host of new products and services—at good prices—that we as consumers are clearly demanding. Speaking for myself, they have allowed me to have an affordable big house, a printer in my office, a pedometer (since thrown out), and a trash can with an electronic eye. There is that unwanted side effect of rapid weight gain, but that's a small price to pay for progress, right?

We explore this price in greater detail in Chapter 6. But first, we go beyond the calories in/calories out discussion to look at other possible culprits in the obesity blame game.

Chapter 4

So Where Else Can We Lay the Blame?

The argument we laid out in the previous chapters explained that the sudden upswing in obesity in America is mostly the result of technological advancements that have made it easier to consume lots of tasty, affordable, high-calorie food, and harder to burn off those calories. In other words, obesity rates increased because it became more expensive, in terms of money and time, to remain thin.

But does the obesity story go further than the "calories in" versus "calories out" equation? In the spirit of full disclosure, this chapter analyzes all the major players in the obesity blame game in order to unravel whether any of these theories can also help explain a portion of the dramatic rise in obesity rates seen over the past several decades.

As we explore below, many of these theories are consistent with our overarching argument that obesity results from technological advancements and a growing economy, albeit not always by changes in prices and opportunity costs. For example, many new pharmaceuticals that successfully treat a broad range of medical conditions from diabetes to psychoses have weight gain as a common side effect. Other theories, including the notion that obesity results from exposure to a chicken virus, clearly fall outside of an economic model.

Blame Mom and Dad

So you might think that until this point of the book, a major component of obesity has largely been overlooked: genetics. In fact, several studies on the genetic component of obesity find that as much as 70 percent of the differences between individuals' body weights can be attributed to biological factors.[1-4] This genetic component helps explain why there are strong racial/ethnic tendencies toward excess weight.

For one, genetics explains why my wife, of Vietnamese descent, can eat all she wants and still shop the children's section at Old Navy. As another example, compare the Pacific Island populations of Nauru, Tonga, Micronesia, and the Cook Islands (with obesity prevalence rates approaching 70 percent) with those of Japan, Vietnam, Indonesia, and the Philippines (all with 20 percent or fewer overweight and 2 percent or fewer obese).[5] It seems hard to imagine that the environment alone could be responsible for such drastic differences in rates of obesity. Genetic differences play a significant role. Genetic differences also explain why Polynesian women in New Zealand are more likely to be overweight than their European-descent neighbors, even when diet and exercise levels are the same.[6]

Even in countries where rates of obesity are lower, children born to obese parents have more than twice the chance of becoming obese as an adult compared with children born to lean parents.[7] So, is this nature or nurture? Research tells us, not surprisingly, that the answer is likely to be a combination.

Although the genetic role of obesity is only just beginning to be understood, scientists are uncovering certain genes that are associated with excess weight. In a recent article in the prestigious journal *Science*, researchers identified one gene, and there are likely to be others, that increases a person's risk for obesity.[8] The authors studied nearly 39,000 white Europeans, 63 percent of whom had either one or two copies of an obesity gene, which they called FTO. People with two copies had about a 70 percent higher risk of being obese than people with none. Those with one copy were somewhere in between. The difference in weight between those with two and no copies of the gene was about seven pounds.

Although weight and the likelihood of being obese are influenced by genetics, environment also plays a major role. For example, studies have found that children's diet and exercise habits follow those of their parents. So if parents engage in obesity-promoting behaviors, then it is more likely that they will pass those behaviors on to their children.[9–11] With that said, two adoption studies point out the strength of genetics when it comes to determining weight outcomes. Both studies investigated the impact of parental body mass index (BMI) on the BMI of adopted and birth children, and both find a much stronger connection between the weight of children and their birth parents than that of adoptees and their adopted parents.[12,13]

Need more evidence? Well, let's take a look at the Pima Indians, a much-studied native tribe of the American Southwest. The Pimas happen to provide, quite by accident, a near-perfect scientific study on the relationship between obesity, genetics, and environment. Their tribal area crosses the Rio Grande, and there are Pimas of essentially identical genetics on both sides of the United States–Mexico border. Although they both have the same genetic makeup, Pimas in the United States are substantially heavier and have a much greater prevalence of diabetes and other chronic diseases than those living in Mexico. Why? Because those on the Mexican side tend to follow their traditional subsistence-farming lifestyle, whereas in Arizona, the Pimas have adopted a largely "American" way of life.

In fact, Pimas in the United States not only have greater rates of obesity than Mexican Pimas, they have higher obesity rates than the average American, or even the average Arizona resident for that matter. So if it were purely the environment that is making the Pimas in the United States heavier, then we would expect their weight to mirror non-Pima Americans in terms of rates of obesity. But this is not the case. In fact, the American Pimas have over twice the rate of obesity as the rest of the U.S. population (69 percent relative to 32 percent).[14] This underscores the interplay between genes and environment. The "American" way of life has made them heavier, but a genetic composition that predisposes them to excess weight exacerbated this effect.

So what is that genetic composition? It is hypothesized that a "thrifty" gene explains why some individuals get heavier in this modern obesity-promoting environment, while others stay slim.[15] The idea behind the theory is this: In the olden days of feast and famine, there was an advantage to being able to get fat. Because much of human history occurred under conditions in which food was scarce, some humans evolved to store excess food intake in good times as fat to serve as an energy store for times of impending scarcity. These people were thus able to increase their survival chances by sustaining themselves on very little food while engaging in very active lifestyles.

Eric Ravussin, a scientist who studies the genetic components of weight gain, has conducted extensive research on the Pima. He hypothesized that the Pima's survival mechanisms evolved to store fat extremely efficiently, a genetic makeup that would have served the tribe well in the harsh desert climates of the Southwest. "The Pima have a genetic liability. But it's only a liability in our environment," said Ravussin. "It was an asset to survival in mankind's history."[16]

But imagine what happens when an individual carrying these "thrifty" genes is introduced to a modern world of purely "feast." You guessed it: He holds on to that store of energy, meaning he gains weight—fast. His genes are no longer saviors; they are detriments because they allow him to rapidly gain weight and store it for a future period of famine—a famine that never comes.

So what does this example tell us? Well, it offers one explanation of why the weight of some groups is more responsive, and thus more adversely affected, than others by a changing environment.

But does it help answer our original question? Can genetics explain the recent rise in obesity rates—the "obesity crisis" we described in the first chapter? The answer, in short, is no. Why? Because it takes generations for genes to mutate.

A far more plausible explanation is that our genetic predispositions are interacting with a *changing* world, and that is causing nearly all groups to gain weight, but some groups—who are more genetically predisposed to weight gain—are gaining faster than others. So, while genes may predispose some people to gain weight, they will do so only if the environment allows for it. One way to think about it is that genes load the gun, but an obesity-promoting environment pulls the trigger.

Then Just Blame Mom
(You Know You Will Anyway)

So we can't blame the sudden upturn in obesity rates on a changing gene pool, but we can still blame Mom. She has always made a good target in the blame game, but there is actually a *bit* of validity to this argument. As discussed in Chapter 2, one factor behind the obesity epidemic is that Mom has backed away from the kitchen counter and headed toward the office. Home-cooked meals are now taking a backseat to the calorie-dense foods in the frozen-food section and at restaurants and fast-food venues. And when Mom and Dad aren't at home, it is much harder for them to monitor what their kids are eating. It's also less likely that kids will play outside after school if their parents are not around to watch them. As we've said, the TV does make a good babysitter.

Like it or not, the segment of the population that has traditionally been in charge of putting dinner on the table—wives and moms—are increasingly working outside of the home. The fraction of women aged 16 and over who were employed rose from 36 percent in 1960 to 48 percent in 1980 and to 58 percent in 2000.[17] Moreover, this rise in women working was not met by an army of new Mr. Moms. Men's work hours have remained fairly stable over the last several decades. In fact, from 1970 to 1990, the typical two-income family increased its annual hours worked by 600 hours—mostly thanks to more women entering the workforce.[18]

There is perhaps yet another reason to point the finger at Mom for the rise in obesity rates, at least in some small part. Thanks to greater opportunities for women in the workforce, many women are choosing to delay childbirth to pursue career and educational goals. The average age for first-time mothers in the United States increased by 2.6 years (from 24.6 to 27.2), between 1970 and 2000.[19] And, although the underlying causes remain unknown, there is some evidence that delayed childbirth increases the risk of having overweight children. One study found that the odds that a child will be overweight increase 14 percent with each five-year increase in the mother's age at pregnancy.[20]

So, go ahead, blame Mom. She's probably used to it anyway. But to be fair, she is only responding to a changing economy that increasingly values the fruits of her labor. Ultimately, it's a strong economy, increased opportunities, and higher-paying job prospects that have lured her out of the home and into the labor market. Sorry kids, but it's economics that is behind this one as well.

Mom has also often had a finger pointed at her for failing to breast-feed her babies—a practice that has been believed to significantly reduce the risk of obesity in children (by an estimated 30 percent).[21] Whether breast-feeding provides lifelong protection against obesity remains an open question. However, a recent Harvard study, published in May 2007 in the *International Journal of Obesity,* found that while breast-feeding has many benefits, it won't prevent a child from becoming obese as an adult.[22]

Even without this research, this is a clear case of a "busted myth." The "Breast Is Best" slogan, in tandem with other breast-feeding education, seems to have made its impact. Although one might suspect that more women in the workforce would lead to less breast-feeding, the data actually show the opposite. Recent data reveal that breast-feeding has been on the rise since the 1970s—rising from 22 percent to 73 percent in 2005.[23,24] So, clearly, reductions in breast-feeding cannot help explain the rise in obesity rates.

Blame the Meds

Once again, we start off a section by brandishing a basic economic principle: the theory of supply and demand. In this case, we—consumers—partly as a result of generous insurance coverage, have demanded newer and better drugs to treat a diverse array of medical conditions. In turn, suppliers—the drug companies—have jumped on the market opportunity. The total number of annual prescriptions for drugs in the United States now stands at about 3.5 billion (and that's just counting those filled in retail chain stores).[25] In 2004, more than 68 percent of Americans were taking at least one prescription drug.[26] In fact, the average American fills 12 prescriptions each year, roughly twice as many as were filled in the early 1990s.[27] Seniors fill an average of 15 to 20 prescriptions each year.[28]

But could the cure be making us fat? It turns out that we may need to look no further than our own medicine cabinets to explain at least some of the recent rise in obesity rates.

Many of the best-selling prescription drugs, including those that treat common conditions such as diabetes, mental illness, and arthritis, have one thing in common: Individuals who take these prescriptions are likely to experience weight gain—and not just a pound or two. For example, in exchange for the ability to have sex without having to worrying about getting pregnant or remembering to take a daily pill, women who use the injected contraceptive Depo-Provera may experience weight gain of up to 11 pounds over two years of use.[29]

Examples abound. Many of the beta blockers commonly prescribed for high blood pressure induce an average weight gain of over 2.5 pounds (1.2 kg).[30] Selective serotonin reuptake inhibitors, a common class of drugs used to treat depression (including the popular drugs Prozac, Zoloft, and Paxil), induce weight gain of up to 20 pounds.[31] Talk about depressing! What's more, these drugs are among the top prescriptions dispensed in the United States in recent years.[32] And it is not just prescription drugs that cause weight gain. Even over-the-counter antihistamines such as Benadryl may promote weight gain.[33]

Table 4.1 lists a handful of commonly prescribed drugs that can cause significant weight gain. However, this list is far from exhaustive. In fact, the popular web site, www.wrongdiagnosis.com, names almost 500 medicines (both prescription and over-the-counter) that include weight gain as a common side effect.[34] Although some of these drugs have been around for decades, most came into common use in the 1980s and 1990s, the same time that obesity rates were on the rise.

So, clearly, some drugs are causing some people to gain weight, but looking at the bigger picture, how large of a role have drugs played in America's obesity spike over the last few decades? We did some analysis to try to answer that question.

First, using nationally representative data from the Medical Expenditure Panel Survey, we compared the weight of individuals with select medical conditions to assess whether those taking medications to treat their conditions weighed more than those who were not. We found that those taking medications to treat diabetes, arthritis, mental health,

Table 4.1   Common Prescriptions with Weight Gain as a Side Effect

Antidepressants	Tricyclics	Gains of 1 to 9 pounds per month; minority of patients gain 33 to 44 pounds in 2 to 6 months[35]
	Selective serotonin reuptake inhibitors (SSRIs)	Average weight gain of between 15 and 20 pounds[36]
Antipsychotics	Conventional neuroleptics	Average gain of almost 9 pounds during course of 3-month therapy[37]
	Second-generation antipsychotics (SGA)	Average 10-pound gain while taking clozapine;[38] 94% of olanzapine users gained weight, and the average gain for long-term patients was 22 pounds over 1 year[39]
Diabetes Treatments	Thiazolidinediones	Up to 17-pound gain in an intensive 3-month treatment course[40]
	Sulfonylureas	Up to an 11-pound gain during 3 to 12 months of treatment[41]
Seizure Medication and Mood Stabilizers	Anticonvulsants	Gains of up to 40 pounds[42]
Steroid Hormones	Corticosteroids	4- to 28-pound gain in over 50% of polymyalgia rheumatica patients (those with severe aching and stiffness) taking for 1 year[43]

stroke, hypertension, cholesterol, injuries, pneumonia, and back problems did, in fact, weigh more than those who had these conditions but who were not being treated with medications. For the 21 percent of the population taking drugs to treat diabetes, arthritis (often treated with steroids), or a mental health condition, the difference in weight between those taking and not taking the drugs was most pronounced and statistically significant. These three conditions, as noted in Figure 4.1, are often treated with drugs known to cause weight gain as a side effect. So, although we cannot guarantee that all of the difference in weight between the two groups is a result of the drug side effects, these results are certainly consistent with the notion that drugs are causing people with these conditions to gain weight.

Under the assumption that all of the difference in weight between the two groups is due to the drugs, our analysis suggests that in the absence of weight gain as a side effect of prescription drugs, obesity rates would be about 6 percent lower than they are now. This means that without the use of these drugs, the obesity rate would drop from 32 percent to about 30 percent. This is not insignificant but it suggests that drug side effects are clearly not the root cause of the obesity epidemic.

So what's the take-home message? For one, consumers are demanding medications to treat a broad range of medical conditions, and the drug companies are responding to that demand by bringing a host of effective new drugs to market. Unfortunately, many individuals will gain weight as a result of taking these drugs. They could always stop taking the drugs. That would make them lose weight, but is it worth the cost (in terms of reduced health)?

Blame the Cigs (One More Theory Goes Up in Smoke)

Two of the most notable trends in public health over the past several decades are the reductions in smoking rates and the rise in rates of obesity. Smoking rates began to drop in the late 1960s after the surgeon general first warned of the dangers of smoking, and, as shown in Figure 4.1, continued to decrease throughout the 1980s and 1990s at the same time that obesity rates were on the rise. These trends have given rise to a puzzling question: Have public health efforts to reduce smoking rates in the United States inadvertently caused increases in rates of obesity?

There is substantial evidence that, at least in the short term, smoking and obesity are not independent. Reductions in smoking and/or quitting altogether often result in increased food consumption and metabolic changes that promote weight gain.[44] As a result, weight gain is an often unwanted side effect of quitting smoking. The 1990 Surgeon General's Report, *The Health Consequences of Smoking Cessation,* concluded that the average weight gain after smoking cessation was about five pounds.[45] One paper suggests that increases in cigarette prices as a result of increased excise taxes and other factors are responsible for as much as 20 percent of the growth in BMI during the past two decades.[46] As a result, the authors argue that rising obesity rates are an unintended consequence of the success of the antismoking movement. Researchers with the Centers for Disease Control and Prevention (CDC) have echoed these sentiments.[47]

Colleagues and I were skeptical that cigarette price increases and resulting reductions in smoking rates could account for such a large percentage of the rise in obesity rates, so we reestimated the original analyses, while including slightly more recent data and a few other statistical improvements. We found that, between 1981 and 2002, the rise in cigarette prices and tobacco control spending are responsible for about 12.5 percent of the increase in BMI among former smokers, a nontrivial

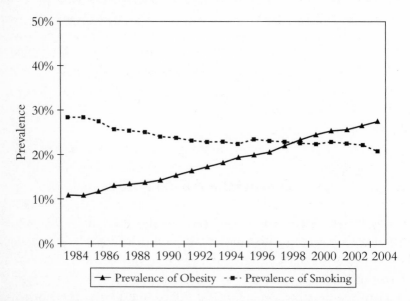

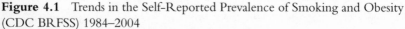

Figure 4.1 Trends in the Self-Reported Prevalence of Smoking and Obesity (CDC BRFSS) 1984–2004

SOURCE: Author calculations based on data from CDC's BRFSS data 1984–2004.

amount, but only 4 percent or less of the increase in BMI for the general population, including smokers and nonsmokers. We find this result much more believable.

Further, despite the positive relationship between cigarette consumption and BMI among former smokers, because smokers tend to weigh less than nonsmokers to start out with, it is not clear whether this weight gain is large enough to move them into the obese range. If reductions in smoking rates were responsible for a substantial share of the rise in rates of obesity, we would expect to see an increasing percentage of the obese population consisting of former smokers. That is not the case. In 1984, 42 percent of obese individuals were former smokers. This figure has changed only slightly in the last 20 years. Although obesity rates are rising, the proportion of obese individuals that consists of current, former, and never-smokers has remained virtually unchanged.

Finally, perhaps the most telling sign that falling cigarette consumption is not responsible for rising obesity rates comes from youth. As noted in Chapter 1, since the mid-1970s, the prevalence of overweight and obesity among adults has roughly doubled, from 15 percent to 33 percent. However, this is smaller than the increase seen for young children, who are least likely to be impacted by cigarette taxes and tobacco control funding. For children aged 2 to 5 and 6 to 11 years old, who are too young to be smoking cigarettes (at least, I certainly hope so), the prevalence of overweight nearly tripled, from 5 percent to 14 percent, and 7 percent to 19 percent, respectively. Cumulatively, these findings suggest that other factors are largely responsible for the rise in obesity rates.

Blame the All-Nighter

Americans are sleeping less than ever. So this probably means we are spending that much more time burning off calories and losing weight. Right? Wrong. Studies show that less sleep, in fact, equals more weight gain.[48,49] Researchers have found that sleep deprivation leads to an increased appetite, slower metabolism, and a higher incidence of type 2 diabetes (because the body experiences a decrease in glucose tolerance).[50–52]

On average, Americans sleep about an hour less per day than they did in the 1970s—a factor that may be partly responsible for the rise in obesity rates.[53] One study found that a person getting only six hours of sleep on average is 23 percent more likely to be obese than an individual who sleeps seven to eight hours a night. If that figure drops down to five hours a night, the person is twice as likely to be obese. A person accruing only four hours a night is a whopping 73 percent more likely to be obese.[54]

But why are we sleeping less? Katie Couric, formerly of *Today*, reported that our lack of sleep could be a "product of a 24/7, over-stimulated and over-scheduled lifestyle."[55] I think another likely answer (for those people who don't have a new baby in the house on top of an aggressive schedule to write a book) is the appeal of staying up late watching some fabulous show on a really crisp-looking television. In fact, those with a television in the bedroom have been shown to stay up later and sleep less.[56]

But if it's not watching television, it is likely that we are staying up late either working or playing on the computer or some other new electronic device. A *Forbes* article reported that according to therapists and psychologists, "around-the-clock access to the office often results in fatigue, a lack of intimacy, resentment, increased conflict, and even premature career burnout."[57]

So, if staying up late is also contributing to making us fat, the underlying cause is likely to be those technological advancements that lure us to burn the midnight oil (instead of calories).

Blame the Air Conditioner (Not Cool)

It has been suggested that your air-conditioning unit may be fattening. Several studies indicate that our increased use of central air is actually slowing our metabolic rate.[58] One of the jobs of our metabolism is to regulate the temperature in our bodies, so when we are hot or cold, our metabolism has to go into overdrive. But when the temperature around us is between roughly 72 and 78 degrees (the thermoneutral zone), our metabolism no longer has to work as hard. Studies find that both animals and people consume more food in a thermoneutral zone and eat less when too hot or too cold.[59] Knowledge of this fact is even used in raising livestock, where temperature control is used to help increase weight gain in animals.[60]

In the United States, air-conditioning prevalence has increased substantially since the 1970s, particularly in the South (homes with central air conditioning increased from 37 percent in 1978 to 70 percent in 1997, while the prevalence of homes without any air conditioning decreased from 26 percent to 7 percent).[61]

Although it is true that, no matter how hot it is outside, Uncle Al's house is always freezing in the summer, I remain unconvinced that we'd experience much of a slim-down effect if we turned off the air conditioners and switched on the fans.

Blame Pollution (It's a Dirty Business)

Pollution is another long shot in the obesity blame game.[62] Technology has provided us with many pesticides, plasticizers, chemicals, synthetics, and flame-retardant materials—all endocrine disruptors. For those of us who didn't major in biology (and that includes me), an endocrine disruptor is any synthetic chemical that mimics or blocks hormones and disrupts the body's normal functions when absorbed.

Many chemicals are known human endocrine disruptors:

- Diethylstilbestrol (DES; the drug initially prescribed to prevent miscarriage).
- Pentabromodiphenyl ether (PBDE; a chemical used to treat fabrics to make them flame retardant).
- Dioxin (a by-product of coal-fired utilities, metal salting, and diesel trucks).
- Polychlorinated biphenyls (PCBs; used in many applications including hydraulic fluids, lubricating and cutting oils, and as additives in pesticides, paints, carbonless copy paper, adhesives, sealants, plastics, and reactive flame retardants).
- Dichlorodiphenyltrichloroethane (DDT) and other pesticides.
- Many other pesticides and plasticizers are suspected of being endocrine disruptors based on limited animal tests.

These chemical compounds have been shown to impact hormones, such as estrogen, to induce a "more fatty body composition" by altering the body's use of nutrients.[63] One reason is that estrogens regulate the size of adipocytes (fat cells) in adult humans and animals.[64] And if their increased presence in the food chain is any indication,[65] then there is reason to believe that their presence in humans is on the rise as well. In fact, one study found that the PBDE concentration in Swedish women's breast milk has almost doubled every five years since 1972.[66]

Still, with the evidence as it now stands, it's a tough sell to name pollution as a major player or, for that matter, even a minor player in the obesity blame game.

Blame That Nasty "Fat Bug"

The next time someone sneezes or coughs your way, you might not just want to worry about catching their runny nose, stuffy head, and fever—perhaps you should also worry about catching their obesity. This may sound surprising, but if you read the dense, nine-page spread in the *New York Times Magazine* last summer, you would have spent a few good hours reading about some new and little-known research being done in the area of *infectobesity* (the term that Dr. Nikhil V. Dhurandhar coined for contagious "fat").[67] The article covered the fascinating work of two scientists: Dhurandhar and Dr. Jeffrey Gordon.

There is now a growing interest in finding viral and bacterial agents that cause (and can potentially cure) obesity in humans. The goal? To either find a way to inoculate ourselves against them or cure ourselves if we've already caught the obesity bug.

Dhurandhar made a name for himself in obesity research when he noticed something strange about a plague that was killing chickens in India. Although the chickens were dying of infection, they weren't wasting away, they were actually gaining weight (and incidentally maintaining low cholesterol and triglyceride levels). Dhurandhar believes this weight gain is the result of a virus that is also contagious to humans. In fact, Dhurandhar found that the people he studied who carried antibodies for the chicken virus weighed an average of 33 pounds more than those who did not carry the antibody. The antibody-carrying individuals also exhibited the same low cholesterol and triglyceride levels as the infected chickens.

These findings brought him to the United States in search of a lab to conduct further research. When our government would not allow him to import the virus from India, Dhurandhar was able to find similar occurrences using several strains of adenoviruses—the "bugs" responsible for all sorts of nagging coughs, colds, and flus.

He has since extended his research to examine antibodies for these adenoviruses in humans. In one study, he looked at 502 volunteers from around the country, of which 360 were obese, and examined them for the presence of an antibody to the virus. Among obese subjects, 30 percent had them; among those who were not obese, only 11 percent had them. Another study with twins revealed similar findings. Out of 90 pairs of twins, those who had been infected with the virus were heavier (an average of 29.6 percent body fat compared to 27.5 percent).

Based on his studies, several pharmaceutical companies are racing to produce a "fat vaccine." However, before you go out and get inoculated, we should point out that in his studies, obesity was associated with low cholesterol and low triglyceride levels. For most obese individuals, their increasing weight results in higher values for both. Moreover, even in his studies, many obese individuals did not test positive for the antibodies, and some of those who had the antibodies were thin. Furthermore, even *if* the association proves accurate, it is not clear whether individuals get the virus and then gain weight as a result, or whether those who weigh more might be more susceptible to the virus. So far, I remain skeptical.

At the same time that Dr. Dhurandhar was looking to viruses to help explain the obesity crisis, Dr. Jeffrey Gordon had a gut instinct that took his obesity research in another direction.

In fact, he became captivated with the human gut or, more specifically, the wonderland of microorganisms our guts contain. Of the multitrillion cells in each of our bodies, Gordon estimates that only 1 in 10 is human—the rest are microscopic organisms like fungi or bacteria. These organisms are everywhere, on every surface of our bodies, but the vast majority call our guts home. We start off in the womb "germ" free, but right from our trek down the birth canal, we begin to adopt many of these microbes from our mother. "Microbes colonize our body surfaces from the moment of our birth," Gordon said in the *New York Times Magazine* article. "They are with us throughout our lives, and at the moment of our death they consume us."

Good thing, too. It may sound like science fiction, but in truth, without these microbes in our bodies, we would be unable to perform many of the tasks necessary for life (i.e., creating the capillaries that line our intestines or producing the enzymes that metabolize cholesterol). But it was the fact that these bacteria assist so much with digestion that caught Gordon's attention. Gut flora help extract calories from the food we eat and help store those calories in fat cells for later use. Gordon wondered why it was possible that two people could eat the exact same foods and engage in the exact same activities yet have two very different weights, and he began to speculate that these microorganisms might be the answer.

When looking at mice that were raised with no microflora in a highly sterile environment, he found they had 60 percent less fat than ordinary mice. Since then, he and fellow researchers have found several specific microbes that are overachievers in that they do an even better job than most of extracting nutrients from food. When these were implanted into mice without other microbes, the mice instantly began to gain weight, and when they were removed, their weight fell.

This is a promising area of research and one that the National Institutes of Health (NIH) believes worthy of government funding. In fact, they have funded several large grants to study this very issue. It is certainly possible that, as with the chicken virus, differences in gut flora may account for some variation in weight across populations and even across individuals and may someday provide inroads to a cure for at least some forms of obesity.

But getting back to the original question: Does gut flora help explain the recent rise in obesity? Once again, I'd say probably not. People have had gut flora since the beginning of humankind. Unless some new research comes out that finds that gut flora has fundamentally changed in the past few decades, it's probably safe to say that gut flora is an intriguing aspect in the obesity blame game and may also partly explain why some people weigh more than others, but it is unlikely to be a culprit in the recent upswing.

It's the Economy, Stupid

Some of these theories have promise, while some seem fairly off the mark. But after considering all of the evidence, I'm sticking to the story we rolled out in Chapters 2 and 3. I have yet to see a hypothesis that does a better job of explaining what's behind the sudden escalation in obesity rates than the simple fact that technological and economic advancements have created an obesity-inducing environment. These advancements (although some of you may disagree with the term) have made it easier and cheaper to eat lots of tasty high-calorie foods, and made it more difficult to burn off those extra calories.

However, as discussed in this chapter, the story does not end there. The advancing economy has given us increased access to other products, including new drugs and technologies, which may also promote weight gain, although not in the conventional manner discussed in Chapters 2 and 3. In contrast, other new drugs and devices work to counteract the adverse health effects that obesity promotes. Yet, as we discuss in the following chapter, these too may be causing people to gain weight.

Chapter 5

Beware: Moral Hazard

One of my best childhood friends, we'll call him Marc, has never been one to plan for the future (as an example, he recently told me that he had unprotected sex with the head of a local Planned Parenthood chapter). Marc's a spur-of-the-moment kind of guy. This carefree attitude is part of why he is so much fun to hang out with, but it also explains why, at age 37, he still lives with his parents.

Marc is anything but obese. In fact, whereas I spent most of the past 20 years either in graduate school or working at a desk job, Marc could be found on mountain bike trails, ski slopes, or surfing at the Jersey shore (to the extent one can really surf in New Jersey). He's in great shape and appears to be one of the happier people you'll ever meet, in spite of having to shack up with the rents.

So why is Marc relevant to this book? Well, it harkens back to a conversation I had with him some years back that really stuck with me. At that time, I was slogging my way through my economics dissertation, and looking for some vicarious fun, I asked Marc if he had been doing any extreme snowboarding of late. He said that he had been "really tearing it up," but that since he recently changed his job (Marc has had more jobs than anyone I've ever met) and did not yet have health insurance benefits, he was "playing it safe" until his insurance kicked in.

Marc didn't know it, but what he was describing is what economists refer to as moral hazard. Usually discussed in the context of insurance, the idea is that the act of obtaining insurance sometimes results in individuals being less careful to protect the insured product, which in this case, is Marc himself. If Marc is showing this kind of rational behavior, then you can bet lots of others are as well. After all, most 37-year-olds don't still live with their parents (sorry to rub it in, Marc).

Although the term connotes immoral behavior on Marc's part, and it is true that Marc has done lots of things his mother would not be proud of (including the tryst with the woman from Planned Parenthood), in this case, there really is nothing immoral about it. Marc is merely changing his behavior because of the increase in costs (to him) that would result from an injury.

For example, say you forgot to pay your car insurance and lost your coverage for a few days while the situation was being rectified. Do you imagine you might drive with a little more care? Or perhaps you'd just park the car altogether until your insurance was reinstated?

Moral hazard, in the context of insurance markets, has been studied extensively. There is overwhelming evidence that moral hazard exists in a number of forms. For example, research tells us that people who have health insurance use more health services than people who do not have insurance. No surprise there, right? Let's look at a few other examples of moral hazard at work:

- In Sweden, the number of days that a worker could receive sick pay was reduced. The result? Fewer sick days.[1]
- Farmers who purchase crop insurance have been shown to engage in riskier growing practices.[2]
- One study found that when banks were forced to share in the financial burden of deposit insurance, it reduced much of their risk-taking behavior, including providing risky loans to individuals with poor credit.[3]

These studies uncover a basic economic theory (which happens to make good common sense): When costs go down, as a result of insurance or other causes, many people will change their behavior in response.

So what does moral hazard have to do with rising rates of obesity in America? Here are two hypotheses.

The first is this: America has more obesity, at least in part, because the financial costs of obesity *to the insured individual* went down after the introduction of programs like Medicare and Medicaid. I'm not sure I buy into this one, but we'll explore the evidence in the next section.

Second, and this one I find much more credible, is that over the past few decades, partly as a result of the Medicare and Medicaid programs as well as generous private insurance coverage, there has been a tremendous increase in the medical, pharmacological, and surgical treatments available for obesity-related diseases and even for obesity itself. So it may be that people are eating more and exercising less, in part, because the consequence—namely, obesity—is no longer so detrimental to their health.

Just Bill My Health Insurance

So let's take a closer look at the first hypothesis: that individuals are less inclined to watch their diet and to exercise because they feel cushioned by their health insurance benefits (in that they have to pay fewer out-of-pocket costs for any adverse health events that might result from their excess weight). It is true that not long after the Social Security Act of 1965 created Medicare and outlined legislation for states' Medicaid programs, obesity rates began to dramatically increase. But this timing could, of course, be purely coincidental.

In reality, testing the impact that health insurance has on Americans' diet and exercise choices is a difficult question to answer empirically. The challenge is that having health insurance is correlated with so many other factors, including education and income, which might also help explain differences in obesity rates across groups. For example, obesity rates for individuals on Medicaid, which has almost no cost sharing, are twice as high as rates for individuals with private insurance, which typically includes premiums, deductibles, and copayments.

On the surface, this certainly seems to support the theory that Medicaid recipients are less likely to watch their weight because they face lower copayments and deductibles than those enrolled in most private insurance plans. However, Medicaid recipients are also likely to have less money. And, as we discussed in Chapter 2, people on a tight budget, like my cousin Carl, are more likely to eat the types of foods that are obesity promoting. This is not because they have greater access to low-cost insurance; it is because they have less money to spend on food. So, although consistent with the moral hazard story, higher rates of obesity for Medicaid recipients are certainly not proof of moral hazard.

What's the picture like for those with private insurance? Again, there is some evidence that supports the moral hazard story. Using data from the 2002–2004 Medical Expenditure Panel Survey (MEPS), we compared the odds of being obese as a function of having purchased private-sector health insurance. We limited the sample to individuals who were not enrolled in Medicare or Medicaid, and adjusted the analyses to control for differences in age, race, and education.

We found that the odds of being obese were 12.5 percent greater for men with health insurance than for men without health insurance. This result is consistent with a moral hazard story suggesting that men make less effort to control their weight after they purchase private health insurance. However, it is unclear whether having insurance is causing men to gain weight or whether obese men are more likely to buy health insurance. Moreover, no significant effect was found for women. So this result, too, provides little evidence to support the idea that health insurance, by lowering the out-of-pocket costs of poor health, is *directly* making people gain weight.

Still with me? Okay, on to Medicare. There is one empirical paper that addresses whether Medicare induces moral hazard on the part of current and future beneficiaries.[4] Although the author does not focus on weight specifically, he found that Medicare induces increases in medical utilization (another form of moral hazard that we mentioned earlier) and small levels of moral hazard in alcohol consumption, smoking, and exercise among the beneficiaries. But he finds no evidence to suggest that individuals younger than age 65 are reducing their exercise levels in anticipation of entering the program and receiving the subsidized health benefits.

Based on these results, Medicare may generate some degree of moral hazard once it is obtained, but it does not appear that younger populations are gaining weight in anticipation of Medicare's covering their future medical bills.

Here's yet another test of the moral hazard question. Currently, 46 states have passed laws mandating that health insurance providers cover diabetes treatment as part of their basic coverage. However, because not all of these states implemented the laws at the same time, these laws provide a natural experiment to test the impact of moral hazard. If insurance coverage is resulting in moral hazard, then we would expect to see higher growth rates in obesity among individuals with diabetes in states where the mandate is in effect.

This is exactly what researchers Klick and Stratman attempted to uncover.[5] They ran a series of models and discovered that the mandates may have increased BMI among those with diabetes by as much as 10 percent. They concluded that: "The true causal effect of passing diabetes mandates is to generate a moral hazard such that diabetics rely more on medical treatments for their disease than on improvements in their diets or exercise patterns." (By the way, someone should tell them that the term *diabetic* is no longer politically correct.)

This paper supports the moral hazard argument, but I would be more convinced if I knew that those with diabetes were actually aware of the state mandates or the extent to which coverage differed in states with and without the mandates.

So, although I remain skeptical, there is limited evidence that supports the hypothesis that more generous insurance coverage may directly increase rates of obesity by decreasing the likelihood that individuals will engage in preventive activities (i.e., diet and exercise). However, it is the indirect effect of health insurance that has likely played a larger role in promoting increased rates of obesity. This is the effect that new medicines and devices, largely funded by health insurance, may have on individuals' diet and exercise choices.

Because health insurance lowers the out-of-pocket costs of care, insured individuals use more health services than they would otherwise—a finding well documented in the economics literature.[6–10] This too, as we mentioned earlier, is basic economics. As the out-of-pocket costs of health services go down, the amount of health services demanded by consumers goes up, and vice versa. My good friend Marc offered the perfect example. Not only does he change his behavior during periods of being uninsured, but he also avoids treatment for his many ailments until his insurance kicks back in. One way to look at it is that he waits until the treatment goes on sale before he makes his purchase.

This form of moral hazard can add up. For example, authors of the Rand Health Insurance Experiment, one of the seminal studies on the impact of private health insurance, enrolled families into health insurance plans with different copayments and deductibles and compared utilization across families.[11] The researchers found that health insurance was directly responsible for about 10 percent of the sevenfold increase in health care expenditures after World War II. Indirectly, however, by promoting new technologies, insurance may have been responsible for a much greater portion of the rise in health expenditures and, likely, some of the rise in obesity rates.

Health insurance creates incentives for suppliers of health services to provide services that they know are likely to be reimbursed. In fact, the period after the introduction of Medicare and Medicaid was known as the Medical Arms Race, as suppliers of health services raced to provide new treatments that they knew would be reimbursed at favorable coverage amounts. This is not to say that many of these technologies might not have been introduced in the absence of insurance, but insurance certainly increased the pace at which these technologies were introduced and became commonly used.

So insurance may have had a small effect on rising obesity rates as a result of lowering the out-of-pocket costs of medical care. However, it may be that it is not these lower out-of-pocket costs that are promoting obesity, but that, thanks to insurance and its impact on promoting advances in medical technology, obesity is no longer as much of a health problem as it was in decades past. This is due, in large part, to the many new treatments that are better able to control the adverse health consequences of obesity-related diseases, and increasingly, of obesity itself.

Is Obesity as Bad as It Used to Be?

Now we move on to my second hypothesis: Are individuals less inclined to watch their diet and exercise because they feel cushioned by new and improved medical treatments?

To answer this question, we need to first take one step back and ask this: Are today's obese individuals healthier than they were in decades past?

This was the question taken up by a recent article published in the *Journal of the American Medical Association* by Gregg and colleagues.[12] The authors of the study noted that while obesity rates have been on the rise, mortality rates from ischemic heart disease as well as levels of key cardiovascular disease (CVD) risk factors have been declining. It is certainly possible that these declines have been driven by reductions in smoking rates or other causes, and that they would have been even larger in the absence of the rise in obesity rates. But it is also possible that obesity has become less of a health problem than it once was, and therefore, even though obesity rates are on the rise, the health consequences resulting from obesity have become less severe.

Gregg used data from nationally representative health surveys that spanned the past 40 years. In each wave of the data they compared cardiovascular disease risk factors between normal-weight and obese individuals. If obesity is no longer as bad for one's health as it once was, then the differences in risk factors across body mass index (BMI) groups should be narrowing over time.

Here's the result: Between 1960 and 2000, the prevalence of high cholesterol, high blood pressure, and smoking levels decreased. However, these decreases were not equal across BMI groups. Reductions in the prevalence of high cholesterol were greater for overweight and obese individuals than for normal-weight individuals. In the early survey waves, obese people had more than a 9- to 12-percentage-point higher prevalence of high cholesterol than normal-weight people, but by 2000, this difference was less than 3 percentage points. Prevalence of high blood pressure also declined more among obese individuals, although the differences were less pronounced. Diabetes prevalence was the notable exception; it increased among all BMI groups.

The authors also found that among today's obese population, the prevalence of high cholesterol, high blood pressure, and smoking are now 21, 18, and 12 percentage points lower, respectively, than among obese individuals 30 to 40 years ago. In fact, obese individuals today have better cardiovascular disease risk factor profiles than normal-weight individuals had 30 years ago.

So, to get back to the question we posed at the beginning of the section, indeed, the health costs of obesity appear to have been dramatically reduced. Given this result, and the fact that it is becoming increasingly costly to diet and exercise, it is no wonder that people are gaining weight. After all, on the surface at least, these results make it seem hardly worth the effort to try and remain thin.

Just Take a Pill or Get a Procedure

What is driving this surge in improved health profiles for obese individuals? The answer, as you might have guessed, is a dramatic improvement in drugs and devices.

For example, in their article, Gregg and colleagues noted that the proportion of the overall population taking medication for high cholesterol and high blood pressure increased among all BMI groups; however, this increase was even larger among obese individuals. The prevalence of treatment for high cholesterol increased from 2.2 percent to 4 percent for normal-weight individuals over the past several decades, whereas the increase was much larger for obese individuals, from 3.5 percent to 9.2 percent. The percentage of normal-weight individuals being treated for high blood pressure rose from 5 percent to 8 percent, while that same figure for obese individuals more than doubled from 11 percent to 28 percent.[13]

As Table 5.1 shows, many drugs have been introduced over the past 40 years that effectively treat cholesterol, blood pressure, and other risk factors and diseases that obesity promotes. Moreover, Americans, both obese and nonobese, are increasingly relying on these drugs to prevent and control cardiovascular disease risk factors and other complications of obesity.

The table reveals that of the top 25 most prescribed drugs on the market today, 10 of them target diseases or risk factors promoted by obesity, and the majority of these drugs were not available a few decades back. This provides further evidence that the health toll imposed by obesity has continued to decline as a result of the introduction of these drugs. While in the past, diet, exercise, and weight loss might have been the primary treatment to help control these risk factors; today, one

Table 5.1 Prescription Drugs Targeting Obesity-Related Risk Factors and Diseases

Generic Drug Name (Brand Name)	Indication	FDA Approval Date	Ranking Based on Number of Prescriptions Filled
Atorvastatin (Lipitor)	Hypercholesterolemia (high cholesterol)	1996	2
Atenolol	Hypertension	1981	4
Lisinopril	Hypertension	1987	6
Hydrochlorothiazide	Hypertension	1963	7
Furosemide	Hypertension	1968	8
Amlodipine besylate (Norvasc)	Hypertension	1992	11
Metoprolol succinate (Toprol XL)	Angina pectoris, hypertension, myocardial infarction	1978	14
Simvastatin (Zocor)	Hypercholesterolemia	1991	17
Hydrochlorothiazide; triamterene	Hypertension	1981	20
Metformin (Glucophage)	Diabetes mellitus	1994	23

SOURCE: www.mosbysdrugconsult.com/DrugConsult/Top_200/.

merely has to take a pill. Many individuals, including Uncle Al, feel that diet and exercise are optional.

Moreover, drugs are only one of the many options available to treat those who suffer from complications of obesity-related diseases or risk factors. For example, during a recent visit from my dad, he pointed out that he and a majority of his friends (he actually only has three) have undergone a surgical procedure known as a cardiac catheterization (or "heart cath") to unclog arteries around the heart. Even though Dad is an exercise fiend, he had one artery that was 90 percent blocked.

And Dad and his friends are hardly alone. Last year, there were over 1.5 million procedures performed in the United States aimed at opening up clogged arteries (percutaneous transluminal coronary angioplasty [PTCA], and other catheterizations with or without stents). As my dad proudly pointed out, his procedure required only one night in the hospital. He was back doing his full exercise routine in a matter of days. Just think how quickly Uncle Al could be back at the buffet!

And why not hit the buffet? It seems like one night in the hospital to have your pipes cleaned plus taking a few pills may be just as effective, if not more effective, in reducing the risk of major health problems as diet, exercise, and weight loss.

In fact, the dirty truth for obese individuals like Uncle Al is that medications are more effective in controlling cardiovascular disease risk factors than losing weight. For example, in a comprehensive review of the literature:

- Avenell and colleagues found that 10 kilograms of weight-loss reduce glucose levels by 0.73 mg/dL.[14] Glucophage, on the other hand, reduces glucose levels by 53.0 mg/dL.[15]
- Aucott et al. found that the same 10-kg weight loss results in reductions of systolic blood pressure by 6 mmHg and reductions in diastolic blood pressure by 4.6 mmHg.[16] Losartan and atenolol trumped these numbers. They showed systolic reductions of 30.2 and 29.1 mmHg and diastolic reductions of 16.6 and 16.8 mmHg, respectively.[17]
- And finally, Poobalan et al. showed that 10-kg weight loss reduces total cholesterol by 8.9 mg/dL, low-density lipoprotein (LDL) cholesterol by 7.8 mg/dL, and triglycerides by 13.3 mg/dL.[18] Atorvastatin blows that away; it shows reductions in total cholesterol of 83 mg/dL, a reduction of 72 mg/dL for LDL cholesterol, and 77 mg/dL for triglycerides. And unlike weight loss, it slightly raises the good cholesterol by 1 mg/dL (or 2%).[19]

Of course, never having gained the weight would have provided the best risk profile, but for the one third of the population that is already obese, that ship has already sailed. For many obese individuals, it certainly appears that taking a few pills and perhaps getting a procedure or two are the preferred options over engaging in an increasingly difficult-to-sustain diet and exercise regimen. Of course, taking the pills *and* losing weight would provide the most health benefit. But for many Americans, and certainly for Uncle Al, the added value of diet and exercise beyond what is achieved from the drugs seems hardly worth the effort.

So this begs the question: With our ever-advancing modern medicine there helping to save the day (at least for many people—certainly not all), are government and the media blowing the magnitude of the "obesity crisis" out of proportion? Although there can be no denying that Americans—and much of the world, for that matter—are seeing skyrocketing numbers on their scales, is it really a "crisis?" Given that new drugs and technologies have been, and will continue to be, developed to cure the diseases that obesity promotes, why are lawmakers, consumer advocates, school boards, the media, obesity researchers, and a good part of the rest of the free world (certainly including Dad) making such a fuss over our growing waistlines? Are we making a mountain out of a molehill?

We begin to hit on these questions in the next chapter.

Chapter 6

So We're Fat—
Who Cares?

The first half of this book touched on the scope of the obesity epidemic and detailed its causes. Let's quickly revisit some of the key facts. First of all, Uncle Al and about 80 million other Americans are overweight or obese. But what's remarkable about the obesity epidemic is not just the volume of Americans who have tipped out of the normal body mass index (BMI) range—it's the velocity at which we're doing it.

Second, unless you buy into the chicken virus story, most people got that way largely because of economics. In fact, our ballooning weight is a product of our economic and technological success. As we explored in depth in Chapters 2 and 3, because of declining food costs and increasing usage of technology, our environment has changed in such a way that we're eating more calories and burning off less. Third, as we discussed in Chapter 5, for an obese individual, the financial and health costs associated with gaining extra pounds has gone down, thanks to the cushion that health insurance coverage and vastly improved medical treatments provide.

The net result: rapid weight gain.

Now, in the second half of the book, we will delve into the implications of this rapid weight gain—and attempt to untangle difficult issues like:

- How big a problem is the obesity epidemic (really)? Is it really even a problem at all?
- Does the rise in obesity justify private and government efforts to try to encourage individuals to change their diet and physical activity patterns?
- If so, how far should (or even can) industry and government go?

Whereas the answers to some of these questions may seem obvious, many, it turns out, at least in the eyes of economists, are more complicated than you might think. So bear with me as I begin to take you down a somewhat twisted chain of arguments and counterarguments to unravel the intricacies of these issues. To begin, let's first turn to, well, who else—Uncle Al.

Is Uncle Al Overweight?

Is Uncle Al overweight? What? What a question! In Chapter 1, we clearly showed that based on BMI guidelines, Uncle Al would be classified as obese. We also documented some of the health problems that Uncle Al is experiencing, most of them, if not all of them, as a result of his extra weight and sedentary lifestyle. On top of diabetes, Uncle Al has developed hypertension (high blood pressure) and high cholesterol, and he suffers from aches and pains in his lower back.

So how could I even question whether Uncle Al is overweight? Didn't I already clearly indicate that he is?

Ahhh, but he's overweight based on government standards. What about the standards that Uncle Al sets for himself?

Let's consider a different question. Suppose at age 25, Uncle Al had the option of choosing to die at age 75 or at age 80. However, choosing age 80 would have required him to make a lifelong commitment to regular exercise and a restricted diet. I suspect he would have chosen age 75 and all the tasty fattening food and limited physical activity that accompanies this decision. Because I try very hard to avoid offending Uncle Al, I have not come out and asked him directly. But the truth is that I don't need to ask. Uncle Al has shown us his choice. He could have led a life that included a more restrictive diet and exercise regimen, but he chose not to.

Certainly, Uncle Al should care about the fact that his excess weight increases his risk of disease and premature death. In reality, I'm sure he does care. But the truth is that Uncle Al cares about lots of other things, too. He cares about being rich, for example. In fact, he spent much of his adult life working his ass off (or perhaps on) at the law firm to attain that goal. This left little time for exercise other than his occasional Sunday golf outings. Uncle Al also cares about fine dining. He and my aunt eat many of their meals at the country club, at restaurants, or order prepared meals to eat at home. As we learned in Chapter 2, these meals are much higher in added sugars, added fats, and calories than home-cooked meals. After all, that's why they taste so good.

So, for Uncle Al, and perhaps for the majority of overweight adults, it is not that they don't care about being overweight; it is that the change in behavior required to lose the weight and keep it off is just too great (and is getting greater all the time).

As noted in Chapter 3, Uncle Al has at various times made efforts to reduce his weight and improve his health. And while these may have been effective at controlling his weight for a while, Uncle Al, like many of us, found that the effort required to fully offset the increase in weight was just too much. After all, Uncle Al's primary goal in life is not to be as skinny as my dad or to live as long as possible. He appears willing to live with some extra pounds and the adverse health risks that might come along with it in exchange for an increased quality of life, which by Uncle Al's definition includes many activities that are obesity promoting. Also, as we talked about in Chapter 5, Uncle Al's generous health insurance gives him afford-able access to new drugs and advanced medical technology, which is a nice cushion to fall back on when those pesky risk factors flare up.

So given these considerations, maybe Uncle Al is not overweight after all. In fact, perhaps he's at his optimum weight once he considers the costs and benefits of what is required to weigh less.

The story of Uncle Al may suggest that obesity is a consequence of gluttony. After all, one does not need all that money or excess. But consider the case of my overweight Cousin Carl. He's a minimum-wage kind of guy. He works long hours and eats out a lot, too. However, he needs to work the extra hours just to pay rent, and that leaves him with little time to exercise. Moreover, most of his dining occurs in fast-food restaurants because he can get a high-calorie meal for pennies on the dollar. Barring a lucky lottery ticket (or a nice inheritance from Uncle Al), I can't imagine him ever being rich, but he, too, is making choices that are leading to excess weight, albeit for very different reasons. So perhaps he's at his optimum weight as well.

And what about me? Focusing on the economics of obesity has renewed my interest in being healthy. Yet, I willingly spend 50-plus hours per week sitting in my office chair banging away on the computer and burning off almost no energy, even though I know it is doing nothing to improve my health.

As we discussed in Chapter 3, people whose work is largely conducted while sitting behind a desk, such as secretaries, lawyers, teachers, and health economists, get very little physical activity during the day. Secretaries, for example, log an average of 4,327 steps, less than half of the often-recommended goal of 10,000 steps a day for optimal health.[1] Teachers get 4,726 steps, lawyers 5,062, and even police officers average only 5,336 steps per day (and who knows how many donuts)—all about the same as I get on days that I do not go out for a run. Letter carriers, by the way, average nearly 19,000 steps per day. Not too shabby.

I sometimes think how great it would be to quit my job and find a more active occupation, but I realize that would entail a huge financial sacrifice that I, and especially the lovely Mrs. Finkelstein, am not prepared to make. What if I came home one day and said, "Hey honey, I've got great news, I quit my job today, but I got hired picking strawberries at Jean's Berry Patch (which, by the way, has great strawberries). I know I'm only making minimum wage, and we'll need to move out of our house in the next few months and sell your new minivan (and the automatic trash can), and God forbid, you might have to get a job, but just think of the health benefits. . . ." That's a conversation that we both hope never happens.

C'mon Now, We're Only Utility Maximizing

Now let's put that same picture into economic terms. Economists would say that Uncle Al, Cousin Carl, and I are not making bad choices about diet and exercise. In fact, we are all utility maximizing. That means that given all the possible choices we could be making, we are choosing those options that make us best off (i.e., the ones that give us the most utility).

These choices concerning how much to eat, exercise, work, and so on are not necessarily made with perfect information or foresight, nor are they made without constraints. In fact, our choices are constrained in many ways, but perhaps the two most binding constraints are time and money.

For Uncle Al, time is the more important constraint. With unlimited time, he would gladly play more golf and get additional exercise, but once he made the choice to work at the law firm, that left scarce time for leisure activities, and exercise had to compete against all the other options available to him. For Cousin Carl, time remains a major constraint, but he also has a much tighter budget constraint than Uncle Al. It is this tight budget that encourages him to spend far less money on food, even though he knows this decision means he is not eating as healthily as he could be. Regardless, both Uncle Al and Cousin Carl are utility maximizers, as am I and most of the rest of us, no matter what our weight happens to be.

In economic terms, we all make choices to maximize our utility given our constraints. However, the factors that we derive utility from (i.e., our preferences) vary from person to person, as do our constraints. For example, Uncle Al loves to play golf. I hate golf, but I like to jog and play basketball. Whereas Uncle Al sometimes chooses to play golf in his free time, running is now my physical activity of choice. Although I like basketball more than running (i.e., I get greater utility from an hour of basketball than an hour of running), I choose running because I can get it done in 30 minutes, whereas basketball is a several-hour affair by the time I drive to the gym, wait for a game, play for a bit, and drive home. I used to choose basketball over running, but now that I have kids, I find it to be too costly in terms of the amount of time required and what I have to give up (i.e., time with my kids) in order to get a game in.

Then there is Cousin Carl, and perhaps lots of other individuals, who would prefer never to exercise at all. Whereas I get positive utility from exercise and Uncle Al clearly loves golf, physical activity may actually make some individuals worse off (i.e., lower their utility), all else being equal. This is not to say that they would never do it. For example, even though my sister admittedly hates to exercise, she still goes walking every morning because she hates being fat even more. That is the same reason she is always going on some crazy diet plan. Diet and exercise are two necessary evils in her efforts to remain thin. The same is true for many of us. It all depends on our valuations concerning exercise, weight, food preferences and other preferences, what trade-offs we are willing to make, and what constraints we face when making decisions that impact our weight and health.

Although I am unable to get confirmation from Cousin Carl or Uncle Al about these trade-offs, I do have data that reveals that, in fact, overweight and obese individuals are quite aware of their elevated risk of disease and premature death. My colleagues and I conducted a nationally representative telephone survey of 1,139 adults to assess whether those who are overweight or obese believe they are at greater risk of both morbidity and premature mortality.[2]

For four of the diseases known to be linked to excess weight (diabetes, cancer, heart disease, and stroke), both overweight and obese individuals reported risks of contracting these diseases that were greater than the risks reported from individuals who were in the normal BMI range. Greatest perceived risks were reported by obese individuals. In fact, obese individuals rated themselves more than twice as likely to get cancer and heart disease, roughly three times more likely to develop a stroke, and four times more likely to develop diabetes than individuals of normal weight. And these analyses included only individuals who were free of these diseases at the time of the survey.

Respondents to the survey who were in the normal BMI range predicted, on average, that they would live to about age 78. Overweight individuals, on average, rated their life expectancy at 75.5, 2.5 years less than normal-weight individuals. Obese adults predicted a life expectancy of 74 years, four years less than the predictions for the normal-weight group. Several published papers that use actual death data produce results for both overweight and obesity that are close to those predicted by the survey respondents.[3-5] In other words, overweight and obese individuals' predictions of a shorter life expectancy appear fairly accurate.

So why is this significant? It suggests that many individuals are making a *conscious* decision to engage in a lifestyle that is obesity promoting, even if they believe that it will result in poorer health and reduced life expectancy.

So are Uncle Al and Cousin Carl at their optimal weight? Could be. Was I at my optimum weight seven years ago when I weighed 194 pounds? I was. Am I at my optimum now, four marathons later and almost 20 pounds lighter? The answer is yes. What changed for me? The main change was my entry into obesity research and the belief that I would be more credible, especially when giving presentations, if I shed a few pounds. In other words, my perceived benefits of weight loss went up, so I lost some weight. This is Economics 101. Was I right? As I'll discuss below, it worked for Jared Fogle (a.k.a. the Subway Guy). Nonetheless, I'll keep the sedentary office job and run marathons to stay in shape, rather than pick strawberries or carry letters for a living.

As an aside, the discussion to date explains why individuals like Uncle Al and Cousin Carl have been gaining weight over the past few decades. In Chapter 1 we showed that, whereas all groups in the United States are gaining weight, those with lower income levels have higher rates of obesity (although admittedly, this gap is shrinking). This makes sense given that the costs of maintaining a lower weight may be greatest for those with lower incomes. However, I've also wondered whether some disadvantaged individuals may weigh more because they feel they have less incentive to maintain a healthy weight. As an extreme example, if you lived in a poverty-stricken, high-crime environment, faced significant discrimination, and had trouble coming up with each month's rent, not to mention food and other expenses, how hard would you work to live to age 78 versus age 74? Or perhaps I have it backwards, how hard would you work to live to age 74?

If life is tough, one way to ease the stress is to eat a big meal, or have a drink, or smoke a cigarette, and the thought that this may be bad for your health in 10, 20, 30, or 50 years is hardly an incentive not to do it. Although it is just a hypothesis at this point, the idea that some individuals weigh more because they feel they have less to live for is certainly consistent with the reality that more disadvantaged groups are more likely to drink, smoke, and engage in other risky behaviors. Even if this hypothesis is confirmed, this, too, is entirely consistent with utility maximization.

Now, Let's Tear This Argument Apart (and Put It Back Together)

As economists are prone to do, the above discussion makes several assumptions. One of these assumptions is that Uncle Al, Cousin Carl, and the rest of us are rational decision makers; we are making the choices that make us best off from our own perspective (we are maximizing our utility) given our preferences and constraints. It does not assume that individuals have perfect information about these choices. However, the decision to acquire additional information is also a choice that individuals can make.

In other words, in its most basic form, utility maximization assumes that every time Uncle Al decides to take his wife out for a nice meal, work extra hours, or ride a golf cart instead of walking 18 holes, he is aware of how these behaviors will impact his future weight and health outcomes, and he is making the best choice for him once all of those factors are considered. If there is some additional information that Uncle Al might want to help him make an informed decision, utility maximization further assumes that he could go out and find that information if he chooses to do so.

For Uncle Al, who is a smart lawyer, this may not be so much of a stretch. I certainly don't know the health content of many of the foods I eat or how many calories I burn in various activities, but I could find out if I truly wanted to. But I'm a pretty smart guy, too. I mean, after all, I have a PhD. (*Note:* This is sarcasm.) What about the average consumer— are they able to acquire this information if they truly wanted to? At least for nutrition content for prepackaged food, the introduction of the Nutrition Facts panel in the early 1990s certainly made this information easier to acquire. And although this information is not readily available for restaurant food, eating out is also a choice that consumers do not have to make.

I suspect that many non-economists will buy into the utility maximization argument in general, but not when it comes to food choices. Their skepticism may be due, in part, to the fact that information on the health content of many foods is hard to come by. The Nutrition Facts panel is available for prepackaged foods, but it is not easily digestible (pardon the pun).[6] Moreover, much of our consumption now occurs in restaurants, where there is often little or no information on the health content of the foods we consume. As a result, people are making food consumption decisions with limited understanding of the health content of these foods.

I agree that we may not know everything there is to know about our food consumption and even our physical activity levels, but a look in the mirror or a trip to the scale should be a pretty good indicator of the repercussions of the decisions. At that point, we can decide whether we care enough to attempt to make the difficult sacrifices required to reduce our weight. Some of these sacrifices would include educating ourselves about health information and the best strategies for weight loss and weight maintenance.

Moreover, if enough of us cared and created a demand for this information, restaurants and other food purveyors, seeking to attract our business, would do a better job of providing it. Subway does. That's how Jared Fogle got skinny. When the Atkins low-carb diet craze was in high gear, many restaurants and food suppliers labeled their products as Atkins approved. A trip to the grocery store reveals numerous products with low-calorie and low-fat labels. So if we want to eat these products, they are there for the taking.

By the way, if I thought losing a few pounds was good for my career, just look at what it did for Jared. I once spoke at a conference where Jared was the star attraction (I got his autograph on a paper I published and later had it framed). He mesmerized the audience by brandishing his giant pre-weight-loss pants held up high for all to see. Judging from his entourage, I am sure he was paid a hefty speaking fee for showing up. It certainly appears that Jared is at his utility-maximizing weight. For him, gaining weight would cost him his career.

There is a second concern about utility maximization for which Brian Wansink and other food psychologists would likely take me to task. I suspect they would probably disagree with the notion that Uncle

Al has *full* control over all of the choices that impact his weight or that he is truly a forward-looking thinker while at the dinner table. Perhaps, as with smoking, Uncle Al has a food addiction that does not allow him to stop eating when he wants to. Or perhaps he is so short-sighted that he does not think about the long-term consequences of his food consumption decisions.

I have young children, and I know they don't consider the long-term consequences of many of their actions, but can the same really be said for Uncle Al? We do know he eats more at a buffet than he would at a sit-down restaurant. We also can guess that he probably would eat stale popcorn at a movie theater if it were free. Maybe, like an addict, he can't help himself. If not, then the utility maximization argument goes out the window and, as we discuss in the following chapter, Uncle Al may need some outside help to ensure he does not overeat.

Although I'm not discounting the notion that there are many psychological aspects related to food consumption, I'm skeptical that the rapid weight gain seen over the past three decades has much to do with food addictions. I'm sticking with the utility-maximization argument and our earlier conclusion that the rise in obesity rates is a result of our current obesity-promoting environment that has increased the costs of physical activity and lowered the costs of food consumption and of being obese.

Why? Because putting aside increases in food availability and falling prices for high-calorie foods, the reality is that I had to scratch my head for quite a while to think up an occupation, berry picking, which has not been automated to the point where people no longer get physical activity doing it. Given that, the choice to enter the workforce—which, for many of us, is not a choice if we want to eat and not be homeless—largely means that we are committed to 40-plus hours a week of inactivity. This stacks the deck against us in our efforts to remain thin.

I could have chosen to pick berries, but is that a realistic option? Combine that with increasingly low-cost, readily available, and tasty food options and the many new treatments for obesity-related risk factors and diseases, and the result is that, for many of us, weight gain seems to be the rational economic choice.

But if Uncle Al and the rest of us are at our optimum weight, why is Dad so upset about it? As I mentioned in the introduction, he just can't stop talking about Uncle Al and his ballooning waistline. And though he claims to not care that Uncle Al is obese, considering the amount of time and energy he puts into talking about him, I'm not really buying it. And, in fact, perhaps he should care.

So Should Dad (and the Government) Care that Uncle Al Is Obese?

In reality, my dad, like someone you know (maybe many people), is a fattist. That is, he is bigoted against overweight people. (He doesn't really like lawyers either, by the way). Like most bigots, he's not the kind who would be outwardly mean to an obese person (or even a lawyer). But, when it comes right down to it, he considers them inferior on some level because they don't "do what it takes" to be thin. And he's hardly alone. It's often been said that prejudice against overweight people is the last-standing acceptable form of bigotry.

I can recall being at an obesity conference where the speaker (an obesity researcher) led off with a cartoon showing an obese person who could not fit through the doorway to get out of a doctor's office. The caption said something about this being his proven technique for weight loss. Needless to say, some members of the audience were very offended.

The media are not any better—how many movies or shows have you seen where obese people are the butt of the jokes? For instance, I've seen a very large woman on CSI suffocate her lover by passing out on him, and I've also noted how movies like *Shallow Hal* (Gwyneth Paltrow is no longer in my top five) and *The Nutty Professor* are liberally laced with fat jokes. Both movies were awful, by the way.

But jokes aside (something hard for Dad since he loves getting a good jibe in about Uncle Al whenever he can), just what is it about Uncle Al's excess weight that bothers Dad and others so much? Well, this is a complicated question with multiple answers, some of which go beyond the scope of this book. But, no doubt, part of his bigotry results from misunderstandings of basic biology and economics.

As we discussed in Chapter 4, much of the variation in weight across individuals is caused by genetics. When Dad or other fattists see overweight people, they typically assume that their weight is due entirely to their unwillingness to diet and exercise. Whereas this may be true for many overweight individuals, for others, due to their genes, maintaining a normal weight is much more difficult. This point is likely lost on Dad and other fattists.

Dad's bias against Uncle Al and other obese individuals is also partly based on a misunderstanding of economic theory (he admittedly got a C in the course in college). "If I were Uncle Al, the first thing I would do is go on a diet," Dad has said on many occasions.

But this is simply not true. Dad thinks Uncle Al is making bad choices. But what he doesn't realize is that Uncle Al is not making bad choices— he just has different preferences. If Dad were truly transformed into his half brother, he would have Uncle Al's body and his preferences, and therefore he would do exactly what Uncle Al has done, which is engage in a lifestyle that is obesity promoting. And although Dad would shudder at the thought, he would even be a lawyer, just like Uncle Al. Of course, he would also have a whole lot more money in the bank.

If Dad were in a position of power (God forbid), he might discriminate, in hiring or in some other way, against Uncle Al and other obese individuals, because of his belief that they are not "doing what it takes" to be thin. Employment discrimination, by the way, is perfectly legal. Michigan provides a notable exception as the only state that prohibits employment discrimination on the basis of weight. Short of that, Dad might try to force Uncle Al to diet and exercise more because he doesn't like the choices he has made that resulted in his excess weight.

To be fair, however, we need to point out that Dad is not so different from the government on many levels. As we'll talk about in the next chapter, governments often take the paternalistic approach that they know better than Uncle Al (or Cousin Carl). And because governments have power, they often pass legislation and enact policies aimed directly at doing what Dad would like to do: force (or, at the very least, encourage) their citizens to change their behaviors.

Forcing individuals to make changes that lower their weight may very well make them worse off (in the utility-maximizing sense). But as we discuss below and in the following chapter, there may be some valid (and some not-so-valid) reasons for employers and government to implement these types of policies for the good of the firm and/or society (although perhaps to the detriment of Uncle Al and Cousin Carl).

In the introduction we briefly mentioned several additional reasons why Dad—and why government—might care about the rapid weight gain of Uncle Al and the rest of the U.S. population: "It's making our businesses less competitive, pushing good jobs overseas, hurting our military readiness, increasing our taxes, and helping to bankrupt the Medicare and Medicaid programs." Is this hyperbole? Let's see.

Just Follow the Money

If you recall, in the introduction I quoted a phrase often uttered by my mom when she sees a severely obese person. "There's someone who could participate in your study," she says. Although, as my dad often points out, she could afford to lose a few pounds herself, she too is a bit of a fattist. (Sorry, Mom.)

The study she is referring to is a paper that colleagues and I published a few years back that quantifies the annual increase in medical costs resulting from obesity.[7] We did not actually enroll participants into a study, as Mom believes, but we did analyze health care expenditures based on individuals' weight. Using nationally representative survey data and statistical techniques, we created three groups of people—normal weight, overweight, and obese—who were similar in other demographic characteristics (e.g., age, race, gender).

The idea is that if these groups of individuals are similar in all characteristics except for their weight, then the difference in medical costs between these groups must be due to differences in weight. We looked at costs separately for those with private insurance, Medicaid, or Medicare coverage. Given the increased likelihood of adverse health conditions among those with excess weight (see Chapter 1), we expected obesity to account for a significant portion of aggregate medical spending.

What we found is that in the absence of overweight and obesity, private health insurance and Medicaid expenditures would be about 8 percent lower than they are now, and that Medicare expenditures would be about 11 percent lower. In total, overweight and obesity increase the annual medical bill by over $90 billion per year—yes, that's billions. This figure represents about 9 percent of all medical spending in the United States.

Because most obese individuals will inevitably be covered by Medicare, and because the Medicaid population has a 50 percent higher prevalence of obesity, the government finances roughly half of the total annual medical costs attributable to obesity, or more than $45 billion per year. As a result, the average taxpayer spends approximately $175 per year to finance obesity-related medical expenditures among Medicare and Medicaid recipients.[8,9]

So maybe Dad has a legitimate reason to be upset about Uncle Al's choices. After all, they are raising his taxes. And just maybe this justifies government funding of obesity-prevention efforts. (Of course, if the interventions don't work, they raise Dad's taxes even more.) We return to this issue in the next three chapters. But the fact that roughly half of the medical costs of obesity are funded by the government means that the other half are funded by the private sector. This, too, gives Dad a legitimate reason to be concerned. Moreover, medical costs are just one of the areas in which private employers are adversely affected as a result of excess weight.

In another paper, we assessed increased medical expenditures and sick days as a result of overweight and obesity among full-time employees.[10] In that analysis, we classified obese individuals into three BMI subgroups. Results from the medical expenditure analysis explain the $45 billion price tag of obesity that is financed by the private sector. The average overweight male has annual medical costs that are roughly $170 greater than their normal-weight colleagues. For overweight women, medical costs are $495 higher. For those in the highest BMI category, the excess costs resulting from obesity exceed $1,500 per year for both males and females.

The excess medical costs result from a greater likelihood of adverse health conditions among those with excess weight. Therefore, it follows that obese individuals require greater time away from work as a result of these conditions. This increased absenteeism can be expensive for an employer that may have to hire additional workers and/or retrain other workers to compensate for the lost work time. The results of the absenteeism analysis are reproduced in Figure 6.1.

Normal-weight men miss an average of three days each year due to illness or injury. Annual missed workdays for overweight and grade I obese men are within half a day of this estimate. Grade II and III obese

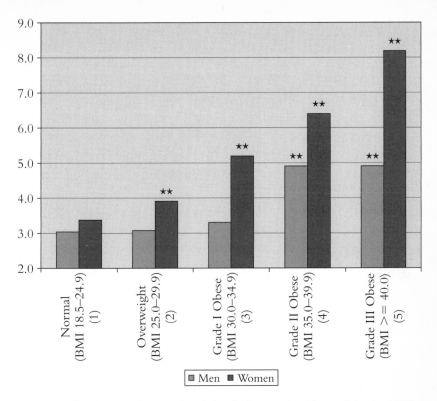

★★Significantly greater than missed work days for the normal weight population (p < 0.05).

Figure 6.1 Predicted Missed Work Days Due to Illness or Injury Among Full-Time Employees by BMI Category
SOURCE: Finkelstein, E. A., I. C. Fiebelkorn, and G. Wang. 2005. "The Costs of Obesity among Full-Time Employees," *American Journal of Health Promotion* 20, no. 1: 45–51.

men, however, miss approximately two more workdays per year than normal-weight men.

Normal-weight women miss an average of 3.4 days each year due to illness or injury. In comparison, overweight women miss 3.9 days, 0.5 more days than normal-weight women; grade I obese women miss 5.2 days, 1.8 days more; and grade II obese women miss 6.4 days, almost double that of normal-weight women. For women with a BMI of 40 or greater (about 100 pounds overweight), work days missed due to illness or injury jump to 8.2 days, almost a week more of missed work each year than normal-weight women.

Based on these results, we show that the costs of obesity alone (excluding overweight) at a firm with 1,000 employees are roughly $285,000 per year, of which 30 percent results from increased absenteeism. Medical expenses and sick leave are not the only costs to employers resulting from obesity. There is additional evidence that obesity increases worker's compensation costs.[11,12] A recent study by UnumProvident Corporation, an insurance provider, found that short-term disability claims attributed to obesity have increased tenfold during the past decade. According to the study, obesity-related disabilities cost employers an average of $8,720 per claim.[13]

And in at least one study, obese employees are shown to be less productive while on the job.[14] That study tracked phone calls at a call center and found that obese women made fewer calls than their normal-weight counterparts. In other words, they were less productive. Although it may not extend to all occupations and certainly does not extend to all overweight individuals, presenteeism, as it is now called, represents a real concern to employers.

Dad is smart enough to realize that his health insurance premiums are higher than they would be if the risk pool did not include any overweight or obese individuals. This provides an additional reason for him to be upset about rising rates of obesity. If Dad were running his own business, you can bet he'd be unhappy about the fact that, on average, two thirds of his employees are overweight or obese. Not only are they exhibiting poor choices, in his opinion (although he might reconsider this statement if their efforts to increase their health came at the expense of their job performance), but they are hurting his bottom line. And whereas Dad can only grumble about obesity and its resulting costs to Mom and the rest of the family, employers have some tough choices to make.

As we will discuss in Chapter 10, some employers are implementing innovative programs in an effort to improve the health of their workforce and their firm's profitability. However, other firms are looking to reduce the impact of obesity and high health care costs by dropping health insurance as a covered option. Still other firms are outsourcing their work to other countries where they can avoid having to pay high health insurance rates.

Whereas Uncle Al's decisions that lead to his excess weight may be the utility-maximizing outcome *for him*, and dropping insurance coverage and/or shipping jobs overseas may be profit maximizing, there are many individuals, across the weight continuum, who will suffer as a result. Would outsourcing still be an issue in the absence of obesity? It would. Would it be as much of an issue? Perhaps not. Regardless, if you were an employer, the rise in obesity rates would certainly represent a major concern.

Here's yet more fodder for employers. A study conducted at Toulouse University Hospital suggests that maintaining a higher BMI can have a negative effect on cognitive function.[15] The study included 2,223 healthy French adults between the ages of 32 and 62. In 1996, they took a battery of standard cognitive tests to assess abilities like memory, attention, and speed of learning. Five years later, the subjects took the tests again. Subjects with a BMI of less than 20 remembered 56 percent of the words, while participants with a BMI over 30 remembered 44 percent of the words, a reduction in recall of roughly 20 percent. Other studies have shown a causal link between obesity and Alzheimer's disease. It has been suggested that the "hunger" hormone leptin, which is produced by fat cells, plays a role in learning and memory.[16] Regardless of the cause, if obesity contributes to presenteeism, through increased illness or cognitive decline, productivity and the firm's bottom line will be adversely affected.

As noted above, employers are taking action to address the obesity epidemic. Aside from outsourcing and dropping health insurance altogether, an easy way to minimize the costs of obesity is simply to pay obese individuals less money. This is by no means discriminatory. If obese individuals are costing the firm more money in terms of health insurance, have greater rates of absenteeism, and are potentially less productive while on the job, then, in competitive labor markets, we would expect to see differences in wages across BMI groups. That is not discrimination—it's profit maximization.

A review of the published literature finds evidence that, in fact, obese women make lower wages than normal-weight women. One study finds that women who are overweight in adolescence have 22 percent ($6,710) lower annual household incomes than do women of normal weight.[17] Another study reports that an increase in weight of two standard deviations (roughly 65 pounds) is associated with a 7 percent decrease in wages for white women, but finds no effect for African-American women.[18] The literature is mixed on the relationship between earnings and weight for men. Some studies find evidence of wage differentials, whereas others do not.[19]

Even if wage differentials exist, it is difficult to discern whether these differences are based on differences in costs or fattism on the part of employers. One study attempted to address this issue.[20] While it is impossible to completely rule out discrimination, if much of the difference in wages were due to medical cost differences, then we should expect to see greater wage differentials between normal and overweight employees in jobs where medical costs are borne by the employer. The authors test this hypothesis by comparing wage differentials in jobs where the employer provides health insurance to wage differentials where they do not. They found that there was a bigger weight-wage gap in industries where health insurance was provided. This suggests that at least part of the wage differential is due not to fattism but to employers offsetting larger health insurance costs with lower wages for obese employees.

And, although the underlying causes remain unclear, there is additional evidence that obese individuals' occupations, primarily women's, differ from those of normal-weight individuals. Obese women work mostly in relatively low-paying occupations and are largely absent from high-paying managerial/professional and technical occupations.[21] For one specific aerospace employer, 65 percent of normal-weight women are in managerial/professional positions compared with only 39 percent of overweight women.[22]

Weight disparities extend to the unemployed as well. Obese women are 2.5 times more likely to report long-term unemployment than their normal-weight counterparts.[23] In fact, a 10 percent increase in weight is associated with an 11 percent increase in time spent on welfare for African-American women and a 16 percent increase for white women.[24] Whether these differences are driven by underlying factors that cause both obesity and poor labor market outcomes or whether they are driven by discrimination, or most likely, a combination, remains an open question.

Aside from employment-related issues, there is at least one more reason why Dad (and all Americans, for that matter) might be concerned about rising rates of obesity. It relates to our ability to recruit individuals into the armed forces and, when necessary, field a competent fighting force. It is an issue that is starting to receive a lot of press. A *New York*

Times headline recently read, "The Military Issues Order to Shape Up."[25] Fox News and MSNBC have also run stories like "Obesity Takes Heavy Toll on Military" and "Are U.S. Troops Too Fat to Fight?"[26]

While we might think that boot camp and rigorous physical training would make being overweight in the military nearly impossible, members of the armed forces have been gaining weight just like the rest of us. As a point of reference, today's soldiers are, on average, 37 pounds heavier than those in the Civil War.[27] More than 54 percent of military personnel are now overweight. But unlike the civilian population, excess weight is more prevalent in men (58.6 percent) than in women (26.1 percent).[28] In fact, over the past few years, thousands of servicemen and -women have been discharged due to their excess weight (3,000 servicemen and -women in 2003 alone).[29]

And because the military recruits from the general population, the fact that Americans are getting heavier makes it more difficult (and more expensive) to meet recruiting targets. For men and women of prime recruiting age, 2 out of 10 men, and 4 of 10 women weigh too much to be eligible to enlist.[30] But there is hope for the slightly overweight individual wanting to join up—the Marines will allow individuals whose weight is up to 10 percent above standards to enlist—as they say, "Send us anybody and we'll turn them into a Marine."[31] (See a more detailed discussion of obesity and the military in the next chapter.)

So the evidence is compelling: Obesity is making us less healthy and increasing our reliance on drugs and medical technologies. As a result, it is putting a financial strain on the Medicare and Medicaid programs. It is raising our taxes, hurting the economy, and perhaps weakening our armed forces. So what could (should) we do? We offer suggestions on what employers can do to address these issues in Chapter 10, but first, we turn to the government's role in addressing the rising tide of obesity. Their role is discussed in the following three chapters.

Chapter 7

The Role of Government

Obesity rates are on the rise because of a changing economy that has increased the costs of being thin. What's more, the changing economy is no accident; it is in response to consumers' insatiable demand for labor-saving devices and affordable, convenient, and tasty food. To be fair, and as we'll discuss in detail in the next several chapters, the rise in obesity rates is not entirely based on supply and demand. Government regulations have also inadvertently made it more difficult for individuals to maintain a healthy weight. Regardless, the economy continues to transform and is now providing new products and services to accommodate an increasingly overweight population.

Given this reality, how should government policy makers address the rising tide of obesity? Should they do nothing and let the economy sort it out? Should they force, or at the very least, encourage Uncle

Al and others to lose weight even though they might prefer not to? I hope I've convinced you by now that the answers are not so obvious. So, what are policy makers to do?

Before tackling this question, let's revisit what the appropriate role of government should be, at least as economists see it. Economists largely believe that government policy should be limited to addressing those areas where private markets fail to reach the optimal allocation of resources.

Are rising rates of obesity evidence of some failure on the part of private markets to meet consumer demands or to optimally allocate resources? As we discuss below, the answer appears to be no. With a few exceptions that we'll discuss in the following two chapters, obesity is largely a result of the success, not the failure, of private markets to supply those goods and services that consumers are increasingly demanding. If true, then, as economists see it, government's role in fighting obesity may be limited.

Government policy makers buy into the market failure role of government, but they also take a broader societal perspective. This is fairly well described in an executive order produced by the Office of Management and Budget and sent to the directors of all federal executive agencies in 2003.[1]

Executive Order 12866 states that any proposed regulation should clearly explain whether the action is intended to address a significant market failure. It further states that if the intervention is not to address a market failure, in order to justify regulation, the agency should demonstrate a *compelling public need*. In either case, the Order recommends that the government consider whether the intervention is likely to do more good than harm. In other words, it should watch out for unintended consequences, which, when it comes to government regulations, are often hard to avoid.

In this chapter, in an effort to identify the appropriate role of government in fighting the obesity epidemic, from a purely economic point of view, we look for market failures that may be partly responsible for the rising rate of obesity. In Chapters 8 and 9 we return to whether there is truly a compelling public need to get Uncle Al and others to lose weight and, if so, we explore the appropriate strategies for government to pursue.

Market Failures

A market failure exists when the private sector cannot reach the optimal allocation of resources on its own. The optimal allocation occurs at the price where the amount of a product or service that consumers demand is equal to the amount that suppliers wish to provide. Although there is not a market for obesity per se, there are markets for many (but not all) of the products and services that influence our weight. These range from the obvious, markets for more and less healthy foods and weight-loss products and services, to those whose influence is less direct, such as markets for lawyers, health economists, and berry pickers, but that nonetheless indirectly affect how much we eat and how active we are in our daily lives.

And all of these markets are formed largely by what economist Adam Smith referred to as an *invisible hand* in his still-relevant 1776 book *An Inquiry into the Nature and Causes of the Wealth of Nations*. Smith wrote:

> . . . every individual necessarily labours to render the annual revenue of the society as great as he can. He generally, indeed, neither intends to promote the public interest, nor knows how much he is promoting it. By preferring the support of domestic to that of foreign industry, he intends only his own security; and by directing that industry in such a manner as its produce may be of the greatest value, he intends only his own gain, and he is in this, as in many other cases, led by *an invisible hand* to promote an end which was no part of his intention. Nor is it always the worse for the society that it was no part of it. By pursuing his own interest he frequently promotes that of the society more effectually than when he really intends to promote it. I have never known much good done by those who affected to trade for the public good.

What Smith was saying is that people's preferences create demand for certain products and services. In response, as if guided by an invisible hand, individuals will realize they can make a profit by providing these products and services for a price and, based on their preferences, will decide which, if any, of these to provide. If markets are working properly, then a price and quantity can be achieved so that the amount that consumers wish to purchase is identical to the amount that suppliers produce.

So let's give a few examples. Adam Smith would say that the increasing numbers of fast-food purveyors in the United States and the world is not a plot by corporate America to make us all fat. Rather, the growth of the fast-food market is merely a response to an increasing demand for these establishments, in part because women's wages have risen (due to increased demands for their labor) and, in increasingly greater numbers, women have responded by leaving the home and entering the workforce.

As another example, Smith would say that the lack of fresh fruits and vegetables in inner city markets is not a diabolical plot to harm the health of those in the inner cities. It is simply a clear-cut matter of supply and demand. After all, if there were money to be made by offering fresh fruits and vegetables in inner city markets, profit-seeking merchants would step up and provide them.

Moreover, the trend toward mechanization and reliance on technology is a market-based response to consumers' insatiable demands to have the latest and greatest products at the lowest prices. If consumers were content to live without these modern conveniences and without tasty, convenient, and affordable food, the obesity epidemic would not exist. For proof, take a look at the Amish, a group that has chosen to live without these conveniences. As we discuss in Chapter 12, they're much less likely to be obese than the average American.

The point is that an increasing rate of obesity is not in and of itself evidence of a market failure. It is possible that rising obesity rates are a result of one or more market failures, but it is also possible (and likely) that, as we discussed in previous chapters, increasing rates of obesity are a natural response to a changing world. In fact, rising obesity rates may be more an indicator of the success, as opposed to a failure, of markets.

So let's take a look at common ways that markets fail to allocate resources appropriately and see if any of these may be responsible for some of the rise in obesity rates. If so, they would be clear targets for government intervention. Common market failures include:

- *Externalities:* Side effects of a market that spill over into society at large (i.e., pollution from an automotive production facility).

- *Market power:* The ability to raise the price of a good or service beyond its competitive level (i.e., monopolies).
- *Public goods:* Goods that are available for everyone to consume regardless of who does or does not pay for them (i.e., public parks)
- *Imperfect (asymmetric) information:* When one person (group) in a transaction has more or better information than the other party and that party cannot acquire that information at a reasonable cost (i.e., used car markets).

Externalities

It is a known fact that many smokers die of lung cancer and other complications of smoking. This however, is not evidence of a market failure. After all, utility-maximizing smokers may be fully aware of these risks and still decide to light up. It is the fact that smoking adversely impacts the health of nonsmokers that generates the market failure. This type of market failure is referred to as an externality, a side effect of an action that influences the well-being of nonconsenting parties.

As economists see it, it is this external (health) cost imposed by smokers that justifies government interventions such as information campaigns, large cigarette taxes, and clean indoor air laws and other restrictions on where smokers are allowed to light up. As of the beginning of 2007, 40 states as well as the District of Columbia have indoor smoking bans on their books (lagging behind are Indiana, Kentucky, Mississippi, New Mexico, North Carolina, South Carolina, Tennessee, Texas, West Virginia, and Wyoming).[2] Many states still allow smoking in bars and other businesses serving alcoholic beverages, but increasingly these states have dates in the near future to phase out smoking in even these locations. Several cities in California are taking it even further. In 2004, San Francisco approved one of the strictest outdoor-smoking bans in the world to date, prohibiting smoking in all city-owned parks and plazas as well as public sports facilities.[3]

These strategies are directly aimed at reducing exposure to second-hand smoke, although it should be pointed out that they, too, come with unintended consequences. For example, not only are smokers worse off as a result of these laws, but many businesses who might want to operate smoking-friendly establishments are barred from doing so, and their profits may suffer as a result. Although the benefits may outweigh the costs, these examples highlight the unintended consequences that result from well-intentioned government interventions.

But is there an externality resulting from obesity? Does Uncle Al's excess weight increase the health risks of those he comes in contact with? Or are the risks associated with his increased body weight his to bear alone? Moreover, if his weight does impose on others, is there a market mechanism to compensate them? If so, then government intervention may not be required.

When people hear that I work in obesity, they often launch into their "horror" stories involving contacts with someone of excess weight. One favorite beef is to describe how terrible it is to sit next to an obese person on a flight and liken this to an externality (of course, they never mention how terrible it must be for that person). In a sense, they are correct. Obese individuals generally take up more than their allocated "airspace" and thus may infringe on neighboring nonobese passengers. They might even do it on purpose. The National Association to Advance Fat Acceptance (NAAFA) has posted on its web site (www.naafa.org) some tips for airline travel that specifically recommend that passengers encroach on other passengers' room/comfort:

> When you get to your seat during pre-boarding, raise the arm-rest between seats. This may give you the inch or two of extra space you need. The chances are that the passenger who will be seated next to you won't say anything; if he does, smile pleasantly and say that you'll both be more comfortable if the armrest is up.

So this appears to satisfy the criteria of an externality, but does it justify government intervention? After all, can't the airlines solve this problem by themselves? In reality, they can. Southwest and several other airlines have policies that require the purchase of two tickets for individuals who cannot fit into a single seat. So, if you don't want to risk being inconvenienced by sitting next to an obese passenger and you don't have the money for first class, fly Southwest. Of course, this is never a guarantee that your neighbor won't continue to impose other "externalities" on you during the flight. Who hasn't had luggage dropped on them, soda sloshed on their pants, or the much-needed nap interrupted by a screaming child?

My friends in the nursing field also tell me that nursing is becoming more difficult and dangerous because of the many overweight patients who have special needs. If true, then perhaps that shift has something to do with the fact that nurses' wages have been increasing in recent years. If the market can compensate nurses for their increased risk and/or provide new products to minimize these risks, then again, there is no role for government.

There is, however, one example of an obesity externality that may justify government intervention: obesity among women of childbearing age. As discussed in Chapter 1, not only does obesity adversely impact pregnant women, it increases the likelihood of adverse health outcomes for their offspring, which is a clear externality.

As we discussed in Chapter 1, obesity in pregnancy raises the risks for a host of negative outcomes: delayed diagnosis, ineffective ultrasounds, increased need for cesarean or instrumental delivery, and increased risk of several conditions that may impact the viability of the unborn child, including preeclampsia, eclampsia, gestational diabetes, and blood loss. In addition, obesity in pregnancy raises the risks for neural tube defects, spina bifida, heart defects, and delivery-related neonatal morbidity. As a result, government action to reduce obesity rates among women of childbearing age may be warranted.

But with the notable exception of obesity in pregnancy, there are no obvious obesity externalities that suggest government intervention is warranted on these grounds. Generally speaking, no person other than Uncle Al himself is likely to be affected by his excess weight.

Market Power

Market power occurs when a single firm (monopoly) or a small number of firms (oligopoly) are the dominant suppliers of goods or services in a specific market. Microsoft, for example, has at times been the target of state and federal antitrust agencies because of concerns that its dominant share of the market for operating systems for personal computers allows it to unduly influence this market. In general, antitrust agencies are concerned that firms will take advantage of this market power by raising prices and restricting quantities beyond competitive levels.

With respect to obesity, the opposite is occurring. Food prices are falling, not rising—a primary factor causing us to consume more calories and ultimately leading to higher rates of obesity. If we wanted to buck this trend, a monopoly in the food industry might do us some good. A monopolist would raise prices and limit choice—just the thing to reverse the rising tide of obesity rates.

Public Goods

Market failures often result around the provision of public goods. To best understand the concept of a public good, it may be easiest to first look at its counterpart, a private good. When we think of goods being traded in markets, we are typically discussing private goods that are *excludable* (consumers can be excluded from consuming the product if they are not willing to pay for it) and *rival* (one person's use of a good limits another's use). Think back to Uncle Al's chicken parmesan dinner in Chapter 2. If Uncle Al isn't willing to fork over the money to purchase it, then the restaurant isn't required to feed him (excludable), but if he does buy it, then no one else can have it (rival), unless Uncle Al is willing to offer up a taste, which is highly unlikely knowing how much he loves this dish.

So a public good has the opposite qualities of being *nonrival* and *nonexcludable*. A classic example of a public good often used in economics textbooks is a lighthouse used to help ships navigate at night.[4] Once a lighthouse is built, the value of it does not diminish as more ships use it. Moreover, it would be nearly impossible to prevent certain ships, say from a rival fleet, from using it.

Public goods are typically underprovided by the private sector. Because it is difficult to exclude others from using the goods, it is therefore difficult to profit off of them. Many possible producers of the good will wait in the hopes that someone else will provide it so that they can enjoy the benefits without having to pay any of the costs. This is often called the "free-rider" problem. For these reasons, public goods represent a market failure. The solution to this market failure is often to have government step in to make the public good available. The taxpayer, in turn, pays the cost.

So is there a public-goods argument related to obesity? For example, it may be that the private sector is producing too few outlets for physical activity and/or not enough information concerning how best to consume a nutritious diet and lead a healthy lifestyle. Whereas it is difficult to know what the optimal level of provision of these public goods is, we do know that the government is heavily involved in providing both. For example, the government provides over 84 million acres of public parks and recreational facilities in the United States, which is over twice as many as there were in the late 1970s, when obesity rates were markedly lower.[5]

Although not without significant controversy (see Marion Nestle's book *Food Politics* [University of California Press, 2002] for a great discussion of this issue), the government produces the Food Guide Pyramid (available at www.mypyramid.gov) and other nutrition and obesity information campaigns. The government-funded Steps to a HealthierUS Initiative, for example, has awarded nearly $100 million to 40 communities to implement health promotion programs with a focus on obesity and related risk factors.[6] The Centers for Disease Control and Prevention also funds obesity prevention programs in communities throughout the United States. In addition, the government finances much of the research and dissemination of information related to the causes and consequences of obesity.

Government provision of public goods in the areas of nutrition, physical activity, and obesity has increased substantially over the past several decades. For example, the National Institutes of Health's budget for obesity research is now $440 million, an almost 250 percent increase since just 1998.[7] Therefore, it is a tough sell to claim that a lack of public goods is responsible for the rise in obesity rates. Could federal, state, and local governments provide more public goods? Certainly, they could. Should they? We'll discuss that in the following chapters.

Obesity and National Defense

Another classic public good is national defense. This is something that would clearly be underprovided by the private sector. And, as noted in the preceding chapter, rising obesity rates are making it more difficult for the military to meet its recruiting targets.

Is obesity truly hurting our military readiness? Perhaps, but the extent is likely to be small. Although it is true that the military is having a tough time recruiting, the cause likely has far less to do with obesity than it does with the fact that those entering the military today have a far greater likelihood of serving in combat, and perhaps dying, in an increasingly unpopular war. The military, with its high-tech training, is very attractive to many individuals during peacetime. However, given that we have now been at war for six straight years with no end in sight, and the fact that the death toll among U.S. soldiers continues to increase, many would-be recruits are looking for other opportunities. So even though the benefits of service have remained largely unchanged, the costs (which may include injury and death) are much greater. As a result, recruiting numbers are down. I suspect that if there is ever again a time when we are not at war, recruiters will find that getting healthy young men and women to enlist will be a much easier sell.

Recruitment aside, what about the extra pounds that our military personnel are carrying around? How does that impact the troops' performance? Well, in actuality, the increasing weight among active-duty members may be no more of a problem than it is in the private sector. As with private-sector jobs, many military specialties have been mechanized to the point where carrying a few extra pounds may not decrease job performance. (Note that while military personnel are increasingly more likely to be overweight, very few fall into the obese category.) Clearly, there are some roles that require individuals to be in elite fighting shape, but there is no evidence that these individuals are the ones who have been gaining weight. Moreover, if there are adverse effects, the military has procedures in place to address these issues.

In fact, the military has instituted new policies aimed at controlling weight. In 1981, the Department of Defense implemented its first "weight directive" to address the growing waistlines of military personnel.[8] While this set the general tone, each branch then developed its own weight-loss program.[9] The Army instituted a required weight-management program for all overweight servicemen in the 1980s—if they do not improve their fitness within six months, they are asked to leave. In 2004, the Air Force upped its weekly workout regimen for airmen, and in 2005 the Navy began requiring overweight sailors to take fitness classes.

In the previous chapter we noted that 3,000 servicemen and women in 2003 alone were discharged due to their weight.[10] In reality, this figure represents only one fifth of 1 percent (1.4 million in active duty, so 0.2 percent) of the total armed forces population. Moreover, given the pressures imposed on today's military, it is certainly possible that some of these individuals fattened up as a way to get out. I've met individuals who gained weight so they could become eligible to receive bariatric surgery, so it's not so much of a stretch to think some soldiers would gain weight to avoid combat. To sum up, today's military faces enormous challenges, but rising rates of obesity falls pretty far down the list.

Imperfect (Asymmetric) Information

Often, one party in a transaction has better information than another. For example, in the case of Uncle Al's chicken parmesan dinner, there were probably lots of things about the meal that he did not know both before and after consumption. I doubt he knew the calorie and fat count, where the chicken was purchased, or exactly how it was prepared, but these concerns certainly did not discourage him from making the order. However, there are times when imperfect information can actually lead to a complete failure of the market. Economist George Akerlof earned a Nobel Prize in economics largely for proving this result. Bear with me as I walk you through his logic.

Akerlof leveraged the used car market to show that, under certain conditions, asymmetric information can lead to an outcome where transactions may actually cease to exist even though there are some prices where sellers would like to sell and buyers would like to buy.[11] In other words, asymmetric information can lead to a market failure.

If you've ever shopped for a used car, you understand the logic behind this result. Suppose a good used car sells for $20,000 but that not all used cars are good. Some may have defects that make them worth, say, $10,000. If you are the seller of a used car, even if it is a bad used car, you might try to find some sucker who will pay you $20,000 for your car. Let's suppose that half the used cars are good and half are bad. In this case, the expected price of a used car should be $15,000, the average of the two values. So a moderately savvy buyer, such as my dad, will not pay more than this amount for a used car. However, this is below the value of good used cars, so owners of these cars would be unlikely to sell them. So a really savvy buyer, Uncle Al, for example, would realize that good used cars are unlikely to be put on the market at a price below $20,000, so anyone selling a used car must have a bad one. As a result, Uncle Al, who is a self-proclaimed brilliant lawyer, will not pay more than $10,000 for a used car. This finding, by the way, is why even almost new used cars sell for so much less than brand-spanking-new cars. Would-be purchasers assume they must have some problem and therefore will need a large price discount to be induced to buy them.

In this example, only used cars will be sold, and at a price of $10,000. However, Akerlof took this one step further and showed that when there is a continuum of used cars available of various qualities above and below this value, there may be no market at all. The presence of cars worth less than $10,000 will scare buyers away from paying this amount. They will require an even greater price break for fear of getting an even bigger lemon. However, as the price gets bid down, owners of the higher-quality cars will decide it is no longer worth it to sell them and pull their cars from the market. With these cars gone, the expected value, and thus the price, goes down even further, and this repeats until only the person with the worst possible car available is willing to sell their car, and nobody would want it.

If I lost you somewhere in this argument, keep in mind that Akerlof did share a Nobel Prize for figuring this all out. The main point to remember is that markets can fail because buyers have less information than sellers. This concept extends beyond used cars. Some have suggested that health insurance for the elderly may be a lemons market. Due to the presence of unobservable high-risk individuals (lemons), health insurers may not be able to offer insurance at a price that elderly consumers would actually want to (or be able to) pay. As a result, the introduction of Medicare may be the best strategy for resolving this potential market failure and ensuring health insurance coverage for seniors. However, as we discussed in Chapter 5, resolving this potential market failure by creation of the Medicare program may have also inadvertently created incentives that lead to greater rates of obesity (watch out for unintended consequences).

Although government intervention may be warranted to solve market failures caused by imperfect information between buyers and sellers,

Akerlof also points out that, under some conditions, potential market failures can be resolved by the private sector. With respect to used cars, he points to warranties and branding as strategies for promoting a broader market in cases where buyers have limited information.

The popular auction site, eBay.com, also faces a "lemons" problem. In this case, buyers risk the possibility that some sellers of ill-repute (the lemons) will not deliver on their promised merchandise. eBay addressed this problem by asking buyers to rate their experience with sellers. eBay then provides that rating to all prospective buyers. This system has created a market where the decision to buy often hinges on the seller's rating. Sellers with poor ratings have a difficult time making subsequent sales and, therefore, have an incentive not to rip off consumers.

Getting back to the point, are obesity rates rising due to asymmetric information? And if so, is government intervention required to solve this problem? The short answer to these questions is, respectively, yes and no. It is true that consumers know far less about the health and nutrition content of the foods they eat than do suppliers, and are probably taking on more calories, fat, and sugar as a result, but the market does not appear to be unraveling (as Akerlof termed it). In fact, the opposite is occurring.

For example, although the government mandates that nutrition information be included in labeling of prepackaged food, it is often difficult to get information on the nutrition content of foods served in restaurants. With that said, the restaurant industry has grown virtually every year since the 1970s, and consumers today are spending a larger portion of their food bill on restaurant foods, even though they offer no nutrition information. As noted earlier, although there are some restaurants that provide this information, most do not. But has that stopped consumers from eating their products? Not a chance. Consumers know a good deal when they see one.

The high demand for restaurant food suggests that for many individuals, obese or not, lack of knowledge about the nutrition content of the food is not enough of a concern for them to forgo consumption. As a result, and as discussed further in the following chapter, government regulation mandating disclosure of this information is not warranted. In fact, this was the finding in a recent report issued by the Food and Drug Administration (FDA).[12] If consumers truly want this information, they will put their money where their mouth is and create a demand for it.

There are, in fact, some consumers who are doing just that, and the market appears to be responding. For example, Subway readily provides nutrition information, and other restaurants are beginning to follow suit. Even McDonald's is now including calorie information on its wrappers in many of its stores.[13] Although obesity rates are on the rise, imperfect information does not present a clear market failure that justifies additional government intervention.

There are circumstances, however, in which, due to asymmetric information, the government has determined that regulation is warranted. One example is the Nutrition Facts panel on prepackaged food. For these foods, the government decided that mandated disclosure was necessary, even though it is certainly possible that the private sector could have produced the optimal level of disclosure without this regulation. It should also be pointed out that introduction of the Nutrition Facts panel appears to have had little to no positive effect on reducing obesity rates.

Similarly, many states have proposed legislation to require menu labeling at chain restaurants, as well as institute sweeping bans of ingredients, most notably trans fats, due to the medical evidence that they contribute to high cholesterol and heart disease. In December 2006, New York City became the first to pass an outright ban on the use of trans fats in city restaurants.[14] The city also approved a proposal to implement menu labeling in restaurants.[15]

But it is important to keep in mind that the mere presence of asymmetric information is not a carte blanche for government regulation. For example, as noted above, an FDA working group reviewed the case of restaurant labeling and decided it was better to let it remain voluntary, even though there is clearly asymmetric information between buyers and sellers. Authors of the report relied on the economic argument that the market, reacting to consumer demands, could solve this problem on its own. As proof, they could point to the recent fact that without legislation, 43 of the top 50 fast-food chains (and with the exception of Quizno's, all of the top 20) already provide nutritional information regarding menu items—some through web sites, others through pamphlets in the store.[16]

Also in response to consumer demands, many manufacturers of prepackaged foods have been phasing out their use of trans fats since the early 2000s, although there is still no legislation requiring it.[17] In fact, about half of the restaurants in New York City didn't use trans fats in their meals even before the ban ever passed.[18] So, even though government regulation may be warranted to protect consumers in cases of asymmetric information, sometimes it is best to let the market solve these problems and avoid the unintended consequences that often accompany government interventions.

Is There a Role for Government?

The above discussion suggests that there are no obvious market failures that are responsible for the rise in obesity rates in the United States. Therefore, government intervention cannot be justified on these grounds. This is not to say that there is not a *compelling public need,* as specified in Executive Order 12866. However, this phrase is certainly open to interpretation. For example, in my first year of graduate school, I had a microeconomics professor, Gene Silberberg, who would ridicule the class if we used the term *need.* He would say that we need air, water, shelter, and food (although certainly not in its current form), but beyond that we need very little. This is a quote I often repeat to my wife when she comes to me with her list of "needs." They tend to go well beyond the big four listed by Professor Silberberg.

I am sure that when it comes to obesity, Dad and Uncle Al would clearly differ on the extent of the compelling public need for government intervention and what strategies might be appropriate. As you might have guessed, I have my own views on these issues, which you'll get to read in the following two chapters. These chapters also discuss the extent to which past government interventions have created market failures and, quite by accident, spawned increasing rates of obesity.

Government has imposed numerous laws and regulations that, either directly or indirectly, influence our food consumption and physical activity decisions, and ultimately our rates of obesity. So, an appropriate role for policy makers in response to the obesity epidemic may not be to solve existing market failures, but to revisit past laws and regulations to determine whether, in their current form, they are doing more harm than good. This is exactly the spirit of Executive Order 12866.

Chapter 8

Weighing the Public Policy Issues (for Adults)

In the last chapter, we concluded that there are no obvious market failures that suggest that additional government interventions aimed at reducing rates of obesity are warranted on economic grounds. Well, I hope you are sitting down for this shocker, but it turns out that the government, more often than not, sets policies with noneconomic factors in mind. These policies are often justified based on a compelling public need as outlined in Executive Order 12866. But how are these needs determined?

Here's one small example. I once conducted a cost-effectiveness analysis for a government program. When the results did not show any effectiveness, let alone cost effectiveness, I naively assumed that would spell the end for the program. I was wrong. Government policy makers liked the fact that the program focused on a low-income population and chose to continue funding it in spite of the lack of evidence that it was doing anyone any good. In other words, policy makers felt that the compelling need to provide a program to low-income individuals was enough to justify continued support even in the absence of evidence of effectiveness.

It has often been argued that a compelling public need of government is to provide services to low-income individuals who otherwise could not afford them. Wide differences in wealth can lead to a wide gap in living standards. Although, as Professor Silberberg made clear, this is ultimately a value judgment, society may come to the view that too much inequality is undesirable and may take actions to redistribute income or to provide goods and services to those who otherwise could not afford them. It is this rationale that motivates government to provide welfare programs, food stamps, and Medicaid, for example, as well as progressive taxes on higher-income households to finance these programs.

In addition to equity concerns, government policy makers often feel the need to intervene in cases where they believe (rightly or wrongly) that the government makes better decisions for individuals than the individuals themselves.

Economists also buy into this concept, but only when individuals are unable to make the decisions that maximize their utility—because of irrationality, addiction, or myopia. But most economists do not believe in intervening to change the behavior of rational, utility-maximizing individuals like Uncle Al or Cousin Carl in the absence of an identifiable market failure. But, as I've often lamented, economists do not run the government.

So can a case be made for publicly funded antiobesity interventions *for adults* on the grounds of equity, irrationality or any other compelling public needs? Let's discuss.

Equity

It is commonly believed that poverty is, in large part, driving higher rates of obesity. If true, then government may be able to justify antiobesity interventions based on equity concerns.

Whereas obesity used to be much more prevalent among those with lower incomes, this trend has been changing over time, and in fact, it is questionable today whether obesity is more prevalent among those with lower incomes once racial differences are accounted for. As noted in Chapter 1, there is a wide gap between the obesity rates of different racial groups in America. So it could be that the perceived low-income/ high-income obesity gap may actually be owed more to racial differences (which could be partly genetic) than to differences in income.

To test this hypothesis, we used nationally representative data for adults to quantify the odds of being obese as a function of family income. We controlled for differences in age and ran separate models for African-American, Hispanic, and white non-Hispanic men and women. The results are presented in Figures 8.1 and 8.2.

For Hispanic and African-American men, these results do not support the hypothesis that lower incomes are causing higher rates of obesity. For Hispanic men, the probability of being obese is about the same for those in the top and bottom of the income distribution, and actually *lower* than the probability for those in the middle of the income distribution. Results are similar for African-American men, although the probability of being obese actually increases with rising family income up to about $100,000 per year. At that point, it decreases slightly.

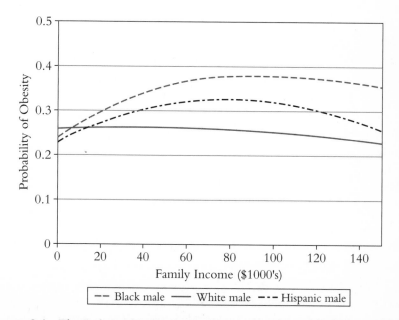

Figure 8.1 The Relationship between Obesity and Income for Males
SOURCE: Analyses based on data from the Medical Expenditure Panel Survey.

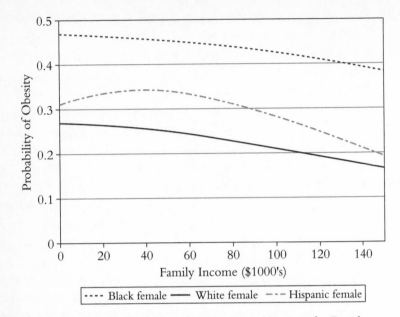

Figure 8.2   The Relationship between Obesity and Income for Females
SOURCE: Analyses based on data from the Medical Expenditure Panel Survey.

Only for white men, do we have the expected result that the odds of obesity decrease as income increases. However, the difference between the richest and poorest white males is only a few percentage points.

Results for African-American and white women are more consistent with the obesity-income hypothesis. For these groups, higher family incomes are associated with a lower probability of obesity. For Hispanic women, this relationship holds for family incomes above $40,000. Below this level, as with Hispanic men, obesity rates increase with higher family income.

Given the increasingly high rates of obesity, there may indeed be a compelling public need for government interventions. However, these results, especially for men and Hispanic women, reveal that it is increasingly tough to argue that obesity interventions are justified on equity grounds.

With respect to food consumption, it is certainly true that Cousin Carl eats a lot of fast food and high-calorie, highly processed food because of its low cost, but Uncle Al has his own reasons for choosing a high-calorie diet. In other words, poor people generally consume diets that fall far short of government recommendations for healthy food consumption, but so does everyone else—even rich people. And don't just take my word for it. A recent survey of 3,500 low-income consumers in the United Kingdom confirms this result. Dr. Alan Maryon Davis, president of the Faculty of Public Health at the British Food Standards Agency, had this to say to BBC news about the survey results: "It's encouraging [that] people in the lowest income bracket are not eating a worse diet than the bulk of the population but, and it's a big but, the bulk of the population is not eating a healthy diet."[1] A big but is right.

If there is a compelling public need to improve dietary intake of Americans, that rationale cuts across the income spectrum. However, policy makers should keep in mind that Uncle Al certainly has the resources to eat healthier if he wanted to, he just chooses not to. They should also keep in mind that once Cousin Carl gets that nice inheritance from Uncle Al, there is little evidence to suggest that he will improve his diet. So if there is a compelling need, Uncle Al and Cousin Carl don't see it.

Diet is only part of the obesity equation. But the argument is equally true for obesity interventions. For example, had I been Hispanic, these results suggest that my weight, as someone whose family income is in the middle of the range, is likely to be greater than that of low-income Cousin Carl or rich Uncle Al. Should obesity interventions focus on middle-income Hispanic or wealthy African American males because they have higher rates of obesity? Few politicians would make that claim.

For those who want to justify government interventions, they may be able to make the argument that the increasingly high prevalence of obesity generates a compelling public need overall (although Uncle Al and much of the voting public would disagree). However, it would be inappropriate to target obesity interventions at low-income individuals on these grounds. At least for men, that is not where the need is greatest.

It should be pointed out that these results focus solely on adults, but as we discuss in the following chapter, the case for government interventions targeted at youth is a much easier sell, even for economists, and definitely for me.

Irrationality

Let's get back to Uncle Al. When Uncle Al goes out to dinner (which he does on most nights) and chooses the chocolate cake over the fruit plate or when he decides he would rather ride in a golf cart than walk the course, is it because he is being irrational, myopic, or has an addiction?

Deborah Cohen, a physician and a senior natural scientist and the coauthor of the book *Prescription for a Healthy Nation: A New Approach to Improving Our Lives by Fixing Our Everyday World* (Beacon Press, 2005), would probably say that Uncle Al is not just irrational—he is as about as helpless "to the current environment's ubiquitous cues" as "Pavlov's dog." She wrote in a column special to washingtonpost.com's Think Tank Town[2]:

> Food marketing efforts are the modern Sirens, leading us inexorably to chronic diseases and sometimes to early deaths. Just as Ulysses was able to defeat the Sirens by having his men plug their ears and tie him to the mast, today we need active protection from an aggressive food industry that is luring us to obesity and illness.
>
> People who are overweight and obese are unknowing victims of a food environment created for corporate profits rather than health.

Brian Wansink, in his book, *Mindless Eating: Why We Eat More Than We Think* (Bantam, 2006), provides compelling evidence focusing on the psychology behind what people eat and how often they eat that strengthens Cohen's extreme views (see Chapter 2 for a fuller discussion). However, even if their contentions about the food industry are correct, when Uncle Al looks in the mirror and sees his growing proportions, it is hard for me to imagine him as an "unknowing victim." I give him more credit than that. I see him more as a smart guy who loves to eat good food and does not much like to work up a sweat in his scarce free time.

Similarly, Cousin Carl eats lots of fast food because it is cheap, filling, tasty, and quick. That choice also sounds pretty rational to me, especially given his money and time constraints. Could it be, as we hypothesized in Chapter 6, that they know exactly what they are doing?

Moreover, even if we do "overeat" in some situations, do we not have the ability to avoid buffets or other food environments that might tempt us to do so or to "overexercise" if we happen to slip? I believe most of us have the ability; we just choose not to exercise it.

So do psychology and marketing play into what we eat and how often? Of course. They play into nearly all of our purchasing decisions. But it's a tough sell to make the leap that food industry practices do not allow adults to make rational decisions related to food consumption, let alone weight, to the point where additional government interventions are warranted. However, as we discuss in the following chapter, kids are a different story.

Compelling Public Need

So if obesity interventions cannot be justified on equity grounds or irrational behavior on the part of consumers, can there be a compelling public need to reduce rates of obesity, even if obesity is a result of utility-maximizing behavior on the part of Uncle Al and others? As noted above, policy makers sometimes take the paternalistic approach that they know better than Uncle Al or Cousin Carl and enact policies aimed at doing what my dad would like to do: force—or at the very least, encourage—citizens to change their behaviors.

Even if policy makers' intentions are noble, government efforts to reduce rates of obesity based on "need" reflect a misunderstanding of the role of utility maximization in individuals' choices related to diet, exercise, and weight.

Government interventions may be successful in getting people to weigh less, but only by encouraging them to make choices they would prefer not to make. In other words, as a result of the interventions, both weight and utility will decrease; individuals will weigh less, but they will be worse off.

As noted in the previous chapter, the government serves a valuable role in providing public goods that, in theory, may reduce rates of obesity. Some public goods, such as parks and recreation facilities, reduce barriers to exercise and therefore increase rates of physical activity, and perhaps reduce rates of obesity (although I am unaware of any evidence to support this last point). But I'm skeptical that other public goods, such as media campaigns that inform or educate the public on the dangers of obesity, will have much of an impact on rates of obesity unless they are combined with more aggressive interventions that change the costs and/or benefits of behaviors related to obesity.

As an example, the Health and Human Services Steps to a HealthierUS campaign is aimed at getting Americans to take small steps to improve their health. Its public service announcements use humor to try to inspire overweight adults to incorporate some of the suggested small steps into their hectic lives. One of their ads featured someone walking over love handles that had fallen off individuals as they became healthier.[3] But these ads have missed the point. Uncle Al may be healthier if he lost some weight, but if it required an extensive diet and exercise regimen, would he be happier?

Unless there is some reason to think he is not utility maximizing—and I don't think there is—the answer is that he would not be. As a result, these messages, without an accompanying intervention that changes the benefits and/or costs of behaviors related to obesity (which may or may not be justified on economic or noneconomic grounds), are unlikely to change his behavior. The same goes for Cousin Carl and the rest of us.

If policymakers are convinced that obesity is a problem worth fighting, then they will need to do far more than just educate the public about the health risks of obesity. In fact, if anything can be learned from efforts to reduce smoking rates, it was that education and information alone were insufficient. Cigarette taxes and smoking restrictions were far more effective policy tools. However, it is likely that the information and education campaigns are what allowed policy makers to introduce the tax hikes and enact the more intrusive policies without being kicked out of office. This may be their most valuable role.

However, aggressive policies to combat obesity currently do not sit well with many Americans. As David White opined in a *Washington Post* article: "Like chugging beer on St. Patrick's Day or smoking after sex, the choice to eat high-calorie foods is not always prudent. But government prohibition of that choice is a confiscation of freedom."[4]

Revisiting Past Policy

Regardless of the merits of government interventions, the political climate around obesity issues is heating up. It's spurred on, in part, by actions such as Surgeon General Richard Carmona's warning us in a much-publicized lecture at the University of South Carolina that obesity is now a greater threat than terrorism,[5] the chest beating and noise making by a wide variety of advocates, and an unprecedented media explosion of obesity-related articles.

In fact, in 2006, Congress introduced more than 75 new bills aimed at curbing obesity. (Just two made it past committee, by the way.)

But before we start exploring possible government actions to address obesity (which we will do in the next section), let's first look at how government policy has affected the obesity issue to date. As we suggested in the previous chapter, government policy makers have already unleashed a slew of laws and regulations that may have inadvertently led to increases in rates of obesity (again, recall the rule of unintended consequences). The past policy decisions of well-intentioned bureaucrats have, as an unintended side effect, profoundly affected the way we eat, engage in physical activities, and ultimately fit into our jeans. Let's look at four prominent examples:

1. Agricultural subsidies
2. Food stamps
3. Medicare
4. The built environment

Big Farma

The story of food production in our country—from farm to fork—is central to the obesity epidemic. And as we write this book, a significant piece of legislation that impacts food production, the Farm Bill, is up for its five-year renewal.

Though historically viewed as a parochial piece of legislation of interest to just midwestern farmers, this bill is now getting a fair amount of attention. And it's not just because the bill involves $300 billion of our taxpayer dollars. In fact, calling this mammoth piece of legislation the

"Farm Bill" is a misnomer. In reality, it addresses a slew of issues beyond subsidies for crops. The bill includes access to healthy food, nutrition programs, sustainable agriculture, rural development, conservation, land stewardship, research and much more (see the discussion about food stamps in the next section). Its influence extends far beyond "the farm" and may, in fact, be partly responsible for the rise in obesity rates.

Whereas the current farm bill does little to support farmers who grow fresh produce, it offers huge economic incentives to produce corn, soybeans, and wheat. In 2006, those three crops alone received a staggering $25 billion in U.S. subsidies.[6] As we discussed in Chapter 2, because these subsidies encourage farmers (or farm corporations) to produce these in lieu of other crops, there is a greater supply of the big three and a smaller supply of the alternatives. This excess supply drives prices down for corn, wheat, and soybeans, and the many products that use these as their prime ingredients, and drives prices up for alternatives, including fresh fruits and vegetables.

These subsidies are at least partly responsible for the relatively high cost of fresh fruits and vegetables and the low cost of many of today's high-calorie corn, soy, and wheat-based products—the building blocks of calorie-dense, nutrient-poor, processed foods. How much less the price of fruits and vegetables would be compared to corn and soy-based products in the absence of the subsidy is an open question, but the laws of supply and demand tell us that if the subsidies were to go away, some farmers would switch from planting corn, soy, and wheat to growing fruits and vegetables and this would affect the prices of each.

So even while the U.S. Department of Agriculture (USDA) has been doing more, over time, to promote health through revised dietary guidelines, food pyramids, and other nutrition programs, more than one fifth of its budget goes toward a farm bill that provides economic incentives to produce the very foods that it is increasingly warning Americans to consume less of (i.e., those with lots of added sugars, likely in the form of high-fructose corn syrup, and added fats, including hydrogenated vegetable oil from soy-based products).

The good news is that with the farm bill coming up for renewal in 2007, there is an opportunity to revisit past decisions and determine whether heavily subsidizing corn and soy-based products remain appropriate given the obesity epidemic. And, encouragingly, for perhaps the first time, nutrition and public health advocates are coming to the same table with farmers, agribusiness, and government to discuss agriculture and food policy recommendations. This bill represents an opportunity to move agricultural policy in a new direction.

Given rising rates of obesity and the fact that these subsidies may be playing a role, government policy makers should strongly revisit whether or not we would be better off if the decision of which crops to grow were left to the laws of supply and demand, as opposed to laws passed by Congress.

Food Stamp(ede)

The Food Stamp Program is another part of the giant farm bill that is up for renewal. The Food Stamp Program, created in 1964 after the U.S. government declared war on poverty, was designed to alleviate hunger by distributing coupons or, currently, electronic benefit transfer (EBT) cards, which can be used at grocery stores to purchase food. It is an entitlement program available to all households that meet eligibility requirements pertaining to income, work, and immigration status. Eligibility and benefits are based on household size, household assets, and gross and net income. In 2006, a family of three with a monthly income less than or equal to $1,798 would meet the gross income eligibility requirement in most places. In 2004, the 24 million people who participated in the program received an average monthly benefit of $200 per household, or $86 per person, or just under $3 per person per day.

According to the USDA's 2007 Farm Bill proposal, the Food Stamp Program is slated for a long overdue name change. The proposal states, "The name does not reflect the Program's mission of reducing hunger and improving nutrition among low-income people."

So the next farm bill might usher in the "Food and Nutrition Program." This new name would be an improvement, I suppose, but the key question is still this: How effective is the program at improving nutrition? Many have questioned whether the Food Stamp Program, designed to provide a nutritional safety net for low-income households, could also be a culprit in the obesity blame game by encouraging the consumption of too much food, or at least, too much consumption of the wrong kinds of food.

Cornell University food security researcher Christine Olson states: "What we find from our studies is that as families become more food insecure, [a measure of inconsistent access to food] the first thing to go from their diets is fruits and vegetables—and the nutrients that go along with them: the vitamin C, vitamin A and fiber."[7]

No surprise there. It is utility maximizing for low-income consumers, like my cousin Carl, to select more affordable, calorie-dense foods that won't spoil when money is tight. So, as long as calorie-dense, nutrient-poor foods are a better deal than more healthful choices, low-income consumers will naturally choose to stock up on the more affordable, less healthy alternatives during periods of financial uncertainty. However, as noted earlier, regardless of income, the diet of most Americans falls far short of government recommendations. It includes more calories than recommended and too few fruits and vegetables.

The Food Stamp Program may provide resources for low-income households to purchase additional foods, but it does nothing to encourage consumption of healthier choices. The fact that the Program distributes benefits only once per month has also been hypothesized to contribute to unhealthy diets. The theory is that soon after the monthly food stamp benefit is issued, food becomes sufficiently abundant so that food-insecure households may overeat. As the month progresses, and participants begin to draw their benefits down, they may start rationing spending and consumption. This cycle of boom to bust, called the "food stamp cycle," may result in binge eating and weight gain.[8]

One study found that women who receive food stamps are significantly more likely to be overweight and obese as compared to those who have similar levels of income but who choose not to participate in the program.[9] A more recent study, however, found that the weight gap between women who receive food stamps and those who do not is vanishing.[10] (Women, by the way, are the primary recipients of food stamps.)

But even if the obesity rates of low-income women on food stamps is, in fact, keeping pace with the rates of low-income women not on food stamps, the fact remains that obesity rates in both groups have been rising rapidly (as it has for men and women in all income brackets).

Although the Food Stamp Program was created more out of equity concerns (i.e., to provide a food safety net) than to resolve an existing market failure, given the rising rates of obesity among its target population, policy makers should revisit the program to determine whether changes should be made, including perhaps revisiting its core mission. The following five strategies have been recently debated to improve the diets—and perhaps reduce the excess weight—among the participant population:

1. *Reduce the benefit.* On the surface, this reform seems to make sense. Since rates of obesity among the target and enrolled population are continuing to increase, thanks to large reductions in the price of calorie-dense food, there may no longer be a need for the program. Consumers can get all the calories they need for just a few bucks a day. Perhaps the program should focus on how to get recipients to eat less, not more. I would endorse this approach if the stated mission were not partly to "*improve* nutrition among low-income people." Reducing the benefit would likely reduce participants' caloric intake, but it would do nothing to improve nutritional intake among the target population. Why? Because as we mentioned above, participants are typically choosing a high-calorie, low-nutrient diet, at least in part, *because* of the constraints of their budget. So lowering the budget will just increase these constraints and put the more healthful (and expensive) food options even further out of reach.

2. *Allow recipients to cash out Food Stamp Program benefits.* This reform would allow participants to cash out their food benefits in dollars and then spend the money however they wish (meaning on either food or nonfood items). This strategy assumes that a utility-maximizing recipient will use the benefit in a way that makes the most sense for his or her family, and this may not be to purchase additional food. If true, this approach would reduce food consumption and perhaps excess weight of some recipients. However, this would make sense only if the goal of the program were to increase the utility, as opposed to nutritional intake, of the target population. As a result, this too is largely inconsistent with the stated mission of the program.

3. *Prohibit recipients from using their benefits to buy foods with limited nutritional value.* Since the current goal of the program is to increase nutritional intake of recipients, then this option seems to make sense. Currently, food stamps cannot be used to purchase alcohol, tobacco,

nonfood items, foods eaten in the store, or hot foods. Why not further restrict the selection to rule out foods of minimal nutritional value? The answer, according to a USDA report, is that it would create too much bureaucracy.[11] The report states that there are "serious problems with the rationale, feasibility and potential effectiveness of this proposal." They further state:

- There are no widely accepted standards to judge the "healthfulness" of individual foods.
- Considering that there are more than 300,000 food products on the market, and an average of 12,000 new products were introduced each year between 1990 and 2000, implementation of food restrictions would increase program complexity and costs.
- Since about 70 percent of all food stamp participants (those who receive less than the maximum benefit) are expected to purchase a portion of their food with their own money, there is no guarantee that recipients would not substitute one form of payment (cash) for another (food stamps).
- There is no strong research-based evidence to support restricting food stamp benefits. Food stamp recipients are no more likely than higher income consumers to choose foods with little nutritional value; thus, the basis for singling out low-income food stamp recipients and restricting their food choices is not clear.

I find these responses troubling. With respect to the first two bullets, many states are creating their own standards for what constitutes a healthy food and are using these standards to determine the foods that can be offered to kids in schools. I see no reason why the USDA could not do something similar for recipients if they wanted to. With respect to the third bullet, under this logic, there is no reason for the program to rule out alcohol or cigarettes, or nonfood items, for that matter. If the USDA recognizes that substitution is a major issue, then giving food stamps as opposed to cash would have no added benefit and the program should strongly consider the second recommendation above.

The final bullet is also troubling given that it suggests USDA has bought into my argument that unhealthy food consumption is not an issue of equity. If the agency believes this to be true, what is the rationale for singling out low-income households and trying to get them to consume healthier diets?

Regardless of these concerns, if policy makers believe that improving nutritional intake should remain a goal of the program, in lieu of restricting which foods are covered by the program and running into concerns over substitution of covered for noncovered items, I recommend that the program implements monetary incentives to influence food purchases.

4. *Use incentives to promote specific foods.* Under this alternative, food stamp recipients would be able to use their status and food stamps to obtain price discounts on healthy products. This would encourage greater consumption of these products in lieu of products that are deemed to be of low nutritional value. Fresh fruits and vegetables, for example, could be purchased at significant discounts, whereas other foods with lower nutrient content, would receive smaller discounts. This strategy would not restrict choice but would provide incentives for individuals to purchase healthier food options. There may also be some positive spillover for non–food stamp recipients if the increased demand for these products encouraged suppliers in low-income neighborhoods to keep fresh produce on hand.

5. *Provide more nutrition education.* Many have argued that an effective strategy to encourage healthier diets and improved health outcomes among beneficiaries is to provide more nutrition education. I'm highly skeptical that this would be money well spent. In the absence of subsidies for healthier products, I doubt that a significant investment in nutrition education would have much of an impact.

Currently, federal nutrition education expenditures are minuscule compared to food industry advertising expenditures, although they have increased rapidly in recent years. In 1992, five states had approved nutrition education programs (NEPs) with a federal expenditure of less than $100,000. In 2002, 48 states had NEPs with federal expenditures of nearly $199 million.[12] This seems like a big number but it pales in comparison to what the food industry spends marketing their products. For example, the ad budget for the top-spending fast-food restaurants alone came in at $2.3 billion in 2004.[13]

Given this imbalance and the fact that these programs do nothing to change the costs and benefits of behaviors related to obesity, it is not surprising that they appear to have had little, if any, impact. It is just not clear to me what we could tell a utility-maximizing, low-income consumer like Cousin Carl that would encourage him to consume healthier products in greater quantities than he does now. I think he could do more to educate policy makers about how to make smart (utility-maximizing) food choices when on a tight budget. This is not just my speculation. Past research suggests that the health benefits of nutritional information programs are modest at best.[14]

We could easily dedicate the rest of the book to debating the merits of the Food Stamp Program and whether or not it is even necessary given today's abundance of high-calorie, low-cost foods. However, at the core of the argument is this point: If policy makers are truly interested in improving nutritional intake among beneficiaries, they are going to have to make healthy choices more affordable. Otherwise, low-income, utility-maximizing consumers will continue to bypass these choices in favor of options that offer a greater bang for the buck.

Wading through the Medicare Morass

As we discussed in Chapter 6, among other issues, obesity is making us all dip into our pockets a little deeper when we pay our taxes. Because most obese individuals will inevitably be covered by Medicare, and because of the high prevalence of obesity among the Medicaid population, obesity costs state and federal governments about $45 billion per year in increased medical spending for these programs. This increases the average tax bill by about $175 per person per year.[15]

So should we all be forced to pay a price because Uncle Al and Cousin Carl (and lots of others) are unwilling to make the increasingly difficult sacrifices required to control their weight? Under our current system of health care financing, the answer is yes, we should pay. Why? Because that is how we, as taxpayers and voters, opted to design the systems. Both Medicaid and Medicare were designed as entitlement programs. That means that all people who qualify for the programs are given equal access. Regardless of whether Uncle Al is obese, smokes, drinks, rides a motorcycle without a helmet, does drugs, or engages in risky sex, he will pay the same Medicare premiums as everyone else who is eligible for the program.

If one is truly upset about the high costs of obesity in Medicare and Medicaid, there is an easy solution: Say goodbye to the "entitlement" aspect of the programs and make obese people pay more money to access the programs. Called an experience-rated insurance premium (charging people based on their expected costs), this extra cost would compensate the program for the higher costs imposed by those with excess weight. There is a precedent for this change. For example, smokers pay a higher fee to receive life insurance, and both smokers and obese individuals often pay a higher fee to receive health insurance in the individual (non-employment-based) market.

So how would this change affect Uncle Al? Well, in a few years he will enter the Medicare program. Results from our obesity cost analyses (see Chapter 6) reveal that if his premiums increased by 37 percent, or about $1,500 per year, the government would, on average, no longer be losing money as a result of his excess weight. At this point Uncle Al would have the option of paying the extra money and maintaining his current weight, or he could attempt to lose weight and pay the lower premiums. If the premiums are set correctly, his decision about whether or not to lose weight will not impact the bottom line of the Medicare trust fund. On average, Medicare will be paying out what it brings in.

Experience rating is easy to implement, virtually costless, and will reduce the costs that Uncle Al and Cousin Carl impose on Dad and others down to zero—regardless of whether they decide to lose weight.

So we could easily solve some of Dad's problems with Uncle Al and Cousin Carl by changing the Medicare and Medicaid programs to charge higher premiums for those who are overweight or obese. (Don't worry, Dad would still find plenty of reasons to gripe about Uncle Al.)

However, if he thought about it, I'm not even sure Dad would support this solution. First, if we raise rates for those with excess weight, why not do it for anyone who is caught engaging in any risky behavior that might increase health care costs down the road?

For example, one call to Dad's automobile insurer will reveal that he is a terrible driver. He drives an automatic with one foot on the gas and the other on the brake nearly all the time. Not only does it sicken those unlucky passengers who ride in the backseat, but it is responsible for at least a few fender benders. So maybe Dad should pay higher rates as well?

Experience rating in publicly funded health insurance programs brings us down a slippery slope. Not only does it remove the entitlement nature of these programs, but it basically gives government a free pass to "tax" any behavior that might increase health care costs down the road. This prospect makes me very uncomfortable.

The point is that we (the societal we) cannot have it both ways. We can drop the entitlement aspect of Medicare and Medicaid and charge experience-rated premiums. In that case, obesity would no longer impose an additional financial burden on these programs (or Dad's tax bill). Or we can address broader societal issues, including funding for Medicare and Medicaid, to resolve concerns over unequal access to health care. However, if we do the latter, then it is inappropriate to use the high costs of these programs as justification for government interventions aimed at reducing rates of obesity. For it is government intervention (i.e., creation of Medicare and Medicaid) that has made these high costs a "problem" in the first place.

By this point in the book, I hope I have convinced you that most individuals have some control over their weight. It should also be clear, however, that not everyone starts on an equal playing field. For example, if you are from Nauru or Tonga, are a Pima Indian, or have the newly discovered obesity gene, you are likely to weigh more than many individuals who have the very same diet and exercise patterns as you do. Should they pay higher health insurance rates for Medicare and Medicaid because they are genetically predisposed toward obesity? Clearly, there are real equity concerns with implementing an approach that sets publicly funded health insurance premiums based on body mass index (BMI).

Moreover, Medicaid is a safety net program designed to provide health insurance to those who otherwise could not afford it. What happens when Cousin Carl can't pay his Medicaid premiums? Do we deny him potentially lifesaving treatment because he made some choices that Dad doesn't like?

Well, Dad firmly believes that Uncle Al should pay higher Medicare premiums on account of his excess weight. However, I do not think that even he would recommend an experience-rated system for all individuals in these programs. So is there anything the government should do to address the high costs of obesity in publicly funded health insurance programs? The answer to this question requires a rethinking of health care financing in the United States.

Not only do state and federal governments finance the Medicare and Medicaid programs, but after World War II, the government passed legislation that allowed employer contributions to health insurance to be excluded from employees' income and payroll taxes. This large tax break is what encourages many employers to provide health insurance to their employees. However, by promoting employment-based health insurance, and given the fact that employees tend to switch jobs every few years, the subsidy also reduces the likelihood that insurers will provide coverage for obesity prevention activities (see Chapter 10 for a more detailed discussion of this issue).

Recommendations for revamping health care financing in the United States go far beyond the scope of this book, but the reality is that the system we have in place now—employer-based health insurance followed by Medicare at age 65—provides few incentives for investments in wellness and obesity prevention. In the ideal health insurance system, enrollees would remain in the system for a long enough time period so that investments in wellness, via financial incentives or other strategies, would have a chance to pay off.

Instead, current government policy provides disincentives for insurers to incorporate obesity prevention programs into their policies. Short of removing the subsidy for employer-provided health insurance, which is something I endorse, government should promote efforts to develop and market new health care financing arrangements that make it profitable for insurers to invest in the long-term health of their insured population.

Until the next generation of health care financing is developed, policy makers would still like not to have to throw so much money at obesity-related health care expenses. They probably consider this goal a *compelling public need*. Dad, and many other taxpayers, would readily agree. Without changing the entitlement nature of these programs or cutting benefits, there may still be cost-cutting strategies that would be a win–win for government and enrollees. For example, some Medicaid programs have begun offering coverage for Weight Watchers. There is not yet any evidence that this coverage will save money, but if it does, that would be something even Dad would support. If it saves money *and* benefits enrollees, why not cover it?

Another example might be for government to mandate or subsidize coverage for certain obesity treatments, wellness programs, or other interventions among the population under age 65. As we will discuss in Chapter 10, these interventions might save money in the long run, but due to concerns about the short time horizon of employers, among other issues, few firms have the incentives to provide them on their own. If the government required every firm to provide the services or subsidized their costs, return on investment would be less of a concern, and this too could be a win-win situation.

It is worth reiterating, however, that if the high costs of obesity to government are the underlying justification for publicly funded obesity interventions, then, regardless of how effective at reducing weight or improving health an intervention may be, unless it is cost-saving, it ultimately raises dad's taxes even more. Moreover, I've yet to come across an obesity intervention that has proven to save money.

The State of Our Neighborhoods

Let's take a brief look back to what Uncle Al's dad, my grandfather, might have called "the good old days." Before the middle of the twentieth century, communities were typically designed to offer pedestrians a convenient way to walk or bike to everyday activities such as shopping, work, and school. Economics was at the core of this design. Homes, employment centers, stores, schools, and government services were built within close proximity. Streets usually had sidewalks and were laid out in a grid to give pedestrians easy, direct routes from place to place. High-density residences helped make local stores financially viable. These traditional communities were called "walkable."[16]

Then, later in the twentieth century, America experienced the rise of suburbia, and the core philosophy behind the "built environment" fundamentally changed. Now cars, not pedestrians, became king. Policies were geared at optimizing automobile travel. Different types of land use were separated by zoning laws, so homes were no longer built within walking distance to stores, employment centers and other conveniences. Residential streets were broken down into long blocks and cul-de-sacs, often without sidewalks, making pedestrian travel difficult. These low-traffic residential streets then fed into multilane, high-speed arterial streets that presented serious dangers to pedestrians. Because the design of suburbs essentially requires the use of automobiles for all trips, these communities are often described as "unwalkable."[17]

Part of the reason that many communities are "unwalkable" is that zoning laws do not allow employment, residences, and retail shops to be located geographically close to each other. Therefore, going from one location to another likely requires a car. This is another example of how well-intentioned government policy has contributed to an obesity-promoting environment.

The connection between sprawl, inactivity, and obesity is more than just hypothetical.[18] Studies show that there is a higher risk of obesity in less walkable communities.[19,20] For example, compare the least sprawling part of the United States, New York City, where people live, work, and shop in the same locations, with the most sprawling area, Geauga County, Ohio, (located in the greater Cleveland metropolis, an area with a population of 91,000 in 2000). Not surprisingly, there is an average six-pound difference in weight between the thinner New York City residents and the heavier Ohio residents.[21]

The good news is that some lawmakers are now beginning to wake up to the reality of how aspects of social planning, such as zoning, school siting (the term used to define where schools are located), sidewalks, safe play areas, and access to fresh foods, collectively called the "built environment," contribute to rising rates of obesity, diabetes, asthma, and other diseases.

For example, school siting is sparking a particularly heated debate in many local communities. In the 1950s, as people moved to the suburbs, districts began building large schools on the periphery of communities. Land was cheaper in these locations, so districts could afford to build bigger, better schools with more space for sports fields. One unforeseen consequence of these well-intentioned policies was the elimination of the schools that had glued "walkable" neighborhoods together.

Many communities are now taking a fresh look at the old "neighborhood" concept. Along with a renewed interest in mixed-use suburban environments, there is now more interest in smaller schools located within walking distance of neighborhoods.

Given my concerns about childhood obesity, I recently moved our family into an "urban village" complete with walking trails to a neighborhood school. My family can now walk from our home to shops, restaurants, a wellness center, a swim club, a grocery store, and numerous parks. I chose this neighborhood for these amenities, but it came with a hefty price tag. The cost of our house is more than double what it was in our old neighborhood. For me, the additional cost is worth it to give our family the chance to lead a healthier lifestyle. My kids are far more active than they were in our old, unwalkable neighborhood.

I must confess, however, that I cannot recall more than a handful of times that my wife has walked the half mile to the grocery store, and many of our neighbors drive their kids the half mile to school every day. I also know that Uncle Al lives in a walkable neighborhood, yet he owns a golf cart for making the trips around his hood. So while changes in zoning will lower the barriers to exercise, only some of us will actually choose to take advantage of the lower costs and increase our levels of physical activity. Others, like my wife and Uncle Al, may still choose the path of least resistance.

The Road Ahead

Due to unintended consequences, well-intentioned government policies are partly responsible for creating an obesity-promoting environment. To solve this problem, government policy makers certainly should revisit these policies. It also appears that they are poised to implement new polices directly aimed at increasing physical activity, improving healthy food consumption, and reducing rates of obesity. But is there a compelling public need for these programs, and can government engineer the desired outcomes? In this section, we look at three policies that have received considerable attention of late. Specifically, we discuss:

1. Menu labeling
2. Obesity lawsuits
3. A fat tax

Hold the Lettuce, Bring on the Lasagna

Which dinner item at Romano's Macaroni Grill would you guess has more calories: traditional lasagna or a chicken Caesar salad?

The answer: the salad. If you got it wrong, you are not alone. Nearly 70 percent of Californians who took a survey in March 2007 failed to identify the low-calorie, low-salt, high-fat, or high-calorie items in a short list of dishes from Denny's, Chili's, Romano's Macaroni Grill, and McDonald's.[22]

The Davis-based California Center for Public Health Advocacy (CCPHA), which commissioned the poll, claims the results contradict the restaurant industry's claims that fast-food restaurants offer plenty of healthy options and consumers just need to make better decisions. "You'd have a better chance at choosing a healthy option by throwing a dart at the menu board," said Harold Goldstein, executive director of the CCPHA, in a report the CCPHA issued.[23]

Even Goldstein missed every question. He said that the fact that lasagna is less caloric than a meal based on lettuce particularly surprised him. "It says 'salad,' so you think it's the best choice," he said.

More than 80 percent of survey participants said they would support a law requiring that restaurants post nutrition information on menus. Why not support this law? From a consumer's perspective, it can't hurt. But tell that to the restaurant owners who have to comply with the law.

The poll's release came a week before the California State Senate voted on a bill that would require restaurant chains with 10 or more locations to list on menus the calorie count, grams of saturated and trans fats, as well as the carbohydrate and sodium content for standard items. Menu boards at fast-food restaurants would only be required to display calorie counts.

California is in good company. Starting in 2001, when the U.S. surgeon general began calling for an increase in nutrition information for foods eaten and prepared away from home, similar bills have been proposed by lawmakers across the country—with varying degrees of success—from Washington, D.C., to Connecticut and New York to places as far flung as Puerto Rico. And, at the federal level, the Menu Education and Labeling Act, which would require restaurant chains with 20 or more outlets to post calorie and other nutritional information adjacent to each food item, was introduced in the House of Representatives in 2003. While the bill simmers in committee, the debate over the benefits of legislating labels in restaurants boils over.

Here's the basis for these bills. Not only is it difficult to make an educated guess about the nutritional value of menu items, but, as we reported in Chapter 2, food away from home is increasingly contributing to Americans' caloric intake. About 46 percent of Americans' household food budgets are now spent on goods prepared outside the home. Every day, about 132 million Americans eat out, reports the National Restaurant Association.[24] And, what we are eating away from home is typically more calorie-dense and nutritionally poor compared with foods prepared at home.

So here we have yet another example of a government intervention that, at least on the surface, seems to make perfect sense. Just give people some more information about the foods they eat in restaurants. Who's it going to harm?

Well, take the Super Duper Weenie in Fairfield, Connecticut, for one. John Pellegrino, a co-owner, said labeling his menu items, which include "the Californian"— a hot dog piled high with chili and cheese— would be costly and difficult. The restaurant's other co-owner, Gary Zemola, put it more bluntly to a *New York Times* reporter, "If you are looking to count calories, what are you doing here?"[25]

Mandatory labeling would, in fact, come at a significant cost, both to suppliers and to regulatory agencies who would have to monitor compliance. Suppliers would be required to finance the costs of providing additional information, and due to the increased cost of labeling, may be less likely to expand or change their existing menus. The restaurant industry also says providing nutrition labeling for all menu items is infeasible because recipes change frequently, and patrons often request customization of their meals and the number of options available for customization is large. For example, according a press release issued by the National Restaurant Association, a sandwich consisting of just five items can be ordered 120 different ways.[26] Throw in five condiment options—such as lettuce, ketchup, mustard, onions, and oil—and now you have more than 3.6 million combinations.

But these concerns could be addressed (at a cost). More pressing is whether there is truly an economic or noneconomic "need" for this legislation. As we've stated in earlier chapters, if consumers truly demanded this information, restaurants would (and many do) provide the information to their patrons. So there is no obvious market failure that this legislation aims to address.

If the legislation is aimed at reducing rates of obesity, that is likely to be an uphill battle. There is, in fact, little evidence that restaurant labeling will even change dining behaviors. A laboratory study of food intake among normal-weight women found that explaining the concept of energy density and providing nutrition information on labels during meals had no impact on energy intake.[27] Similarly, a controlled experiment in a restaurant setting in England found that provision of nutrition information had no effect on overall energy and fat intake.[28]

Nutrition labeling, in general, appears to have done little to stem the rising tide of obesity. America hasn't slimmed down since the 1994 introduction of federally mandated nutrition facts on most packaged food. Quite the opposite—we've gotten fatter.

Many factors, such as whether the information is important to a large number of consumers (or extremely important to a small group of consumers), the relative health effects of specific attributes listed on the labels, whether consumers will expend the time and effort to read the labels, and the ease with which information can be used by individuals, will determine whether labeling alters behavior enough to make significant differences in food purchases and ultimately rates of obesity. For many, the answer is that labeling is unlikely to influence their food choices.

In March 2004, The Food and Drug Administration's (FDA's) Obesity Working Group (OWG), weighed in on this issue in a report entitled "Calories Count."[29] The report recommended that restaurants should not be *mandated* to provide nutrition labeling. Instead, the OWG recommended that the FDA *encourage* restaurants to provide more readily available nutrient content information at the point of sale.

The OWG also recommended that FDA encourage consumers to request nutrition information in restaurants. The report stated, "Because restaurants respond to consumer demand, such demand may help create an impetus for more restaurants to provide such information." (By the way, you may not be surprised to find out that the working group included several economists.)

In essence, the OWG report encouraged the market to sort the labeling issue out by itself—relying on the laws of supply and demand to bring us to the optimal level of provision of nutrition information. Not surprisingly, I agree with this recommendation. If consumers were to start dining in great numbers at those restaurants that voluntarily offer nutrition facts on their menus, other restaurants would soon follow.

Similarly, by the way, if demand for healthier meals and smaller portions were higher, then restaurants would respond by revamping their menus. But I'm not holding my breath on this one.

The McLawsuits

In early 2002, Caesar Barber, a 57-year-old maintenance worker from the Bronx, New York, filed suit against McDonald's, Pizza Hut, Kentucky Fried Chicken, and Wendy's. Barber weighed 272 pounds, suffered from diabetes, and had experienced two heart attacks. He blamed his poor health on these fast-food companies.

> I can trace [my health problems] all back to the high fat, grease and salt, all back to McDonald's, Wendy's, Burger King—there was no fast food I didn't eat, and I ate it more often than not because I was single, it was quick and I'm not a very good cook. It was a necessity, and I think it was killing me, my doctor said it was killing me, and I don't want to die.[30]

Barber sounds like a utility maximizer to me. I suspect he knew long before his doctor pointed it out that the food was unhealthy. How else would he explain his weight of 272 pounds and his two heart attacks? But he also knew that fast-food restaurant fare was cheap and convenient—not to mention, tasty. It certainly seems to me that Barber, Uncle Al, and Cousin Carl have a lot in common. They all could have done things differently and weighed less, but they chose not to. It is certainly not the fault of the fast-food companies that Barber made these choices. In Barber's own words, these venues were a necessity for him (of course, Professor Silberberg would disagree), suggesting he would have been far worse off had they not existed.

So that's the story, case closed. The courts apparently agreed—Barber's lawyers withdrew the case only a few months after the initial filing. But the Barber case is just one in a recent slew of litigation aimed at "Big Food."

Perhaps the most intriguing of the recent lawsuits is *Pelman v. McDonald's Corp.* The case was initially filed in the Southern District of New York in 2002. The suit involved Ashley Pelman, age 14, and Jazlyn Bradley, age 19. Pelman and Bradley said that on most school days, their breakfast, lunch, and snacks consisted almost entirely of McDonald's Happy Meals, McMuffins, and Big Macs. Ashley Pelman was 4'10" and 170 pounds (a BMI of 35.5) and Jazlyn Bradley was 5'6" and 270 pounds (giving her a BMI of 43.6). The teenagers alleged the food caused them to develop diabetes, coronary disease, and high blood pressure and cholesterol.

Although the case has seen several dismissals and appeals since the original filing, it largely hinges on the plaintiffs' claim that they were unaware of the dangers of eating at McDonald's. The plaintiffs argued that their excess consumption resulted from deceptive marketing practices and that McDonalds acted negligently "in selling food products that are high in cholesterol, fat, salt and sugar when studies show that such foods cause obesity and detrimental health effects." They further argued that "McDonald's failed to warn the consumers of McDonalds' products [that] a diet high in fat, salt, sugar and cholesterol could lead to obesity and health problems."

Although we may not have heard the last of Ashley Pelman and Jazlyn Bradley, all of the plaintiffs' claims were initally dismissed (though after multiple appeals and amendments to the complaint, three claims remain against McDonald's). In an early dismissal of the case (prior to the appeal), the presiding judge stated that "as long as a consumer exercises free choice with appropriate knowledge, liability for negligence will not attach to a manufacturer."

In other words, the judge recognized that utility-maximizing consumers like Uncle Al and Morgan Spurlock (of *Super Size Me* fame) may optimally choose to eat at McDonald's every day, even with full information of the adverse health consequences. However, he did state that if the plaintiffs could show that the additives to McDonald's products were harmful and the public could not reasonably acquire this knowledge in order to make an informed choice, the case might have merit. He then allowed the plaintiffs to file an amended pleading, suggesting he did not think the case was frivolous.

Unlike Uncle Al, I'm no lawyer, but this case troubles me for a couple of reasons. First, for Pelman and Bradley to win the case, one of the findings they would have to show is that it was their excess consumption of McDonald's that made them obese. If, like Caesar Barber, they ate at many food venues, it would be difficult to prove that any one establishment was the cause of the excess weight. But if they ate only at McDonald's, I find it hard to believe that they could not associate their excess weight with their daily consumption of McDonald's fare.

Bradley was 19 years old and 270 pounds. Even under the most deceptive advertising practices, if all she eats is McDonald's, and her weight balloons, wouldn't you think a 19 year old could make the connection between her weight and her food consumption? If she is mentally unable to make that connection, then, in my view, no amount of information McDonald's could provide would help her make more informed decisions. I would argue, then, that McDonald's should not be held responsible for her current weight and health problems.

Ashley Pelman was only 14, but the same logic applies to her. Even a 14 year old should have the ability to equate her food consumption, physical activity, and weight outcomes. And if she can't, one must question whether her parents (and her school) bear at least as much responsibility as McDonald's for her current weight and poor health.

I would also be willing to wager that neither of these defendants was physically active at the time that their weight was increasing and that they watched hours of television every week. So even if they did eat at McDonald's every day, it is still hard to lay the blame entirely on McDonald's doorstep. As we will discuss in the next chapter, these issues also point to the role government plays in educating youth about the benefits of healthy food consumption and physical activity and encouraging, if not forcing, youth to be more physically active.

Although neither Caesar Barber nor Ashley Pelman and friends have been successful in their efforts to collect damages as a result of their excess weight, these kinds of cases are a major concern for fast-food companies. They are fearful that lawyers—emboldened by their success with the tobacco industry—have next set their sights on the food industry. As a result, food purveyors have been hard at work lobbying Congress to pass legislation to insulate them from these types of lawsuits. Congress has responded with a series of legislation. One example, known affectionately as the "Cheeseburger Bill," or more formally, the Personal Responsibility in Food Consumption Act of 2003, was first introduced in the House by Senator Ric Keller (R-FL), to prevent the obesity lawsuits that many claimed were subverting the democratic process.[31] But is this bill appropriate?

The bill would "prohibit new and dismiss pending civil actions by any person against food manufacturers, marketers, distributors, advertisers, sellers, and trade associations for any injury related to a person's accumulated acts of consumption of food and weight gain, obesity, or any associated health condition."[32]

The bill concluded that "because fostering a culture of acceptance of personal responsibility is one of the most important ways to promote a healthier society," obesity lawsuits "are not only legally frivolous and economically damaging, but also harmful to a healthy America."

A very few exceptions were made to "preserve lawsuits based on violations of express contracts, knowing violations of laws governing food marketing or labeling, and lawsuits brought by the federal government for unfair trade practices, false advertising, or adulterated food."

The bill overwhelmingly passed in the House but failed in the Senate a year later. Proponents of the bill were not easily dissuaded, however, as the bill was reintroduced early in 2005, passed the House later that year, but again died in the Senate. But the lack of success at the national level is not mirrored at the state level. In fact, from 2003 to 2006, while eight states rejected "frivolous lawsuit/personal responsibility" legislation, 23 states passed these laws, and decisions for another four are still pending.

These bills are worrisome. Do we really want to insulate the food industry from obesity legislation? If you believe my story that the rise in obesity rates is a result of utility-maximizing behavior on the part of consumers, then it would be difficult for consumers to prevail in these cases. Given that, any suit filed would only serve to tie up the courts and impose undue costs on both plaintiffs and defendants. Of course, the legislation is more concerned with the costs to the defendants, the industry it is aiming to protect. However, I would argue that these costs are only undue if the suit is unsuccessful. But how could we learn that until the suit has been decided? With this legislation in place, we would never know.

Even in the McDonald's suit, the presiding judge saw enough merit in the case that he allowed it to be amended and refiled. I would recommend that rather than restrict the ability to sue food purveyors, the plaintiffs would be required to pay the defendants' legal costs if the suit is unsuccessful. This added disincentive, similar to what occurs in many European countries, should be sufficient to dissuade consumers from filing frivolous obesity lawsuits.[33] If it does not, then maybe the suits are not so frivolous after all. Moreover, it is possible that the threat of a successful lawsuit (and a financial judgment), will motivate food companies to change their practices. The following examples, although not directly related to obesity, provide support for this claim:

- In 2003, a lawsuit was filed against Kraft Foods in California, to stop the sale of Oreos to children because they contained trans fats. The lawsuit was eventually dropped because Kraft lowered the amount of trans fats used and began offering a low-fat version of their famous cookie.[34]
- In 2006, a Los Angeles woman filed suit against Kraft, claiming fraud because their guacamole contained less than 2 percent of the one ingredient thought to be the base for any guacamole—avocado. They have since changed the name from "Kraft Dips Guacamole" to "Kraft Dip—Guacamole Flavor."[35]
- McDonald's paid out $8.5 million in 2005 for not keeping their promise to reduce the amount of trans fats used in their cooking oil.[36]
- Both Pizza Hut and McDonald's had to answer to vegetarian and Hindu groups when it was discovered that meat flavoring was used in foods labeled as "vegetarian." McDonald's paid out $10 million in 2002 for calling their French fries and hash browns vegetarian when the vegetable oil contained "essence of beef" for flavoring. Pizza Hut, by the way, claimed they never called the "Veggie Lover's Pizza" vegetarian, and never paid out for using beef flavoring in the cheese.[37,38]
- A lawsuit was filed in 2005 against Kraft and several other dairy producers to stop a multimillion-dollar ad campaign that claimed milk could facilitate weight loss because it was based on unsubstantiated scientific evidence. After the suit was filed, Kraft discontinued use of these ads.[39]

Note that it was the mere filing of a lawsuit that encouraged Kraft foods to reduce the amount of trans fats in Oreo cookies, change the name of their guacamole (flavored) dip, and stop advertising milk as a weight-loss product.

So while I agree that policy makers should increase the costs of filing frivolous lawsuits, in my opinion, the European approach, in which the plaintiffs would be required to pay the defendants' legal costs if the suit is unsuccessful, would serve that purpose better than an outright ban.

What about a Fat Tax?

So the Cheeseburger Bill may not be such a great idea. As an alternative, some argue that we should impose a small, or perhaps even a not-so-small, sin tax, also called a "fat tax" or "Twinkie tax," on unhealthy foods just like we do on cigarettes and alcohol. The theory is that this tax would serve two purposes. First, the money raised could be used to finance obesity prevention programs, offset the costs of obesity to Medicare and Medicaid, or perhaps to subsidize the price of healthier options. Second, since falling food prices, especially for fattening foods, are partly responsible for the obesity "crisis," taxing these foods should reduce their consumption, and, in theory, lower rates of obesity.

There is a precedent for this strategy. Sin taxes on cigarettes and alcohol have successfully reduced their use. In fact, although public health advocates who tout the success of antismoking campaigns are loath to admit this, rising cigarette taxes are responsible for the vast majority of the reductions in smoking rates witnessed over the past few decades.[40]

Implementing a sin tax to address obesity is hardly a new idea. Kelly Brownell, a PhD psychologist and director of the Rudd Center for Food Policy and Obesity at Yale University, has been pushing food-related sin taxes since the 1980s. He would like government to use revenue from junk-food taxes to subsidize healthier food choices and fund nutrition education campaigns.[41-43]

The tax, says Brownell, would be a proactive response to a food industry and consumer culture that increasingly promotes high-fat/low-nutrition products as the cheapest, tastiest, most convenient, and most available dietary options.

There's little doubt that fat taxes have the capability to raise significant funds. Brownell estimated in 2000 that a national tax of just one cent per 12-ounce soft drink would generate $1.5 billion annually. A national tax of one cent per pound of candy would generate $70 million. A potato chip tax is worth $54 million and taxes on other snack foods, fats, and oils would be good for $190 million. The grand total of junk-food taxes would approach $2 billion per year.[44]

By the way, a "Twinkie tax" is not just academic talk. You might be surprised to learn that a few states have already implemented Brownell's "Twinkie tax" concept. For example, West Virginia taxes one cent for each bottle or can of soda sold. All revenue is placed into a state "Special Medical School Fund."[45] In 2004, Indiana put into effect a tax on "non-nutritive beverages" (defined as soft drinks and diluted fruit juices) at a rate of $2 per gallon of syrup or about one cent per can. The revenue goes into a long-term care continuum fund.[46] While the added income stemming from both of these taxes goes toward health-related areas, neither tax directly targets obesity prevention. And notably, neither tax is aimed at reducing obesity levels. It's essentially used as a means to generate revenue for the state.

Small taxes aimed at generating revenue are one thing, but a tax aimed at altering consumption enough to impact rates of obesity is much more complicated. There are a number of associated concerns. Let's take them one at a time.

Is There a Market Failure that These Taxes Are Meant to Address?

As we discussed in Chapter 7, there is no obvious market failure that would be resolved via a fat tax. Cigarette taxes reduce exposure to secondhand smoke, and alcohol taxes reduce rates of drunk driving—what would fat taxes reduce? The answer, in large part, is that they would reduce the buying power of consumers who eat fattening food (another good example of an unintended consequence for a well-intended government action). And because people on lower incomes spend a higher proportion of their income on food, this type of tax is largely regressive in nature. One would be hard pressed to justify a fat tax based on equity concerns. A fat tax would be more likely to hurt, not help, the finances of those with limited incomes. If the tax were large enough, it could reduce disposable income for many consumers. But for the most part, Cousin Carl would be the one to suffer the consequences for this tax—not Uncle Al.

What Would We Tax? Narrowly defined taxes, on carbonated beverages, for example, if they were large enough, would very likely reduce consumption of these foods, but they would also likely increase consumption of substitutes products (e.g., energy and sports drinks) that may be no healthier than the taxed products. Even a tax on fat may not have the intended effect if consumers (and suppliers) switch from high-fat to high-sugar products.

Moreover, what is the justification for taxing carbonated beverages, for example, and not taxing other unhealthy foods such as candy and French fries? And what about also taxing activities (e.g., television and video games) that are likely also partly responsible for the rise in obesity rates? And come to think of it, should we try to come up with a way to tax every possible obesity-inducing culprit (see Chapters 2, 3 and 4)? For example, maybe people who work sedentary jobs should pay higher taxes than people whose jobs are more physically demanding.

It certainly seems problematic to target one sector, or one or two food categories, in the obesity blame game and to not address other areas that are also prime suspects. Even a fat tax is problematic given that an excess of calories is ultimately what is causing rising rates of obesity.

Would a Sin Tax Actually Reduce Obesity Levels? Due to the consumer's ability to substitute one food product for another, the reality is that a food sin tax would need to be broad based and large if it were to have any chance of serving as a deterrent and impacting rates of obesity. Even then, there is little evidence to suggest that this strategy would be successful. One study suggests that a 100 percent tax on unhealthy foods would only reduce average BMI by 1 percent.[47] So we could, at least in theory, tax away obesity, but given the large drop in food prices (primarily for high-calorie foods) over the past few decades, it would need to be a hefty tax indeed. Ironically, a large enough tax might generate a renewed mission for the Food Stamp Program.

Is There a Financial Justification for the Tax? One might argue that even without a market failure, the government should tax unhealthy food to make up for the high costs of obesity in the Medicare and Medicaid program. However, as we pointed out earlier, if the government is truly upset about these costs, it could charge a higher rate for obese individuals enrolled in these programs, or even drop the programs altogether. The problem with attempting to solve these problems with a "Twinkie tax" is that many nonobese individuals will wind up paying the tax on top of paying for the costs of obesity in the Medicare and Medicaid programs. For example, Dad and I are already, in part, financing the public-sector costs of obesity through our taxes. Is it fair that we should also have to pay more for our Big Macs and Cokes (in truth, I consume these on occasion, but Dad does not) when we are, at least for the moment, not even overweight?

Kelly Brownell and others might argue that the tax would be so small as to not adversely impact consumers. If true, it merely represents a hidden tax. At this point, one must question the point of the tax. It clearly won't serve as a deterrent to unhealthy eating. And, as noted above, many of the current food-related sin taxes do not even go toward obesity prevention. So if the tax simply serves as a convenient way for state governments to drum up some extra cash, it really can't be construed as an antiobesity measure.

Is There a Compelling Public Need? According to the voting public, the answer, in short, is no. Most Americans just plain don't like the idea. A 2005 joint study by researchers at Harvard's Kennedy School of Government and Princeton's Woodrow Wilson School of Public and International Affairs, found that food taxes were the least popular health initiative, with only 27 percent agreeing to support a snack tax proposal and only 6 percent strongly supporting the tax.[48] In fact, nearly 60 percent of respondents disagreed or strongly disagreed with using snack taxes to subsidize the production and distribution of healthier foods. Although support for these taxes appears to be on the rise, more recent surveys reveal that the majority of Americans remain opposed to sin taxes on food as a means to control obesity.[49]

These discussions, put together, reveal that not only is there no clear market failure that would be corrected through the implementation of a sin tax, this strategy is also unlikely to effectively reduce rates of obesity unless it were implemented on a very large scale, in which case it might increase food scarcity among low-income families. Oh, and by the way, most Americans are not in favor of the idea. So bottom line? This is another example of a government intervention that would likely cause more harm than good.

There is one important caveat to this discussion. A targeted food tax would be appropriate if it "undoes" a subsidy that artificially lowers the costs of some product (e.g., corn or corn by-products) below its market value. In this case, one type of government intervention (i.e., the tax) may be warranted to undo the adverse effects of another (i.e., the subsidy). Of course, the simpler action, as we discussed in the food bill section, would be to remove the subsidies and let food prices be set by the laws of supply and demand. A change of this nature, however, might fall into the category of "fat chance."

Summing Up

There are no clear market failures that suggest additional government interventions are warranted to reduce obesity rates among adults. Short of resolving market failures, the high costs of obesity to Medicare and Medicaid are often presented by policy makers as the underlying motivation for many publicly funded antiobesity initiatives. However, because these programs were purposely created as entitlements, this justification, too, is not compelling.

So is there a role for government when it comes to addressing obesity among adults? First and foremost, because rising obesity rates are likely due, at least in part, to past government actions that inadvertently changed the costs and benefits of behaviors related to food consumption and physical activity, policy makers should focus their efforts on revisiting past policies to determine whether, when it comes to obesity, they may be doing more harm than good.

In addition to revisiting past government policies that may have contributed to an obesity-promoting environment, government policy makers should continue to provide those public goods that would be undersupplied by the private sector. These include provision of parks and recreational facilities, and information about the benefits of a healthy diet and exercise, among others. However, it should be noted that, as was learned from the fight against tobacco, information campaigns, unless they pave the way for more intrusive interventions that change the costs and/or benefits of behaviors related to obesity, are unlikely to have much of an impact.

Policy makers should continue to debate other antiobesity initiatives, but appropriate policy should either resolve an existing market failure or address a compelling public need. The fact that Uncle Al and millions of other adults have chosen a lifestyle that leads to excess weight does not, as economists see it, provide a compelling public need for government intervention. Moreover, the "need" for three additional measures on the table, menu labeling, legislation related to obesity lawsuits, and fat taxes, is also not compelling. However, when it comes to youth, as we discuss in the following chapter, additional government policy is sorely needed.

Chapter 9

Weighing the Public Policy Issues (for Kids)

I am writing the introduction to this chapter in what has to be one of the most appropriate settings possible: I am huddled over my laptop in the middle of Chuck E. Cheese's in Durham, North Carolina. My seven-year-old son has a double-header today—two birthday parties in a row. That's four hours of video games, Kool-Aid, pizza, and candy. Lucky him. Unlucky me.

In fact, as I left the house this morning, grumbling, naturally, about the excessive amounts of added sugars and fats my son would consume and the lack of physical activity he would get today, my wife reassured me: "He will get plenty of exercise running around Chuck E. Cheese's."

But watching my son hit the video games, it's obvious that he is burning off more tokens than calories. In fact, today is likely to be one of many days when his calories-in/calories-out balance tips in the wrong direction. And he's not alone. Excuse me as I start to rant (and I admit, the indescribable noise level in here is making me irritable), but the sight of all these young children, a number of them overweight, downing pizza, cake, candy, and iridescent red punch, and then running off (but only a few yards) to plug more tokens into games and rides has put me in a mood.

Today happens to be the first beautiful day of spring. In three hours I might be able to begin enjoying it, but for now, it's me, my laptop, and Chuck. And it's not just this day. With 26 kids in my son's class, not to mention the kids on the soccer team and in the neighborhood, birthday parties are nearly a weekly event.

Of course, any good economist (or any of you who have read this far into the book) will point out that I didn't have to take my son to the party. I could have taken him to a park to kick around a soccer ball or out to shoot some hoops (which would have been my strong preference). But then I would have faced the wrath of both my son and my wife—and I wouldn't have been able to squeeze in the time to work on this chapter. So, though I'm complaining, this decision, along with the one to steal a slice of greasy pepperoni pizza off of a kid's plate (which, truthfully, was pretty tasty), is utility maximizing for me. The costs (to me) of not taking my son to the party were just too great.

As parents, we face these kinds of choices (going to the party, not stealing the pizza) on behalf of our kids every day. And unlike me, few probably ever consider the darker side of birthday parties. I must confess that on the drive over, with my wife out of earshot, I had a talk with my son about how to eat and drink healthily while at a birthday party (I know, I'm obsessed). I honestly think he gets it. But the truth of the matter is that if destiny were in my son's hands, every day in his young life would be spent at Chuck E. Cheese's or similar venues.

I'm quite certain, with the possible exception of my son, that there's not a kid here worrying about the effect that greasy pizza and sugary juice will have on his or her waistline and future health. But at this young age, that's probably not something they should be worrying about. That's what parents are for. But when parents fail, and we are failing (for proof see Chapter 1), that's where government may want to step in on behalf of America's youth.

And now, in the face of the childhood obesity epidemic in America, local, state, and federal government agencies are becoming increasingly involved. But are their efforts justified? Are they likely to have the intended effects? We explore these questions in this chapter.

First, a Step Back

In Chapter 7 we discussed how there are no obvious market failures that appear to be responsible for the rise in obesity rates. And in Chapter 8, we covered the role of government in addressing obesity among adults. We argued that the primary response should be for policy makers to reconsider past policies that may have unintentionally led to higher rates of obesity.

Government does, however, have a much stronger case for obesity interventions when it comes to youth. In this case, there is a compelling public need, including:

- To protect youth from making decisions they might grow up to regret (myopia).
- To provide youth with information and education that would allow them to make more informed decisions (public good).
- To ensure that all youth have the ability to engage in healthy behaviors (equity).

"Where will our soldiers and sailors and airmen come from? Where will our policemen and firemen come from if the youngsters today are on a trajectory that says they will be obese, laden with cardiovascular disease, increased cancers and a host of other diseases when they reach adulthood?"

—Richard Carmona, the U.S. General Surgeon[1]

As we discussed in Chapter 1, with rates of childhood obesity tripling since the 1980s to around 15 percent, we're raising a generation of children who have the frightening honor of belonging to the first group in history that may have a lower life expectancy than their parents. In fact, the Centers for Disease Control and Prevention (CDC) has predicted that if current trends continue, as many as 30 to 40 percent of today's children will get diabetes in their lifetimes.[2] The long-term health consequences for childhood obesity may be greater than for underage drinking and smoking.

As hard as it is to quit smoking, weight loss may be even tougher. As a result, as noted in Chapter 1, a child who becomes overweight at an early age will have a very difficult time controlling his or her weight later in life. Past diet and exercise decisions, if they lead to excess weight, are very hard to reverse. Therefore, there is a compelling public need for government intervention (and active parenting) at an early age and through adolescence to minimize the possibility of children growing up to regret the diet and exercise choices they may have made as myopic, uninformed youth.

The classical economic model assumes that individuals are capable of weighing the short- and long-term costs and benefits of their decisions and making the choices that are best for them. As a parent of young children, I am the first to admit that kids are not forward-looking thinkers. They often make decisions without considering the consequences a few minutes ahead, let alone a few months or years, down the road. For example, left to his own devices, my son would choose to watch Cartoon Network and eat candy all day long, and he would never do his schoolwork. In the short term, these are utility-maximizing decisions for him, but were he to think long term, it is likely that he would make decisions to invest more in his future.

Because of this myopic behavior and the potential benefits to society (positive externalities) that could result through regulation, there is a compelling public need to interfere in the affairs of youth in many areas. Mandatory schooling, and minimum drinking, smoking, and driving ages are a few of the many government interventions targeted at youth. These regulations are aimed at restricting the choices of youth for the greater good of society.

Whereas one could potentially argue that these same motivations apply to adults, they have a greater understanding of the long-term costs and benefits of their choices or could acquire that knowledge if they chose to do so. They also have a greater cognitive ability to make utility-maximizing choices and have fewer constraints on their behavior than do youth. As a result, the *need* to interfere in the affairs of youth does not directly translate to adults.

Admittedly, some utility-maximizing youth may optimally choose to drink, smoke, and drop out of school at early ages and never regret this decision. However, the government has decided to limit their ability to make these choices to protect those who would grow up to regret having done so. Of course, these concerns also provide a justification for active parenting, and when it comes to diet, exercise, and obesity, there is considerable debate about what role should remain with the parents and where government should step in.

For example, in Chapter 3 we noted that kids who watch a lot of television are more likely to be overweight. We also noted that the link between TV viewing and childhood overweight is not exactly clear. Regardless of this uncertainty, you won't be surprised to learn that I limit the amount of time that my kids are allowed to watch television and play on the computer. To do this, I use an economic approach. I tell my kids that they can watch TV and play on the computer as much as they want, but the deal is that for every minute they spend in front of the TV or on the computer, they need to spend one additional minute engaging in physical activity. I then leave it up to my kids to decide how best to allocate their time. When I'm around, this strategy works surprisingly well, although it requires a fair amount of oversight on my part. When I'm off working, at a conference, or writing this book, I suspect the screen time at my house is substantially higher and physical activity much lower. With only one adult to look after two kids and a baby, the TV, as I've said, turns out to be a pretty handy babysitter.

The government could certainly help me out by yanking Cartoon Network off the air (sorry kids), by limiting the number of commercials for junk food, or even by airing messages to tell kids to turn off the TV and go get some exercise. In reality, our government takes a light hand in regulating food marketing to kids as compared to some other countries (see the food marketing section below). However, it has taken a stab at using the airwaves to encourage kids to be more physically active. "VERB™ Its what you do," was a large-scale national marketing campaign that targeted more than 21 million multiethnic American tweens (aged 9 to 13) through edgy TV, print, and Internet advertising as well as some school and community activities. The goal? To increase kid's physical activity by portraying exercise as cool. After the first year of the campaign, research published in *Pediatrics* reported that the average 9- to 10-year-old youth engaged in 34 percent more free-time physical activity sessions per week than did 9- to 10-year-old youths who were unaware of the campaign.[3]

The study was unable to show that the greater levels of physical activity were *caused* by the program, but it suggested that the program may be having a positive effect. It turned out to not matter. In 2006, after a five-year ride, the plug got pulled from the CDC program due to lack of federal funding.

In any case, irrespective of the success of VERB or other government efforts, isn't it my wife's and my job to determine how much exercise my kids get and how much TV they watch? And although my kids lobby incessantly for sugared cereal, soda, candy, and other foods of minimal nutritional value, my wife and I are the ones who ultimately do the purchasing (although any good advertising agent will tell you that the kids are clearly able to influence our purchasing decisions). So maybe it is the parents' job to ensure that their kids are healthy and active.

Here's the problem: As reported in Chapter 1, the rapid increase in rates of childhood overweight suggests that many of us are failing in that role.

Americans are only recently warming up to the idea of active government interventions when it comes to obesity, and, as noted in the preceding chapter, most of the support is for interventions aimed at youth. As recently as 2001, a nationally representative sample of U.S. households found that "most Americans [were] not seriously concerned with obesity, [expressed] relatively low support for obesity-targeted policies, and still [viewed] obesity as resulting from individual failure."[4]

Then, as the waves of media and government attention increased, the tide began to turn. More recent surveys show that public sentiment has shifted, especially when it comes to kids. Youth-focused interventions have now become much more politically viable. For example, in a survey that my colleagues and I conducted in 2005, respondents said that they consider childhood obesity to be as serious as other major childhood health threats such as tobacco use and violence.[5] This study demonstrated that there is now strong public support for interventions aimed at reducing obesity among children and adolescents. It also showed some of the specific school, community, and media interventions that the public supports and opposes (see Table 9.1).

Table 9.1   Support for Childhood Obesity Intervention Strategies

Intervention	Percentage in Favor
School Vending Machines	
Increase promotion of healthy foods	85.4%
Increase cost of less healthy foods	45.3%
Allow only the sale of healthy foods	70.9%
Remove all vending machines from schools	35.9%
School Cafeterias	
Increase cost of less healthy foods	44%
Restrict availability of less healthy food	74.5%
Allow only the sale of healthy foods	67.4%
School Curriculum	
Require more physical education	82.3%
Require teaching of healthy eating and exercise	93.9%
Weight evaluation in schools	
Recording weight on regular basis	49.5%
Send parents a health report card of children's weight on regular basis	57.1%
Marketing of Less Healthy Foods	
Restrict less healthy food ads during kids' TV programs	75.3%
Prohibit less healthy food ads marketed to kids	47.9%

SOURCE: Evans, D., E. Finkelstein, D. Kamerow, and J. Renaud. 2005. "Public Perceptions of Childhood Obesity." *American Journal of Preventive Medicine* 28, no. 1: 26–32.

The remainder of this chapter describes the pros and cons of a number of these interventions. Because an evaluation of all the interventions currently on the public policy table could easily be a book in and of itself, I focus on the issues that have inspired the most discussion and/or may hold the most promise. These include the following:

- Parental oversight of children's eating habits (can extreme cases be construed as child abuse?)
- Competitive foods in the school cafeteria
- Vending machines in the school cafeteria
- Fresh produce in the school cafeteria
- Body mass index (BMI) report cards in schools
- Physical education in schools
- Food marketing to children

Child Abuse?

There is now a heated debate in many communities, in the United States and abroad, about whether or not parents who let their kids get too fat are committing a form of child abuse. In one case in the United Kingdom, British authorities threatened to take an 8-year-old boy weighing 218 pounds (nearly four times his ideal weight) into protective custody unless his mother improved his diet.[6]

Connor McCreaddie's mother said he steals and hides food, frustrating her efforts to help him. He eats double or triple what a normal eight year old would have, she said. "He likes processed foods and if I try him with any salad, vegetables, fruit, he just refuses to eat it or spits it out," the mother told BBC Radio. "When a child won't eat anything else, you've got to feed them what they like," which, according to the boy, is lots of chocolates and junk food.

Connor said he was frequently bullied and that a five-minute walk left him breathless and vomiting. At night, he had frequent nosebleeds and difficulty breathing.

As sad as this story is, it gets even worse. "I've asked the doctors to check him, but they can't seem to find anything wrong. . . . In a way I hope that he has a disease or syndrome, so that he can be given a tablet or treatment that will make it all stop," his mother said.

Sound familiar? That is what Uncle Al does.

Few in the medical community would dispute that this boy does have a disease, and that it was likely caused, or certainly exacerbated, by his mother's inability to address his eating habits. However, at least for now, there is no magic pill that will cure what ails him. Sadly, Connor and others in his situation face a tough road ahead. As discussed in previous chapters, they will likely face significant discrimination, have many health problems, have a more difficult time landing a good job, and are likely to have an early demise.

So should Connor be removed from his mother's custody? In my view, what his mother is doing is a form of child abuse that needs to be addressed. This situation is no better than if she let Connor smoke and drink. As a result, there is a compelling need for government intervention. In this case, the threat of removal seems to have been sufficient, at least for the moment. As a result of government efforts, Connor started on an exercise program and began eating healthier foods. As of the writing of this book, his weight was down slightly, probably, in large part, because of the threat that he would be removed from his mother if it did not improve. Hopefully, Connor's weight will continue to decrease. However, if it is shown that his mother has ceased to make efforts to improve Connor's food intake and physical activity levels, policy makers would be justified in following through on the threat of removal, for Connor's own good.

School-Based Regulations

Much of the debate surrounding government involvement in the childhood obesity epidemic focuses on school-based interventions. And there's a reason: Kids spend more than half of their days in school. It's by far the biggest opportunity for public policy to influence America's kids (one way or the other). Moreover, public schools are a place where parents relinquish oversight responsibilities to school administrators, who are, after all, government employees.

School cafeterias are usually the first culprit to be pointed to for the rise in obesity rates. And again, there is a reason. Often, what the lunch ladies serve up doesn't look all that different from the birthday fare my son received at Chuck E. Cheese's. So the solution should be simple, right? Get the junk food out—bring the healthy food in. Alas, nothing is simple when it comes to obesity.

In fact, the great school lunch debate is incredibly complex. And it's riddled with surprises and often contradictory data. For example, if the schools live up to their reputation as an obesity-promoting environment, one might expect kids would either lose weight or at least maintain their weight over the summer, when they are, in theory, eating better and exercising more. A recent study found that kindergartners and first-graders gain more weight during summer vacations than during the school year.[7] And we are not talking about just a growth spurt here. The study found that during the summer, children gain weight at twice the rate as during the school year.

The study authors do not claim to know why kids gain extra weight during the summer, but they do suspect that their findings might deflect some blame from the schools. "Schools have been getting a bad rap," said study author and Indiana University Bloomington Professor Brian Powell. "This isn't to say that schools can't improve—but we found that kids' weight gain is more under control during the school year than during summer break. This suggests that instead of thinking of schools as the problem, schools appear to be part of the solution."

The study results are interesting, but I'd like to see a similar study that evaluates weight gain over the summer for students attending middle and high schools—since we know the school lunch picture usually gets worse as availability of junk food increases with school grade levels.

Regardless of this study's findings, there is no question in my mind that most schools are not the panaceas of health and nutrition that they could be. So the question remains: Can public policy improve this picture? We discuss some of the most prominent targets for school-based interventions below.

What! No Cokes or Cookies?

It is no secret that what goes into the school lunch has long been a battleground for legislators, researchers, consumer groups, food suppliers, and school boards—not to mention parents.

But, in fact, it might be the lunch's "competitors" that are the more appropriate target for government intervention. *Competitive food* is the term used to describe foods and beverages sold in school that are not part of federal school meal programs—in fact, they literally "compete" for a student's lunch money. Competitive foods are sold, sometimes throughout the day, sometimes just within certain hours, in the a la carte lines in the cafeteria, in vending machines, snack bars, and school stores in 98 percent of secondary schools, 73 percent of middle schools, and 43 percent of primary schools.[8]

While not all competitive foods are unhealthy, the vast majority are highly processed foods and drinks that are high in added fats and added sugars. The reason is simple: These foods have a greater demand and higher profit margin than healthier foods. Fresh fruit, for example, is more expensive to ship and store and often has to be thrown out if it is not consumed within a limited time frame. So schools earn more profits by offering highly processed foods at the expense of healthier alternatives.

But why does the school cafeteria need to worry about making a profit? The answer is that most schools count on profits from the cafeteria to fund other school activities. Cafeterias are not only asked to cover their own costs, but as local and state budgets have declined, they are increasingly asked to make up for shortfalls in other areas.

I recently spoke with a former account representative for Sodexho, a large company that operates the lunchroom in many cafeterias across the country. He said his (former) company has a bad rap for feeding kids unhealthy foods, but in reality, it was the schools driving the decisions.

He said that nearly every time he spoke with a principal or member of the school board, it was the same story: "We want our cafeteria to offer healthy foods," they would say.

"Great," he would respond. "We can do that."

He would then go on to show them the cost and revenue projections from this approach versus the alternative of putting in the competitive foods (and drinks), and adding French fries, chicken nuggets, and similar fare to the lunch line. Nine times out of ten, the high-profit-margin, highly processed competitive foods found their way into the schools. From the decision maker's perspective, the prospect for profits to cover the costs of running the cafeteria and to finance other school activities was more important than the health benefits that could be achieved through healthier lunch options.

Currently, federal guidelines only exist for foods sold as part of the federally reimbursed school meals programs. These foods must meet federal nutrition guidelines (an issue, by the way, that is also hotly contested). Competitive foods provided by the school, however, do not need to meet these federal requirements. To help close that loophole, Congress commissioned the Institute of Medicine (IOM) to write the first set of recommended guidelines for the sale of competitive foods in schools. The resulting IOM report, with its much more stringent regulations, added to the momentum for national legislation to get competitive food out of schools.[9] The report, which was issued in the spring of 2007, said less nutritious items should be replaced with healthier foods such as fruits, vegetables, and low-fat dairy products. It emphasized adding snacks with more whole grains and less sodium, saturated fat, and added sugar.

"The difference between the current USDA and new IOM school food standards is night and day," said Center for Science in the Public Interest (CSPI) nutrition policy director Margo G. Wootan in a press release. "Congress should support parents and protect kids by having USDA bring its disco-era nutrition standards in line with modern science."[10]

Modern or not, the question we still must ask is this: Would more regulation actually improve the nutritional intake of America's youth? There is some evidence to suggest that it would, at least while kids are on the school grounds. Two recent studies conducted in middle schools show that fruit and vegetable intake is higher among students at schools where unhealthy competitive options are not available when compared with schools that offer these options.[11,12]

Of course, as suggested above, there is a downside to additional regulation. It will limit the school's ability to finance the cafeteria and other school activities, which may include after school programs that promote increased physical activity. For example, in 2002, Oakland, California, was the first major school district to ban certain foods deemed of low nutritional value. This decision cost the district an estimated $650,000 in lost revenues annually.[13] Other schools have made similar changes and not only lost needed revenue, they have faced complaints from parents who like having these options available for their kids' lunches.

Despite the obstacles, there is increased public support for restrictions. If you recall from Table 9.1, 74.5 percent of respondents in our survey supported restricting the availability of less healthy foods in the cafeteria. And so the seeds of change have been planted. Consistent with the IOM recommendations, 21 states now have policies that place restrictions on competitive foods. For example, the West Virginia Board of Education, one of the most aggressive states when it comes to childhood nutrition, prohibits the sale or serving of the following foods and beverages at school during the school day (e.g., between the arrival of the first child at school and the end of the last scheduled instructional period):

- Chewing gum, flavored ice bars, and candy bars.
- Foods or drinks containing 40 percent or more, by weight, of sugar or other sweeteners.

- Juice or juice products containing less than 20 percent real fruit or vegetable juice.
- Foods with more than eight grams of fat per one-ounce serving.

In addition, soft drinks are prohibited at elementary and middle schools. Soft drinks may be sold in high schools but not during breakfast and lunch periods. On top of these regulations, local schools and school districts are also implementing their own restrictions.

If I were the superintendent of a school district, I would implement a policy similar to that of West Virginia. Schools in my district would not profit at the expense of their students' health.

So if you're a concerned parent, here's my advice. Lobby your school board to enact policies similar to that of West Virginia, and lobby your legislators for the resources required to adequately fund school programs. If that is too much work, do what we do: Pack your kids a lunch.

But I Want My Coca-Cola!

The preceding discussion focused largely on what is served during the lunch hour. But there is also considerable debate about the role of vending machines on school campuses. These machines are typically stocked with candy, chips, and, you guessed it, soft drinks.

Perhaps nowhere can the power of the childhood obesity debate be seen more clearly than in the actions taken around soft drinks in schools. As recently as two decades ago, vending machines in schools were uncommon. But as schools began to recognize their revenue potential, many districts, struggling with budget shortfalls and searching for innovative strategies to obtain external funding in the presence of budget shortfalls, installed vending machines to pay for computers, sports programs, and after-school activities. As of 2000, soft drink vending machines were available in most secondary schools (76 percent) and middle schools (55 percent), and even in a substantial proportion of primary schools (15 percent).[14] Most schools restrict the times the vending machines are available.

Many school administrators sign agreements with soft drink vending machine service companies and soft drink distributors to receive a percentage of the profits from the sales in their school. In addition, some school administrators sign "exclusive pouring rights" contracts or other types of agreements with soft drink distributors. These agreements specify additional payments or equipment that schools will receive from soft drink distributors in exchange for exclusive sales rights, placement of a minimum number of vending machines, marketing opportunities within the school, or other agreements that aim to increase sales to students. These agreements transform the school's role from being a provider of vending machines to being an active soda marketer.

Until recently, these agreements were conducted largely without the review, knowledge, or input of the school board or parents and with little to no oversight concerning how the profits were being spent.

Then this practice came under fire—at both the local and national level. Consumer groups, parents, and others rallied against the sale of "liquid candy" in the schools. And research revealed that the widespread availability of soft drinks was displacing healthier beverage choices such as water, low-fat milk, and 100 percent fruit juice.[15] Studies also began linking soft drink consumption with childhood obesity.[16]

So what happened? While legislators, consumer groups, parents, and school boards argued bitterly, former President Bill Clinton got to work. His nonprofit organization, the Clinton Foundation, sidestepped the feds by negotiating directly with suppliers. In May 2006, the nation's largest beverage distributors, Coke, Pepsi, and Cadbury Schweppes, in tandem with the Clinton Foundation and the American Heart Association, announced a halt to nearly all soda sales to public schools. The companies pledged to work to implement the changes at 75 percent of the nation's public schools by the 2008–2009 school year and at all public schools a year later.

So that's the plan, but I have to say I'm not entirely convinced it will happen on this timeline. Nonetheless, regardless of the rollout, it is clear that schools were already moving in the direction—state by state, district by district—of getting the soft drinks out of the schools. So the beverage companies, being no fools, probably realized they were better off jumping on this train and getting some positive press rather than fighting the current (and getting flamed by the public). Not surprisingly, the beverage distributors are still hoping to maintain their presence in the schools. They reported that they plan to replace the high-calorie, sugary drinks in school vending machines with bottled water, unsweetened fruit juices, milk drinks, and sugar-free sodas—all served in smaller portions.

Regardless, if it reduces excess caloric intake among the student body, it's a step in the right direction.

The extent to which the soda bans, and similar strategies, will reduce excess caloric intake among youth, however, remains an open question. My suspicion is that the answer might be less than you might think. For example, take the case of Adam Drenkard, a 17-year-old senior, who, as a *New York Times* article reported, used to stop at his high school store for a daily soda before his after-school activities began.[17] When a new school nutrition law went into effect in Connecticut that banned soda in his school, he simply began driving to a nearby gas station instead. "I get 15 or 16 sodas sometimes just for kids here," he said.

Resourceful kids like Adam minimize the intended effect of these policies. And he's hardly alone. For example, I've heard that when schools ban chocolate, bustling young entrepreneurs will buy chocolate bars in bulk and sell them during the school day.

In the extreme, students may not decrease their consumption of the less healthy products during the school day and/or may increase consumption after school to fully offset the effect of the policy. However, this is unlikely to be the case. By raising the costs of the soda and other banned products (that is, by making them less accessible), we should expect to see a decrease in overall consumption, perhaps not to the degree it would if our kids weren't so enterprising, but a decrease nonetheless.

An additional policy that bans the sale of these products on school grounds (by anyone) might help minimize the role that Adam and other young entrepreneurs play in limiting the impact of the restrictions. In my district, I would enact such a ban.

Bring on the Broccoli (and Make It Cheap)

The flip side of getting the less healthy options out is bringing more healthy options in—and getting students to eat them. In other words, bans are one thing, but getting kids to eat healthier choices is a whole separate story (as any parent well knows). A separate intervention seeks to expose students to greater quantities of fresh produce marketed in a way that is appealing.

So here we get back to the usual problem for most school districts: cost. Not only are the healthier products typically more expensive and with lower profit margins, they require far more labor to get the products into the mouths of the students. The increase in costs and labor can result for the following reasons:

- Food service employees must negotiate with different distributors for the best prices and ensure that the fruits and vegetables are delivered in good condition.
- There is a higher likelihood of waste if students do not consume the produce before spoilage occurs.
- Food service staff preparation time for fresh produce is greater than what is required to stock processed foods. Food service is often short-staffed and relies on prepackaged foods and quick preparation methods to meet volume and time demands.

Schools are responding to these challenges with a wide array of solutions. At one extreme end of the spectrum, there is Ann Cooper, director of nutrition services for the Berkeley, California, school system, who has become a media superstar in her own right as the "Cafeteria Crusader."[18] When Cooper (or Chef Ann, as she is known) came to Berkeley, the school cafeteria was similar to most around the country: The bread was white, the meat was highly processed, the fruit was canned. Then Cooper closed deals with local suppliers. So now, not only is the produce fresh, the rolls are whole wheat, the dairy is hormone and antibiotic free, all of the Mexican food is made by a locally owned Hispanic-owned company, and the baked products come from a local, female-owned company.

Cooper's staff of 53, accustomed to reheating food from outside vendors for the 4,000 lunches, 1,500 breakfasts, and 1,500 snacks served each day, learned how to make meals from scratch.[19] The school went from 95 percent processed foods to 95 percent made from scratch with fresh fruit and vegetables offered at every meal and a salad bar in every school[20] (though I have to add that salads aren't necessarily great beacons of health if they are doused with creamy dressing and bacon bits).

As you may well have guessed, Berkeley has an unusually well-funded school lunch program. They have to—all these changes are not cheap. According to Cooper: "It costs about 18 percent more per kid per lunch—which is about 50 cents a day—more than what we get in reimbursements from the Feds and the state. That's not just for food; it includes labor—but not overhead, which adds another 50 cents."[21]

And there's the rub. Few communities can tap money and resources like Berkeley. Relying on donations and parent and volunteer support to bring food into the cafeteria on a daily basis is simply not sustainable in the long run for the vast majority of schools. So, instead, is there a middle ground?

I applaud the efforts of Berkeley, but the reality is that schools can only go as far as their budgets will take them. In the end, schools should be encouraged to produce a range of meals and competitive foods that meet federal and state nutrition guidelines but that have enough appeal so that students will continue to purchase them.

The good news here is that the Feds are, to some degree, making moves to improve the federal guidelines for the school meal. In 2005, the USDA set new dietary guidelines that called for some of the biggest changes in recent years, including greater consumption of whole grains, fruits, vegetables, and nonfat dairy products, such as skim milk. The USDA did not, however, require that schools follow these requirements. But in April 2007, the USDA proposed, for the first time, requiring schools to bring their cafeteria menus into compliance with the latest U.S. dietary guidelines.[22] The USDA also proposed spending $6 million to provide guidance and technical assistance to school food professionals to bring cafeteria meals in line with the guidelines.

The reality is that even within the guidelines, some foods (e.g., fruits and vegetables) offer more health benefits than others. Therefore, an additional strategy to encourage consumption of the healthy foods might be to price them below market value (even at a loss) and to increase the price of some of the less healthy options to make up the shortfall. This strategy may be necessary to get kids to consume the healthier options.

If I ran the cafeteria, the price of the fresh fruits and vegetables and other healthier options would be subsidized to reduce their costs. The price tags on the least healthy foods would be hiked up to finance the costs of the subsidies. This strategy would operate under the very same principle that I will outline in Chapter 10 when I describe my hypothetical corporate cafeteria: A successful obesity prevention program needs to do exactly the opposite of where the economy is taking us by making it cheaper and easier to be thin—not fat.

And, in fact, there is research to back up the idea that decreased prices will result in increased consumption. One study, for example, showed that reducing the price of fresh fruits and vegetables effectively increased sales of the targeted items by fourfold and twofold, respectively, among high school students over a three-week period.[23] No surprise here—even kids respond to economic incentives.

F Is for Fat

Reading, writing, and arithmetic aren't the only things some schools are measuring these days. Seven states—Arkansas, California, Illinois, New York, Pennsylvania, Tennessee, and West Virginia—now require BMI report cards that give parents information about whether or not their child is overweight or at-risk for being overweight based on current guidelines. The hope is to rouse the parents (who are very likely over-weight themselves) to take action. Legislators in other states have BMI report cards on the table as well, and some individual school districts have also adopted the practice of their own accord.

In 2003, Arkansas became the first state to enact BMI report cards, when the legislature directed public schools to weigh and measure children and calculate their BMI. Act 1220, which mandated the measure, requires that Arkansas public schools:

- Annually report each student's BMI to his or her parents and pro-vide families with information about the importance of nutrition and physical activity.
- Bar student access to food and beverage vending machines in elementary schools.
- Create local school-district-level advisory committees to raise aware-ness about physical activity and nutrition and develop school-based policies that create a healthier learning environment.
- Disclose food and beverage contract agreements, including revenues and expenditures.

Arkansas credits its program with helping to slow the rise in child-hood obesity in their state. Although the number of overweight children in the state did not drop, it did level off, a promising result in a state where obesity rates have grown steadily over the past decade and have consistently ranked well above the national average. Today, a shocking 37 percent of Arkansas children and adolescents are overweight or at risk.

The former governor, Mike Huckabee, championed the program (not surprising given the 110 pounds he dropped after being diagnosed with diabetes). But now there's a skinny new governor in town, and he's got some different ideas. Governor Mike Beebe said the school weigh-ins and report cards had "a lot of negative, unintended consequences" and hurt some children's self-esteem.[24]

He favors less frequent testing and letting parents drop out of the program more easily. At the bequest of the new governor, in the beginning of 2007, the Arkansas House approved a controversial bill that would repeal the BMI report cards altogether.

Americans seem to be pretty evenly divided over this issue. In our 2005 survey (see Table 9.1), about half of respondents supported recording student's weight on a regular basis and 57.1 percent of respondents favored sending parents a health report card of children's weight on a regular basis.

Although there could be a downside to the report cards, I think the Arkansas bill that revokes the report cards is a mistake. Yes, weight is a highly sensitive issue, and if the screenings are not handled with care and confidentiality, there is the potential for stigmatization. But let's face it—the findings that these BMI screenings reveal, by and large, are already known by the other students. And they do not need this information as an excuse to be mean. In fact, as we discussed in Chapter 1, a large body of research tells us something we already know: Overweight kids are often the target of teasing and discrimination by their peers and others.

So the sad fact is that many of these kids are already having a tough time in school—and that's without BMI report cards. Although the self-esteem of some overweight youth may be hurt by the report cards, these same kids are the ones who could stand to benefit most from the program.

Moreover, the reality is that without this information, many parents would not take action to reduce their children's weight. I find this hard to believe, but the literature reveals that the vast majority of parents of overweight youth do not even recognize that their child has a weight problem. In a 2003 study, for example, only 10.5 percent of parents with overweight children perceived their child's weight accurately, compared with 59.4 percent of other parents.[25] Although many parents may ignore the report cards altogether, this is a case where the potential benefits of the information outweigh the costs.

If I were in charge, in addition to providing BMI reports, I would also include health report cards that incorporate results from the President's Challenge physical fitness test and other measures of fitness, including sit-ups, shuttle run, 600-yard dash, pull-ups (flexed-arm hang for girls), and other measures of fitness. These levels and percentiles would be provided to parents, along with an interpretation of results and strategies for increasing physical activity and finding additional resources. From there, parents could make informed decisions about whether they want to take action to improve their children's fitness ability and nutritional intake.

I was surprised to recently find out that my children's school actually provides this information. My son, a first-grader, and my daughter, a kindergartner, recently came home with report cards that showed their scores and percentiles for the President's Challenge, along with their grades for their traditional classes. Although my kids are not overweight, they are admittedly not very into sports, and fared fairly badly in the fitness areas. However, as a result of these tests, we now do sit-ups and push-ups most mornings. I try to make it fun, but I will admit that I bribe my kids (like a true economist) to keep working hard to improve. And by the way, I don't do it with candy (surprise, surprise). Pokemon cards work well for my son, and my daughter is young enough that the prospect of stickers is still a powerful motivator. Both have shown much improvement over the last few months, and I credit the report card for starting us on this path.

I'm sure that many parents will not even look twice at the report card. But as I stated above, the potential to induce children into more active and healthier lives outweighs the negatives Governor Beebe worries about. Parents may not want to hear that their kids are overweight (and the kids may not like having it pointed out), but ignoring it doesn't make the associated health risks go away.

No Child Left without a Big Behind

Although I love sports, I never liked having to do Physical Education in the middle of the school day. The reason is that I sweat a lot, and I was always embarrassed about still being sweaty a period or two later. I also do not recall learning much in health class that stuck with me. However, in the wake of the childhood obesity epidemic, even with this knowledge, I believe PE and health education (that focuses on the benefits of a healthy diet and exercise regimen) should be included as part of the core curriculum in all schools (and not just once a week as is commonly the case). Without these requirements, youth will be less likely to make educated decisions about their own diet and exercise choices. Armed with this information, many youth will still grow up and choose a weight trajectory similar to that of Uncle Al's, but at least it is an informed utility-maximizing decision. Similarly, many kids will grow up and choose never to do algebra, but we still teach the subject.

I'm hardly alone in my opinion. In the survey that colleagues and I conducted in 2005 (see Table 9.1), 83.3 percent of respondents favored requiring more physical education and 93.9 percent favored requirements to teach healthy eating and exercise.

Now let's look at reality. It's not such a rosy picture. My kids engage in far less physical activity in school than I did. As a first-grader, I had recess three times per day and PE three times per week. My kids, by contrast, have recess once per day and PE twice per week. There are numerous studies documenting how physical activity in schools has diminished over the years. One much quoted study, for example, conducted by the 2006 Shape of the Nation, found that the percentage of students who attend a daily physical education class dropped from 42 percent in 1991 to 28 percent in 2003.[26]

Remember the law of unintended consequences? Many schools have been forced to cut back on PE, health, and recess because of the enormous pressure caused by the No Child Left Behind Act. The policy holds schools accountable for test results in reading and math from grade school through high school. If standards aren't met, teachers can get cut, and schools can even be shut down.

The No Child Left Behind Act has been pointed to as a culprit in the diminishing PE curriculum and is said to be unintentionally sapping schools of time and resources for exercise as educators focus more on test scores and rigorous academic coursework. Some jokers have even taken to calling the act "No Child Left without a Big Behind Act" or "No Child Let Outside Act."

Though it is likely that the No Child Left Behind policy has played a role in eroding the PE curriculum, so far the evidence has been more anecdotal than substantive. So the policy's impact remains an open question.

An additional concern is not just how much time students spend in PE, but what they are doing while they are in the class. While most states require some sort of physical education, the majority do not have specific curriculum requirements or end-of-grade testing for physical activity analogous to No Child Left Behind, which is something I would support. As a result, with the exception of a few strict states, decisions concerning what activities should be undertaken is often left up to local school districts, individual schools, or even teachers.

PE classes have been widely criticized for taking a "Roll out the balls and let them play" approach in which there is little to no organized activity and no assurance that students are physically active. In fact, a 2005 research paper found there is little evidence as to whether more PE, *as it currently exists*, even affects physical activity or weight.[27] The researchers suggest a focus on revamping the curriculum prior to increasing the time spent in PE. What good is gym class if the time that the students spend there does not increase their physical activity?

So, if I were in charge, what would I do? For one, I would enforce minimum PE and nutrition education requirements, knowing full well that these requirements *may* hurt test scores in core courses (and possibly hurt the school's evaluation for No Child Left Behind). Students would be required to take PE at least three times per week (which still falls short of government fitness recommendations) unless they participate in a sponsored school sport. The PE curriculum would also be strengthened to ensure kids are engaging in some minimum standard of physical activity. And as noted above, students and schools would be graded in fitness the same way they are graded in other subjects via No Child Left Behind.

The reason I would so strongly advocate to have a structured PE program is this: We cannot rely on kids to do any physical activity outside of school. Though there are an estimated 41 million American kids participating in organized, extracurricular youth sports like soccer, baseball, and football, not every child is able to take part in this sometimes expensive organized play. And, as we've discussed, a disproportionately large percentage of overweight kids come from low-income families, and many live in communities where there are no safe places to play and exercise.

One study found that the problem of lower levels of physical activity outside of school particularly affects teenage girls in urban areas, "where privacy, safety and cultural issues affect participation."[28] That finding might not be much of a surprise if you recall the charts we showed you in Chapter 1 that revealed that the obesity epidemic is particularly profound for minority and low-income women.

For some kids, physical education at school may represent their one and only opportunity to engage in any physical activity. As a result, I would endorse these programs despite pressures from No Child Left Behind or other constraints. And, in fact, PE programs may actually improve test scores. Several studies have found that students who get more physical activity tend to have better concentration, reduced disruptive behaviors and higher test scores in reading, math, and writing.[29]

Your Mouth Will Really Groove

For all the hours that kids spend in school, they still find plenty of time to sit in front of the TV. And, as shown in Figure 9.1, there is a clear racial divide in television viewing, with African-American children watching far more television than Caucasian children, a finding that once again follows right in line with racial differences in rates of childhood obesity.

With rampant television viewing in mind, one of the first ways that Vivien Morris, a nutritionist with Boston Medical Center, engages with the overweight children who come to her for weight loss help is to sing the opening stanza of an advertising jingle, Morris told a reporter with the *Boston Globe*.[30]

"And then I see if they can complete it," said Morris. "If I say, 'You deserve a break today,' they will say, 'McDonald's.' That's as familiar to them as anything else in their lives."

This is testimony to far more than just the power of a jingle. Turn on the TV on a Saturday morning—or most mornings, for that matter—and kids start consuming a steady diet of advertisements for Chuck

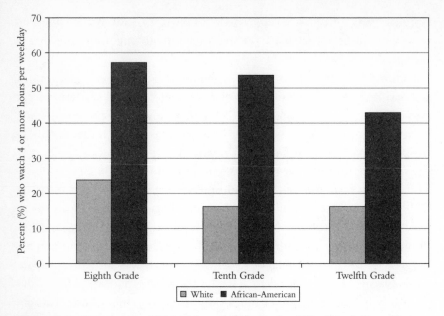

Figure 9.1   Percentage of 8th, 10th, and 12th Graders Who Watch Four Hours or More of Television on Weekdays, by Race, 2004
SOURCE: Child Trends original analysis of Monitoring the Future data, 2004.

E. Cheese's, Burger King, and rapping SpaghettiOs that promise "your mouth will really groove."

All told, the food and fast-food industry spends roughly $1 billion per year on advertising to kids.[31] These advertisements largely focus on foods of minimal nutritional value. A 2007 report by the Kaiser Family Foundation found that the typical 8 to 12 year old is bombarded with 21 food ads a day on television.[32] Teenagers see slightly fewer—17 a day, or about 6,000 a year. Children ages 2 to 7 see the fewest—12 a day, or 4,400 a year.

TV ads are one influence. Then there are the ads in magazines, in the schools, in retail food outlets, in movie theaters, on the Internet, and in video games. In fact, there are ads in just about every venue that somehow touches kid's lives.

We know that these advertisements impact children's food choices (or the advertisers would not do it), and there is some evidence that they may promote obesity. Several studies have found a significant association (not causation) between the proportion of children who are overweight and the number of advertisements per hour on children's television, especially those advertisements that encourage the consumption of energy-dense, nutrient-poor foods.[33]

In the face of rising rates of childhood obesity, policy makers are increasing pressure on broadcasters and advertisers to rein in their ads. The public also seems to largely support ad restrictions. As shown in Figure 9.1, our survey revealed that 75.3 percent of respondents supported restricting less healthy food ads during kids' TV programs.

Advertisers are showing some signs that they are feeling the heat. The Kellogg Company announced in June 2007 that it would voluntarily phase out advertising its products to children under age 12 unless the product meets specific nutrition guidelines for calories, sugar, fat, and sodium.[34] Kellogg also said that it would stop using licensed characters or branded toys to promote foods that do not meet those same nutrition guidelines.

And in November 2006, 10 major food and drink giants, including McDonald's, Coca-Cola, and PepsiCo, agreed to adopt new voluntary rules for advertising. The companies said they would devote at least half their advertising directed to children to promote healthier diets and lifestyles. This is considerable when you consider that the Kaiser study's review of more than 8,800 food commercials failed to find a single ad promoting fresh fruits or vegetables to children.[35]

Other countries have taken a more aggressive stance against food advertisers. In Great Britain, for example, policy makers have banned ads for foods high in fat, salt, or sugar in programming aimed at children under 16, and have prohibited the use of premiums or children's characters in food ads to young people. Other European countries have enacted similar legislation.

In contrast, the United States does little to regulate advertising to children. Current law restricts the amount of time devoted to advertising during children's programs to 10.5 minutes per hour on weekends and 12 minutes per hour on weekdays. Additional proposals designed to limit children's exposure to food advertising include:

- Requiring all broadcasters to air advertisements for healthful foods such as fruits, vegetables, and whole grains to counter ads for high-fat snack foods and sugar-sweetened beverages.

- Limiting advertising for certain types of foods (high-fat, high-calorie, low nutrient) in certain locations and at certain times (e.g., during child television programming).
- Banning in-school advertising.
- Forcing advertisers to clearly distinguish between advertising and program content across all media targeted toward children.

The goal of these interventions would be to reduce children's exposure to commercial pressures at a period in their lives when they are least able to make informed choices. It has been shown in numerous studies that, developmentally, children are less capable than adults of distinguishing between advertising and program content, and they are also less able to recognize the persuasive intent of advertisements and less able to critically evaluate advertising claims than adults.[36]

Although these proposals have merit, there are several arguments against imposing regulation of advertising to children:

- It is the role of parents, not advertisers, to limit their children's exposure to advertising or to the advertised products.
- The networks will claim that lost revenue from advertising will limit their ability to air youth programming, and that some programs might need to be canceled due to lack of profitability.
- Advertisers will argue that not only will advertising restrictions unjustly hurt their profitability, advertising is intended to sway consumers from one product to another rather than to increase overall consumption.
- There are first amendment concerns about whether or not the government has a right to restrict what is broadcast on the public airways.
- It is one thing for government to educate youth and control what goes on in public schools, but it is another to control what goes on in the privacy of a child's home.

It is the last point that holds the most sway with me. Food advertising may promote childhood obesity, but so too may television viewing, computer use, and a host of other sedentary activities that occur within a child's home. Should the government implement regulations on all of these? I would say no. However, I would recommend that the government continue to work with food industry leaders to establish stringent criteria of what constitutes appropriate food advertising to children on child's programming and in other media outlets. Policy makers should also consider additional strategies to encourage, but not require, the food industry to voluntarily conform to those criteria.

As a final recommendation, I would implement a simple color-coded scheme (similar to the terrorist threat level) that would alert parents to the health content of processed foods, especially those foods marketed to children. Green could identify the healthiest products, and red could indicate products with minimal nutritional value. Some parents may have the ability to comprehend the information on the Nutrition Facts panel, but many, including myself, do not. I believe that this kind of pared-down scheme might do more to improve the health of children (and their parents) than advertising or any other restrictions.

In Closing

Did you know that mangos are the world's most popular fruit, while strawberries are the United States' most popular berry? Seventh- and eighth-graders at the Mitchell Senior Elementary School in Atwater, California, absorbed this fact while making fruit smoothies with a visitor from Jamba Juice.[37]

The smoothie lesson was hosted by teacher Patty Stroming, who has taught a class about food at the school for over a decade. When Stroming first started teaching the class, curriculum focused more on cooking and less on overall health, she told a reporter with *The Merced Sun-Star*. The curriculum has changed over the years, she said, especially since the Atwater Elementary School District passed a wellness policy.

"The whole focus (of the class) is nutrition and wellness," said Stroming. "Helping to give them opportunities to make good choices for a healthy life."

As an aside, I hope Stroming encouraged her students to start making those good choices at the Jamba Juice counter. Smoothies from Jamba Juice can range from 160 to 900 calories. In fact, many of them contain more calories than a Big Mac—540 calories without cheese.

In any case, the reality is that if Mitchell Elementary is like any other school in the country, many kids who attend Stroming's class will grow up and become obese. However, proper nutrition education, along with the strategies presented above, will allow tomorrow's adults to make informed diet and exercise choices. If they, like Uncle Al, knowingly choose a path that leads to excess weight (and a successful law practice), that is something that I can live with. However, if that path is chosen for them, because of uninformed short-sighted decisions they made as youth without any parental or government oversight, or because they lacked adequate resources to engage in physical activity or healthy eating, then that is something that I think is unacceptable. And based on the survey responses presented above, much of the American public appears to agree.

Chapter 10

The Employer's Dilemma

The previous two chapters focused on the role of government in addressing rising rates of obesity. Now let's return to the private sector and consider the role of employers.

Let's start with a basic fact of life: Employees and dependents make diet and exercise choices—and all choices for that matter—to maximize their own utility. In other words, they make the choices which they believe best serve their own interests—not necessarily the best interests of their employers. (Go figure.) So, when Cousin Carl packs on the pounds by eating lots of affordable and tasty fast food, he does not worry about how his excess weight might contribute to his employer's increased health insurance costs, reduced output, and lowered profitability.

But here's the conflict: Whereas employees (and dependents) are in the business of maximizing their utility, nearly all employers are in the business of maximizing their profits. They want to make money—and as much of it as possible. (Again, go figure.) As Uncle Al always says, you can never have enough money.

And nonprofit firms are actually not so different. For example, my company is a nonprofit research firm that competes for government grants and contracts. Some of our competitors are universities or other nonprofit research firms, whereas others are for-profit. If we were not as efficient with our money as our for-profit rivals, our costs would go up and we might find ourselves out of business. Nonprofits are not allowed to make profits by law, so in our company we "optimize net revenue" instead. If you don't see the difference between that and profit maximization, then you are getting my drift.

But this is not to say that businesses, both for-profit and nonprofit, will not invest in the health of their workforce. Quite the contrary. As we saw in Chapter 6, an unhealthy workforce is clearly bad for business. However, a business is likely to invest in its workforce only to the extent that corporate executives believe it is profit maximizing for them to do so. As the costs of obesity and health insurance increase, so, too, do the benefits of these investments (assuming they work). Therefore, it is not surprising that investments in health promotion are on the rise at businesses across the country. As we discuss below, however, there are several reasons why businesses are hesitant to make large investments in the health of their workforce.

Why Don't Businesses Invest More in the Health of Their Workforce?

While most companies claim to offer some form of health promotion program, these programs are often limited in scope and do little to encourage participation. For example, the 2004 National Worksite Health Promotion Survey revealed that only about one fourth of the firms that offer health promotion programs provide any form of incentives to encourage employees to participate.[1]

So why aren't employers doing more to address rising rates of obesity? Here are five underlying reasons:

1. *Employers have little financial incentive to invest in obesity treatment for younger obese individuals who have not yet developed costly complications.* Although the prevalence of obesity is growing rapidly among youth and young adults, Figure 10.1 shows that the medical costs of a

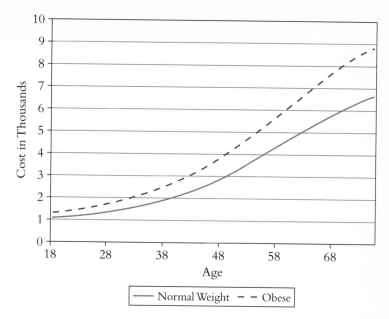

Figure 10.1   Annual Medical Expenditure for Normal Weight and Obese
Employees in the 2001–2003 Medical Expenditure Panel Survey
SOURCE: Finkelstein, E. A., and D. S. Brown. 2006. "Why does the private sector underinvest in obesity
prevention and treatment?" *North Carolina Medical Journal* 67, no. 4: 310–312.

young obese individual are only slightly higher than that of a
normal-weight individual of the same age. In fact, the annual
medical costs for an obese individual do not become statistically
greater than the costs for someone of normal weight until they
reach their early to mid-30s.

Although the risk of type 2 diabetes and other obesity-related
diseases are becoming increasingly greater among overweight youth
and young adults, these conditions are still relatively rare among this
group. Because overweight and obese young employees are not (yet)
tugging at the pocketbooks of their employers in large numbers, firms
have little financial incentive to invest in obesity prevention and treatment for them, no matter how high the prevalence of obesity.

2. *Employers rarely look further than five years down the road (if that) when
   considering an investment in employee wellness.* One may argue that
   focusing solely on current costs of obesity is short sighted. But is it?

Individuals in today's economy tend to switch jobs roughly every four to five years.[2,3]

As a result, employees rarely remain with the same employer for more than a few years. This suggests that an employer who finances the initial costs of obesity prevention and treatment is unlikely to garner the long-term benefits of their employee's improved health—a future employer will instead. This leaves employers feeling that it is not worthwhile to invest in obesity prevention and treatment since the anticipated return is likely to be received by another business—possibly even a competitor.

Current restrictions on the coverage of gastric bypass surgery is a great example of the outgrowth of this issue. Gastric bypass surgery is the best known treatment for severe obesity. This surgery reroutes the large intestine to bypass the stomach and requires the patient to make lifelong changes in diet.

A recent meta-analysis of all the available literature on the surgery showed that:

- The mean percentage of excess weight loss was 68 percent for patients undergoing the surgery.[4]
- Diabetes was resolved or improved in 86 percent of patients.
- Hyperlipidemia improved in 70 percent.
- Hypertension was resolved or improved in 79 percent and obstructive sleep apnea was resolved or improved in 84 percent.
- And contrary to what has been reported in the popular press, the surgery is no riskier than many other invasive procedures and, given the risks of being severely obese, perhaps less risky than not getting the procedure at all. A common measure of surgery risk, 30-day mortality rates, shows that 30-day mortality was less than one half of 1 percent for those undergoing the procedure.[5] Compare this to a 1.8 percent 30-day mortality risk for coronary artery bypass surgery.[6]

Yet, despite the proven health benefits of the surgery, most employers and insurers refuse to include the roughly $25,000 treatment as a covered benefit. One reason is that the treatment is not a cost-cutting measure. We've analyzed the data and found that even under fairly optimistic assumptions, it would take 10 years or more for firms to recoup this investment through reductions in future medical expenditures and reduced absenteeism.[7] In 10 years, most employees are likely to be long gone.

As an aside, if the government were to mandate that all health insurance plans cover select obesity treatments, including bariatric surgery, this *could,* at least in theory, be cost saving to employers and reduce the burden on the Medicare Trust Fund. You might remember we discussed this issue in Chapter 8.

3. *The existence of the Medicare program further reduces the private sector's incentives to invest in obesity treatment.* Even organizations that are able to keep their populations enrolled for long periods of time, such as public-sector employees, are unlikely to fully invest in obesity prevention and treatment because of the existence of the Medicare program, which assumes responsibility for primary health insurance coverage for almost all Americans once they reach age 65. The chronic nature of obesity-attributable diseases implies that a significant percentage of the costs of obesity occur after age 65. In fact, the data used to generate Figure 10.1 reveal that of the roughly $58,000 cost of obesity incurred between the ages of 18 and 75, 38 percent accrues after age 65.[8] Employers are unlikely to consider these costs when determining the optimal amount of money to invest in employee wellness.

On a similar note, retiree health insurance benefits are becoming increasingly uncommon. This, too, reduces employers' incentives to invest in the long-term health of their workforce. For example, suppose a medical treatment was available for a one-time cost of $40,000 that guaranteed that an obese individual would have the same medical cost profile as someone of normal weight for their entire life. A profit-maximizing employer that considers an individual's entire cost profile would provide coverage for this treatment. However, if employers consider only the time period up to age 65, the cost of the treatment is greater than the roughly $36,000 in savings (62 percent of $58,000) that would accrue to the employer, and therefore employers are unlikely to make this investment. Of course, if individuals are switching jobs prior to age 65, the existence of Medicare is of secondary importance.

As an aside, in Chapter 5 we argued that existence of Medicare may have indirectly increased rates of obesity by encouraging development of new medical technologies that reduced the (health) costs of obesity. Now we are saying that in the absence of Medicare, employers might increase their investments in employee health. Should we do away or scale back the Medicare program and/or the subsidy that encourages employers to provide health insurance? As we explained in Chapter 8, there are some good reasons for considering both of these changes and making significant changes to health care financing in the United States today if we want to encourage an increased emphasis on prevention as opposed to treatment.

4. *The fourth reason points to what economists call adverse selection.* Adverse selection is the concern that the "wrong" type of individual will join the company. As an example, a professor and mentor of mine named Paul Heyne, the person who taught me most of what I know about economics, once told me that it was not uncommon for life insurance firms in New York to locate their offices on the upper floors of walk-up office buildings (that is, buildings with no elevators). This measure kept those who were not healthy enough to walk a few flights of stairs from applying for the insurance. Thus, the company was able to avoid these bad risks. In this case, the so-called bad risks are obese individuals who are more likely to experience higher medical expenditures and greater absenteeism.

Along similar lines, in 2005, an internal memo sent to Wal-Mart's board of directors, which went public—to the chagrin of executives—proposed numerous ways to minimize spending on health care and other benefits.[9] To discourage unhealthy job applicants, M. Susan Chambers, Wal-Mart's executive vice president for benefits, suggested in the memo that Wal-Mart arrange for "all jobs to include some physical activity (e.g., all cashiers do some cart-gathering)." The message they were hoping to send was this: If you are not healthy enough to push a bunch of carts around, please do not apply. From a profit maximization perspective, this strategy makes good sense.

The case of bariatric surgery also provides a great example of adverse selection as it relates to obesity. At $25,000 a pop, would you like to be the only employer in town whose insurance plan offers coverage for the procedure? Probably not, as those wanting the procedure might flock to your business solely because of this coverage, and, as noted above, without significant cost sharing, you would be unlikely to recoup the benefits of this investment—not a good formula for profits.

The notion of adverse selection is the reason given by many states' Blue Cross & Blue Shield programs and other private health insurers as to why they dropped coverage for the procedure.[10–12] Those who did not completely drop coverage, such as United Healthcare, have placed stringent criteria that potential recipients of the surgery need to meet before coverage is to be provided. The criteria often include waiting periods, evidence of failed efforts at traditional weight-loss programs, a psychological assessment, and an attestation that the patient will comply with all stages of treatment. Many plans will also cover the costs of the procedure only if it is performed by a practicing physician at a designated "Center of Excellence." These are clinics that see the most patients and have evidence of successful weight-loss outcomes and fewer complications.

From an economic perspective, these strategies effectively minimize the risks posed by adverse selection and the high costs associated with the procedure. And there is good reason for implementing these strategies. Since I've been on the obesity speaking circuit, I have met at least a handful of formerly obese individuals who successfully shopped for a health plan or employer that provided coverage for the procedure. In fact, that's why they are no longer obese!

Then there's the flip side to adverse selection—that's the effort employers make to attract the "right" individuals, the low-risk individuals who are young and healthy. That may drive some employers, including the one I work for, to build a fitness center or a jogging trail, for example, even though there is limited evidence that these investments result in any cost savings. In my experience, many of the users of our new fitness center, including myself, are the same ones who used to belong to a gym. But it certainly is a great sell to exercise enthusiasts who are in the market for a new job. Whereas these assets would hardly lure someone like Uncle Al or Cousin Carl to join the company, I would be hard pressed

to leave my job for a company that does not offer these benefits.
And I always use the gym as a selling point when I am recruiting
new college graduates.

There is at least one more reason why employers may not
implement obesity prevention and treatment programs. *Hint:* It
was alluded to in Chapter 6.

5. *The fifth reason has to do with fattism or discrimination on the part of
   employers and employees.* Note that the discussion up to this point,
   including the discussion in Chapter 6 about paying obese people less
   money or not providing coverage for bariatric surgery or other
   obesity treatments, has nothing to do with discrimination. Reducing
   wages to offset for higher medical expenditures and/or absenteeism
   or not covering select treatments makes perfect sense from an
   economic perspective. These are profit-maximizing strategies for the
   firm. However, when it comes to lack of coverage for obesity treatments, what is a tougher sell is why employers are able to get away
   with it. Why is bariatric surgery, for example, treated so differently
   than other procedures that are, in some cases, more costly and less
   effective? Bariatric surgery is not a good investment for employers
   or health plans, but neither is open heart surgery or cancer treatment, yet these are covered.

   You might argue that heart surgery or cancer treatment are
   necessities whereas bariatric surgery is optional, but there are plenty
   of clinicians who would disagree with that statement. And given the
   elevated risks faced by those who are severely obese, I am inclined to
   agree with them.

   I suspect that some employers limit coverage because they, like
   my father, are fattists, and because, in the current environment, they
   are able to limit obesity coverage options with minimal pushback
   from employees (many of whom may also be fattists). However, as
   the prevalence of obesity continues to increase and a larger percentage of employees are requesting coverage for these treatments, this
   may become a more difficult task.

   Each of the reasons discussed above may explain why employers
   are likely to limit investments in obesity prevention and treatment.
   But when it comes to employee wellness programs, there is an additional reason why employers are hesitant to buy in.

The Dirty Secret about Employee Wellness Programs

As we stated in the opening paragraph, employers are out to make a buck. If there is a profit-maximizing way to minimize the costs of obesity and health insurance, then companies will do it. So why aren't employers, large and small, falling over themselves to implement broad-based employee wellness programs that target obesity and related risk factors?

The answer is that there is little evidence that these programs actually save employers any money. (*Note:* To clarify, I am not here questioning whether these programs *improve health*—though that, in fact, is questionable too—but I am questioning whether they *improve the financial health* of the company [i.e., increase profits]).

I know that my colleagues will read this as blasphemy and point to dozens of articles that *prove* that employee wellness programs result in cost savings. And, indeed, there are plenty of published papers that show that each dollar spent on worksite health promotion programs can yield $3, $4, or even $16 in savings.[13] There are even whole literature reviews devoted to showing that, on average, worksite health promotion programs save employers money.[14] I'm familiar with them all (mainly because these are the papers that get dropped on my desk when I complain about the lack of substantive evidence about this issue), but I have to go on record and say I'm skeptical that this is really the case.

In reality, the science backing up these papers is, at best, mediocre. Many of the evaluations of worksite wellness programs compare medical and other costs for individuals enrolled in the programs against those individuals not enrolled. However, they often only briefly allude to the fact that those who sign up for these programs are often the healthier bunch (just like the individuals who use my company's gym are by and large the same ones who were already working out before the company built the gym). Therefore, although those who enroll in the program might have better outcomes in every dimension measured, these outcomes would have been better in the absence of the program. So attributing all, or perhaps even any, of the better outcomes to the program is clearly problematic.

Other studies attempt to solve this problem by comparing outcomes before and after initiation of a wellness program. This design is an improvement, but real life is not a perfect laboratory, and often other factors are changing that may be equally or more responsible for the change in outcomes. For example, we know that smoking rates have been on the decline in the United States for the past several decades and that a reduction in smoking rates translates into improved health outcomes. We also know that, at least on paper, employee wellness programs have been on the rise. However, a pre/post-analysis cannot distinguish whether the reductions in smoking rates are a result of rising cigarette taxes, for example, or a result of the introduction of employee wellness programs.

There are designs that would tease out these effects, but the point is that nearly every study in the current literature falls short of the rigorous designs required to make strong statements concerning the benefits of implementing these programs.

And you don't need to take my word for it. A current review article assessed the clinical and cost outcomes for 12 recently published worksite-based studies.[15] Of the 12 studies included in the review, four had no comparison group at all. Therefore, there is no way to tell what might have happened in the absence of the intervention. Not surprisingly, these four "showed" the greatest benefits of the wellness programs. As with the smoking example above, they attributed all positive changes over time to the program. It is one of these four that claims the savings of $16 for each dollar invested in wellness.

Do you believe it? I don't. Seven of the 12 studies had a control group but no randomization. They compared the joiners to nonjoiners and tried to attribute any differences to the program. As we discussed earlier, this is likely to produce inaccurate results. In only one study was a rigorous evaluation design employed that would substantiate strong conclusions about the benefits of the program. In this study, the program centered on smoking cessation in the workplace. Using this rigorous design, the program was found not to increase cessation.

Dr. Kenneth Pelletier, the author of this review article, has published a series of similar review papers in the past and notes that the research designs are not only weak, they are getting weaker. He writes: "When corporations and health plans are demanding more evidence-based outcomes, this decline in rigorous research marks a serious challenge to the field of health promotion and disease management."

Yet, he also states that these results present "guarded cautious optimism about the clinical and/or cost effectiveness of these worksite programs." Sure he's optimistic, but it's not his money that is financing these programs.

Authors of the studies cited in the literature reviews, like many in the wellness field, have a vested interest in seeing worksite wellness programs expanded. It's not only their passion, but it is how they make their living. That is the second problem I have with the health promotion literature. Nearly everyone involved in the evaluation has a vested interest in ensuring that the results come out favorably. If you were a human resources representative and you were able to convince your boss to front the money for a wellness program and an evaluation, you can bet you'd want the results to make the program look successful. Heads, including your own, might roll if the CEO finds out it was a waste of money.

In addition, the evaluators and the implementers in these studies are often one and the same, and they, too, are likely to have a vested interest in showing positive results. Otherwise, they might find themselves with one or perhaps many fewer clients. I am sure that message has been conveyed more than once.

But it doesn't stop there. If you are the evaluator and you want to have any chance of getting your results published, which most certainly do, you have a significant incentive to find some positive results to report. I can tell you from firsthand experience that it is nearly impossible to get a paper published that says a program didn't work. Who wants to read about that?

Moreover, health promotion journal editors may not want to publish negative articles because it sends the "wrong" message about health promotion. These concerns lead me to strongly suspect that much of the research on programs that were shown to be ineffective wound up in somebody's trash can. I know a few of my studies have. Whether the majority or the minority of this research gets trashed is anyone's guess, but it certainly makes me wonder whether the business case for these programs is as great as the published literature suggests.

Maybe I should keep these thoughts to myself. It's a risky career move for me to question whether these programs are as good an investment as my colleagues suggest. For example, I was recently asked by a person who works for a public health organization to give a talk about the return on investment for worksite health promotion programs. I said "Sure, I'll give the talk, but I want you to know that I believe there may not be any return on investment for these programs."

Her response: "Well, um, we don't want you saying that."

Soon after our conversation ended, I received an e-mail saying that my services were no longer required. Gee, I wonder why. Well, the simple fact is that she, too, has a vested interest in seeing these programs expanded, as that is part of the mission of her organization, especially if it can be done on someone else's dime.

I should point out that one does not need to fudge the data to get the results they are looking for (although I am sure that it has happened). However, anyone involved in evaluating these programs knows that many assumptions are required. Some assumptions are more optimistic than others, and these can make the difference between a program that pays for itself in 3 years or in 30 years. Given the vested interest in seeing that these programs are successful by nearly all parties involved, it is the results based on the optimistic assumptions (such as assuming all changes over time are due to the program) that often find their way into the press release.

So it appears that nearly everyone has a vested interest in seeing employee wellness programs expanded. I'm sure the employees do, assuming the programs are free for them and not seen as overly intrusive. I love the new gym that my company built. But that is because I get all of the benefits while paying none of the costs. Was it a good investment for my employer? Well, that's anyone's guess.

So What's an Employer to Do?

Having said all that, the simple fact is that health care costs are rising, and obesity is responsible for an increasingly large percentage of those costs. In a recent analysis, economists from Emory University assessed the percentage of health care costs that were attributable to obesity between 1987 and 2001.[16] They found that, due to the higher percentage of obesity in the population and the higher costs associated with treating obesity-related diseases, obesity was responsible for 27 percent of the rise in inflation-adjusted per capita spending over this time period. They note that increases in obesity prevalence alone accounted for 12 percent of the growth in health spending. So doing nothing to address rising rates of obesity and health insurance costs is unlikely to be a profit-maximizing approach. As a result, employers, both large and small, are increasingly taking action.

How much to invest—and perhaps even more important, *how* to invest—largely depends on the specifics of the company. If it is a company with low turnover and/or that strongly believes that wellness programs can help attract and retain a healthier workforce, then it is certainly possible that a significant investment in employee wellness could pay off. If it is a small employer who may not have the resources to make large up-front investments, or one with high turnover, then sinking big money into employee wellness may not be money well spent, no matter how effective the program turns out to be. (Again, let me emphasize that this is an analysis based purely on *economics*—not on the health and well-being of employees.)

The reality is that many employers are investing in wellness programs that focus on the wrong things. If I ran my own company, I would implement a wellness program that is grounded in economic theory (surprise, surprise). In other words, I've (hopefully) made the case that people have gained weight because it has become more expensive, in terms of money and time, to exercise and eat a healthy diet. So, for a wellness program to be effective, it should implement policies that lower the costs of these activities and/or increase the payoffs of maintaining a healthy weight beyond the weight loss itself (which, for many, including Uncle Al and Cousin Carl, is not enough incentive on its own). In other words, a successful obesity prevention program needs to do exactly the opposite of where the economy is taking us. It needs to make it cheaper and easier to be thin—not fat. From an employer's perspective, it also needs to be profit maximizing before many will sign on.

Let's look at some examples of investments that may be effective and potentially cost saving. Building a fitness center or walking trail is one example. If one has access to these facilities without having to leave the worksite, then it becomes easier (i.e., cheaper) to exercise. Therefore, it should encourage more exercise among employees. As noted earlier, these strategies may also help attract and retain the "right" kind of employees and keep them healthier over time. Of course, some employees will merely switch from their current gym to the worksite, but having it on campus and free increases the chances that even these individuals will exercise more (and, as a side benefit, these employees may spend more time at the worksite, thus perhaps increasing the number of hours they work).

However, these are costly investments and may not pay off financially. An example of a lower-cost strategy is to offer healthy foods in the company vending machines and cafeteria. However, access may not be enough to sufficiently shift consumption. It may be necessary to encourage consumption of the healthier options by subsidizing their costs and/or by adding a "tax" to the less healthy alternatives. Note that this type of strategy is easier to justify for businesses that are looking for profit-maximizing strategies to reduce health care costs than for the government, which is assumed to consider broader societal factors prior to enacting regulations of this sort.

Can you really change people's eating habits by using incentives? In a company cafeteria or vending machine where choices are limited, the answer is yes. French and colleagues[17,18] examined the impact of reducing the price of low-fat vending-machine snacks in 12 secondary schools and 12 worksites. Modest price reductions (10 to 25 percent) on selected vending-machine snacks led to increased sales of healthy products and decreased sales of unhealthy products. In fact, a 25 percent reduction in the price of healthy choices resulted in a 50 percent increase in their sales.

In a second study by the same group of investigators, Hannan et al.[19] examined the purchase patterns for seven foods under conditions in which prices of three high-fat foods (French fries, cookies, and cheese sauce) were raised and prices of four low-fat foods (fresh fruit, low-fat cookie, low-fat cereal bar, and baked chips/pretzels) were simultaneously reduced. Sales of high-fat foods slowly declined during the study period.

So in *my* hypothetical company's cafeteria, the salad bar and other healthier options would be subsidized to reduce their costs. The price tags on the least healthy foods would be hiked up to finance the costs of the subsidies. Along similar lines, in our vending machines, the baked potato chips would cost less than the regular potato chips, but the carrots and fresh fruit would cost even less.

But I would not stop there. Economic theory suggests that financial incentives can motivate people to alter a behavior by changing the costs and benefits associated with that behavior. What gets us up in the morning to go to work day after day if not the incentive of getting paid? So if you pay people to be healthier, maybe they will.

In my company, I would set up a system that provides financial or other incentives for employees who can show clear evidence that they have taken active steps to improve their health. Incentives may be offered to increase employee participation, to encourage changes in behavior, or both. Incentives may include small gifts, days off from work, discounts on services or health insurance premium credits, lotteries toward vacations or other prizes, or cash payments. I would provide cold, hard cash to those who could present evidence that they improved their health. Table 10.1 provides example of some of the ways that companies are currently using economic incentives to motivate behavior change.

In my company, I would implement an approach similar to the one taken by VSM Abrasives. VSM is a Missouri-based company that makes, you guessed it, abrasive products. They have implemented a strategy that provides cash payments and a free day off of work to employees who can maintain or move toward a healthy weight. Although its program has not been rigorously evaluated, VSM claims it has resulted in substantial weight loss and cost savings. It would be nice to see the actual data, but for this type of program, even if it doesn't work, there really isn't much to lose. If nobody loses any weight, then nobody gets paid. I might combine the incentives with other strategies, such as Weight Watchers, Jenny Craig, or a subsidized gym membership for those who want them. But I would only subsidize the cost of these or similar programs if successful weight loss or weight maintenance goals are achieved. Otherwise, it's just not money well spent.

So does it work to pay people to lose weight? I guarantee you it would—if the price were right. Of course, if the price were too high, it would not be profitable for firms to offer it up. But there is evidence that even modest incentives can work. Studies have proven that weight-loss programs that included financial incentives resulted in greater weight loss than programs without financial incentives.[20–23]

Table 10.1 Types of Incentives Offered by Employers

Employer	Reward Criteria	Incentive
Adventist Media Center	Log miles by walking or convert other exercise times into miles	One paid vacation day for logging 1,000 miles; smaller rewards (water bottles, pens, mini-flashlights, T-shirts, CD cases, and stopwatches) for mileage achievements
Blue Cross Blue Shield of Michigan	Enter in the 10-week "Dump the Plump" contest as a member of a team	Winning teams won cash prizes collected from employee entry fees
Cigna Corporation	Complete exercise program	Prizes and gift certificates
Dell Inc.	Annual health risk assessment and complete a wellness program for managing health risks	$75 annual premium deduction for the assessment; $225 cash for completing the wellness program
Freedom One Financial Corporation	Periodic weight-loss challenge to meet one of three goals: (1) lose 25 pounds, (2) reduce body weight by 15%, or (3) reduce body fat by 15%	Win cash bonuses, paid days off, or tropical vacations
Hoffman-LaRoche	Participation in 12 health-related activities	$25 gift certificates for each activity completed
Humana	Virgin Life Care: use Virgin-run kiosks to track exercising, blood pressure, body fat and weight, and health and fitness goals	Earn HealthMiles, which can be redeemed at stores like Best Buy, Home Depot, and Target
Johnson & Johnson	Complete health risk appraisal and enroll in one of a choice of wellness programs	Up to a $500 rebate on medical premiums
Motorola	Sign up at a gym or wellness center	$240 cash reimbursement of enrollment fee
Providence Everett Medical Center	Complete wellness challenge(s) and limit medical claims and sick leave	$250 to $325 for completing the challenge and meeting wellness goals
Quaker Oats	Complete health risk appraisal and screening and take lifestyle pledge	Up to $300 allocated across numerous activities

Company	Requirements	Reward
Stanford University	Complete online assessment then earn points for participating in activities and classes (points vary for each)	$100 for completion of online assessment, $150 for earning 200 points
Star Tribune	Complete health assessment and three health education courses, exercise, and forswear risky behaviors	Health premium credits
Synovus Financial	Complete health risk appraisal and screening, and attend a health club three times a week	Reductions in annual health premiums for screening and complete reimbursement for health club membership
Texas Health Resources	Participate in disease management programs, medical screenings, and exercise	Earn points to save up to $260 a year in health insurance costs
University of Minnesota	Complete assessment, then enroll in healthy living course or work with a provided health coach	Both the employee and his or her spouse (partner) can earn up to $130 per year
VSM Abrasives	Climb onto the shipping scale and get weighed four times a year	$25 for maintaining or moving toward a healthy weight, paid day off for maintaining a healthy weight for one year
We Energy	Complete health risk appraisal, outline personal goals, and/or complete wellness challenge(s).	Gain points for different activities and earn up to $200 to $300 in cash per year

Colleagues and I have also done some exploratory research on the effect of incentives on weight loss, and found promising results.

We recently completed a three-month pilot study where we paid some individuals roughly $7 per pound to lose weight.[24] Another group of individuals, the control group, received no incentives. Whereas only about 4 percent of those in the control group lost 5 percent or more of their body weight at three months (5 percent is about where real health benefits start to happen), this figure climbed to 17 percent among those in the incentive group. We are just beginning to embark on a longer-term study to see if this weight loss can be sustained, but based on these results, incentives have promise, even if it's only $7 per pound. As an employer, I would happily pay $7 per pound if I could make that back in lower health insurance costs and reduced absenteeism.

And employees do seem to welcome the introduction of these kinds of incentive programs. In fact, in our pilot study, 82 percent of employees were in favor of incentive-based wellness programs tied to weight.

If I were to implement this strategy, some of my overweight or obese staff might argue that they exercise and eat right but just can't lose weight. And as we explained in Chapter 4, genetics certainly plays a large role in variations in individuals' weight. For these individuals, I would offer alternatives, such as completing a series of fitness events throughout the year. These might include walking, running, or biking races, but they would have to be of reasonable distances so that I could be convinced that their participation must have required a significant level of effort to improve or sustain their health.

Others may have a medical condition that precludes them from participating in weight-loss activities. To ensure I do not run afoul of disability laws, I would entrust the staff to develop reasonable alternatives for these individuals.

I would, however, insist that incentives be tied to things that matter. Otherwise, I might lose money even if employees make the behavior changes. For example, it is not uncommon for some companies to tie incentives to participation, such as attending a series of wellness classes. However, if individuals attend the classes, perhaps while eating a bucket of fried chicken, but never make any changes in behavior, would I really want to reward their participation? The answer is no, this is not a good investment. There may be some value in having them attend the session, but what truly matters is sustained changes in behaviors that promote health. That is what should be rewarded.

Regardless of whether your business chooses to implement a wellness program with all the bells and whistles or something on the cheap, there are dozens of vendors out there ready to provide those services. I should know—I get calls from these vendors almost weekly asking me to endorse their "proven" approach to weight loss and employee health. They often try to convince me, as well as their potential clients, I'm sure, that since my study showed obesity in worksites to be so expensive, their wellness program must therefore be cost saving. As I hope I've convinced you by now, that is a leap of faith, to say the least.

However, I am impressed that many of these programs are embracing an economic approach to wellness and increasingly trying to lower the costs of healthy behaviors and incorporating incentives into their programs. So it is certainly possible that they may be good investments for some firms. If your firm is considering working with one of these vendors, I suggest you ask the following questions:

- First, ask to see the evidence (and I use the term loosely) that their program "works." If they can't produce any, that is a red flag.
- Second, ask how much of their fee they would be willing to put at risk. In other words, if their programs are truly going to save you money, tell them you'll pay some amount up front and then split the savings with them down the road. If they are unwilling to risk losing some of their fee if positive outcomes are not achieved, then that is strike two.
- If they agree to this, then they should also agree to allow a third party (perhaps even me) to evaluate the benefits of the program. Otherwise, that is strike three.

If you can find a vendor willing to meet these three conditions, go ahead and hire them.

For those of you who go down this path, it is important that you don't set your expectations too high. After all, most of your utility-maximizing employees are not going to drastically change their lifestyle for $7 per pound, or whatever you happen to throw at them. The goal of these programs is to find those employees whom you can influence at a reasonable cost, and hope to have a positive impact on them. Your wellness program is not going to cure obesity or drastically reduce health care costs for your organization, but if you can keep your employees health risk profile from getting worse, even if you don't improve it, you are doing better than most.

So that covers the wellness programs, but what about coverage for obesity products and services. Would I provide coverage for bariatric surgery? How about for obesity drugs? There are currently only a few on the market, but I know many more are on the way.

The truth is that, as we discussed above, coverage for bariatric surgery is unlikely to be a good investment. There is one paper that suggests that the surgery could pay for itself in as little as four years, but that papers uses cost data from the Canadian Health Care system and is really not relevant for the U.S. market.[25]

As noted above, our own research suggests that 10 years or more is likely required for the procedure to pay for itself unless significant cost sharing occurs.[26] And that assumes there are no adverse events following surgery and that the recipient does not require other procedures as a result of losing so much weight (for those who lose a lot of weight, excess skin might need to be surgically removed).

The decision to cover bariatric surgery at traditional copayment levels is not profit maximizing. However, I would expect some of the health benefits of the surgery to be passed along to the employer in the form of lower future medical expenditures and/or increased productivity. Therefore, I would provide coverage for the procedure. However, if possible, I would offer coverage with a greater degree of cost sharing (i.e., a higher copayment) than for other medical services. For example, whereas the employee copayment may be 20 percent for general medical services, for bariatric surgery and other obesity treatments, I might raise it to 50 percent.

I am not sure whether a 50 percent copayment is profitable or not, but if these treatments are at all effective, then it must be of some benefit to my business. Therefore, I would be willing to share some of the costs. To ensure that this coverage does not put me at risk for adverse selection or extremely high health insurance costs, I would also impose annual spending limits on treatments for obesity related products and services. Employees who want these services will not like the higher copayments or spending caps, but it is certainly better than no coverage at all. I would continue to revisit the cost-sharing levels to determine the profit maximizing coverage amount. I would employ a similar approach for other obesity treatments that will undoubtedly be coming to market in the coming years.

Okay, so who wants to come work for me now? If you do, you'll see that I practice what I preach. Not only have I run four marathons over the past three years, but I do a lot of preaching about the benefits of a healthy diet and regular exercise. For proof, just ask my family, the parents of my son's soccer team, or those who work with me. I know my preaching is annoying, but in fact, creating a corporate culture of wellness, from the CEO down, is a key to success.[27] After all, disappointing the CEO can be costly.

Could These Programs Get Me in Legal Hot Water?

Before you go ahead and change your company policies based on my advice, talk to Uncle Al or some other lawyer and make sure nothing you are proposing goes against federal or state laws. On the federal level, there is something called the Health Insurance Portability and Accountability Act of 1996 (or HIPAA for short) that you need to understand. If any part of a wellness initiative is linked to plan benefits, premium discounts, or reduced copayments or deductibles, HIPAA rules apply. These rules prohibit health plans from discriminating against individuals on the basis of health status–related risk factors. There are terms under which incentives based on weight are okay under HIPAA, but you can avoid HIPAA entirely if you provide cash directly, as opposed to premium discounts or other benefits linked to the health plan. That is why my company would stick with cash payouts.

If you ignore my advice and decide to link your incentives to your health plan, my read of HIPAA reveals the following (but remember, I'm an economist, not an attorney):

- It is okay to make health plan enrollment or receipt of benefits contingent upon completion of certain activities (e.g., participation in health classes), but it is not okay to make plan benefits contingent on meeting certain weight loss or other goals.

- It is okay to offer incentives for weight loss or weight maintenance (e.g., premium discounts) but the incentives cannot exceed 20 percent of the cost of employee only health coverage.
- You need to provide an alternative way for employees to obtain the incentive if they have a medical reason as to why they can't obtain the incentive via the primary mechanism (note that my recommended approach also incorporates this feature).

And HIPAA may not be the only relevant statute. So before you get yourself or your company in legal hot water, make sure a competent lawyer like Uncle Al reviews and signs off on your approach to wellness.

In the next chapter we discuss, from a business perspective, the plus side of rising rates of obesity.

Chapter 11

The ObesEconomy

We detailed some of the adverse financial consequences that obesity imposes on the economy in Chapter 6. There is a flip side, however, that also deserves mention. We call it the ObesEconomy. The rise in obesity rates has created a demand for all sorts of products and services. And suppliers are scurrying to fill that demand and make a hefty profit along the way. Weight-loss programs, diet books, and natural food stores all promise fast fixes to the nation's obesity problem—fixes that are being eaten up by those looking for the magic-bullet solution to excess weight. The weight-loss industry, which includes diet pills, pharmaceuticals, surgery, books, foods, and other products and services, is now a multibillion-dollar industry.

Even reality television is cashing in on America's obsession with weight loss. For example, NBC's hit show *The Biggest Loser* (think: *Survivor* meets Richard Simmons) pits obese contestants against one another. These contestants are isolated "on the ranch" to see who can lose the most weight strictly through diet and exercise. Viewers tune in to nail-biting weekly weigh-ins to watch the contestants shrink faster than Anna Nicole Smith did on TRIMSPA (and apparently Valium, Provigil, Xanax, Vicodin, and who knows what). In fact, the first finale of *The Biggest Loser*, which aired January 11, 2005, became a ratings heavyweight, scoring NBC's highest rating in nearly three years for that time slot. In Chapter 12 we'll discuss why these contestants seem to fare so much better than the average Joe who goes on a diet.

The Discovery Health Channel regularly showcases monumental weight loss among the morbidly obese in documentaries such as *Half-Ton Man*. This particular show followed Patrick Deuel's journey as he drops down from 1,072 pounds to just south of 500 pounds to become, as Deuel quipped, "the Quarter-Ton Man." Not too shabby.

Weight-loss products, services, and television are just one facet of the ObesEconomy. Owners of www.SuperSizeWorld.com, an online vendor of "plus size" products, who claim to be the "life support for the larger lifestyle," say it best on their home page: "Whether obese people are planning on weight loss or whether they plan to accept their size doesn't matter. They still deserve products to keep them safe and comfortable."

Entrepreneurs are responding to the demands of increasingly overweight consumers and also to increased demands for innovative weight-loss strategies. The economy is adapting to a population where so-called *normal* weight is anything but normal. So, in the end, obesity is a problem for some, but for others, it is an opportunity to fill a demand and make a handsome profit along the way.

Just How Big Is the Weight-Loss Industry?

The weight-loss industry is a $49 billion per year industry.[1] Diet centers and programs; diet camps; prepackaged foods; over-the-counter diet drugs; diet patches; fat blockers; starch blockers; magnet pills; bulk producers; algae, weight-loss books and magazines; electrical muscle stimulators; nutritionists; commercial and residential exercise clubs; sugar-free, fat-free, and reduced calorie food products; and imitation fats and sugar substitutes are everywhere, and they are increasingly profitable.

Then there are appetite-suppressing eyeglasses. The glasses have colored lenses that claim to project an image to the retina that is said to dampen the desire to eat. Don't want to wear glasses? There are also special earrings that are custom fitted to include pressure points that, like acupuncture, also are claimed to dampen food cravings. There is no evidence that either work, but, as we discuss below, that only serves to put them in good company with nearly all of the other weight-loss products and services on the market.

An estimated 50 million Americans will attempt to lose weight this year. And, as shown in Table 11.1, they have a lot of diet plans to choose from. Commercial diet programs such as Weight Watchers, Slim Fast, LA Weight Loss, Nutri-System, and Jenny Craig are the most popular. However, they are facing increasing competition from Web-based programs, including eDiets, Anne Collins, IShape, Jillian Michaels, and others. Many of these not only provide structured diet and exercise programs, but they market their own foods that often include home delivery services. These meals typically range from $10 to $40 per day.

Do these diets work any better than the magic glasses? The truth is that there is scant evidence to suggest that any of them result in sustained weight loss. A systematic review of major commercial weight-loss programs in the United States showed that there was insufficient evidence of the effectiveness of most programs.[2] Weight Watchers was the only program with a well-documented success rate: participants lost 5 percent of their initial weight in the first six months of the program. Regardless of the lack of evidence, it is estimated that 7.1 million Americans have signed on to commercial weight-loss programs and that this market will grow 11 percent in the next few years.[3] Weight Watchers alone generates about $1 billion per year in revenue, and new centers are appearing throughout the nation.[4] However, these are hardly the only games in town.

Rice diets, liquid diets, cabbage diets, and others all have their following. Some of these require extensive and expensive inpatient admissions as part of the program. For example, the Duke Rice Diet Clinic offers a four-week program with physical examinations, routine lab work, daily classes and activities, meals, and medical care for $4,800 plus lodging. Average stays at the center are four to eight weeks.[5] This is just one of the many lifestyle programs that provide support to adults trying to lose weight.

Table 11.1   Diet Plans and Programs

3-Day Diet	F Plan	Peanut Butter Diet
Abs Diet	Fit for Life Diet	Peel Away the Pounds
Anne Collins Diet	Food Combining	Diet
Apple Cider Vinegar Diet	Glycemic Impact Diet	Perricone's
Atkins Diet	Grapefruit Diet	Prescription
Best Life Diet	Greenlane Diet	Protein Diet
Beverly Hills Diet	Hay Diet	Protein Powder Diet
Biggest Loser Club	Health Management Resources	Raw Food Diet
Bill Phillips' Eating	Herbalife	Rice Diet
for Life	High Fiber Diet	Richard Simmons Diet
Blood Type Diet	Hip and Thigh Diet	Russian Air Force Diet
Bob Greene's Diet	Holford Diet	Scan Diet
Body for Life	Hollywood 48 Hour Diet	Scarsdale Diet
Burn the Fat—Feed the Muscle	IShape	Seattle Sutton's Healthy Eating
Cabbage Soup Diet	Jenny Craig	Seven-Day Diet
Cambridge Diet	Jillian Michaels	Slim Fast

Carbohydrate Addicts
Caveman Diet
Celebrity Diet
Change One
Chicken Soup Diet
Chocolate Diet
Cleveland Clinic Diet Program
DASH Diet
Denise Austin
Detox Diets
Diet Divas
DietWatch
Dr. Weil's My Optimum Health Plan
Eat Right 4 Your Type
eDiets

LA Weight Loss
Lindora—Lean for Life
Liver Cleansing Diet
Macrobiotic Diet
Maker's Diet
Medifast
Mediterranean Diet
Metabolism Diet
Michael Thurmond's Six Week Body
  Makeover
Negative Calorie Diet
NutriSystem
OptiFast
Ornish Diet
Overeaters Anonymous

SlimKids
Sommersizing
Sonoma Diet
SparkPeople
Subway Diet
Sugar Busters
Take Off Pounds
  Sensibly (TOPS)
The Cookie Diet
Three Hour Diet
Trim Kids
Warrior Diet
Weight Watchers
WeightLoss4Idiots
Zone Diet

SOURCES: Free Dieting—The Weight Loss Guide. *Diet Plans*. Available at www.freedieting.com/diet_plan_reviews.htm. Accessed on February 18, 2007; and The Diet Channel. *Diet Index*. Available at www.thedietchannel.com/diet-index.htm. Accessed on February 18, 2007.

Overnight camps strictly for overweight youth are another hot trend in the ObesEconomy. There are now well over a dozen summer camps in the nation specifically targeting overweight children. Among them are Tony Sparber's New Image Camps, Camp Shane, Camp Wellspring, Camp Kingsmont, and Camp La Jolla. For about $7,500 a summer, a child can expect to get about 1,500 calories a day and spend three to four hours a day doing physical activity.

In addition to commercial products and on-site weight-loss programs, dietitians and nutritionists are increasingly sought after to assist individuals attempting to improve their diets and lose weight. Many have their own practices, while others work as consultants in fitness centers, hospitals, or physician offices. Six-month customized plans from dietitians cost about $800 on average. Since becoming a nutritionist does not require a college degree, entry into this occupation is fairly easy. There are currently over 50,000 nutrition/dietitian jobs in the United States, and the median salary is over $44,000 per year. The Bureau of Labor Statistics predicts that jobs in this area will grow faster than the average for all occupations at least through 2014.

Work It Out

As individuals try to reduce the effects of lower food prices and more sedentary jobs, it's no surprise that the health and fitness industry was listed as one of the 13 hot businesses for 2005 by Entrepreneur.com.[6] There has been significant growth in the number of health clubs in the United States (see Figure 11.1). Fifty large companies capture more than 30 percent of the market. The average fitness center earns about $3 million a year.[7]

Increasingly, fitness centers are catering to overweight populations, including children. ProMaxima Fitness and Hoist, for example, both manufacture and distribute kid-friendly fitness equipment.

Then there's a new class of fitness centers such as Curves and Planet Fitness that target individuals who feel uncomfortable attending a typical "muscle head" gym. For example, Curves offers women a comfortable environment with predesigned 30-minute workouts. It promotes healthy lifestyles for women trying to get on track with a weight management plan.[8] Planet Fitness advertises itself as a "Judgment Free Zone." It boasts a comfortable environment to build an active lifestyle.

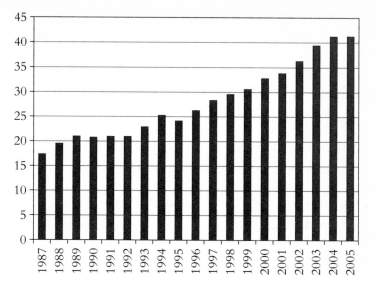

Figure 11.1   Health Club Growth—Number of Health Club Members by Year (million)

Source: International Health, Racquet & Sportclub Association. 2005 IHRSA/American Sports Data Health Club Trend Report. Available at http://cms.ihrsa.org/IHRSA/viewPage.cfm?pageId=804. Accessed on February 18, 2007.

Just Take a Pill

For those who are unable or unwilling to lose weight through diet and exercise, pharmacological and surgical interventions are increasingly available. A common, although not particularly effective, approach is over-the-counter diet pills. As shown in Table 11.2, there are many to choose from. Any watcher of late-night television has been tantalized with products that allow you to: "Eat all you want and still lose weight." Or perhaps you'd like to "melt fat away while you sleep." But if you think these products sound too good to be true, you are probably right. The Federal Trade Commission recently indicated that over-the-counter diet pills are, like most of the weight-loss plans, the glasses, and the earrings, largely ineffective.[9,10]

In addition to little evidence of effectiveness, many of the over-the-counter weight-loss products carry some adverse health risks. To understand this, we have only to look to ephedra, an herbal supplement used to lose weight and increase energy. The supplement was

Table 11.2   Over-the-Counter Diet Pills

Ab-Solution	Endurox	Lipitrex	Suvaril
Plus	Energy Reserve	Lipo	Syntrax Beta
Accel	Enhanced ClA	LipoSlim System	Syntrax
Accuslim Fat	Ergolean MC	Lipovar	Subdue
Burner	Estrin-D	Mega Fat Burner	T3
Adenergy	Estrodex	Meltdown	Taraxatone
Alli	Fahrenheit	Metabolic Thyrolean	Therma Slim
AM Cleanse	Fat Blocker	Metabolife	ThermaZan
Anorex	Fat Burners	Metabolift	Thermics
Carb Blocker	Fat Converter	Miracle Burn	Thermo
Carb Cutter	Fat Cutter	Musculean	DynamX
Carb DynamX	Fblock Xtra	Nitrix	Thermonex
Carb Helper	Formastat	NoPhedra	Thinfat
Carb Intercept	Glucolean	NOS Matrix	Thyro-Cuts
Cardio Stack	Glucomannan	NOX2	ThyroSlim
Cblock	Guarana	NOX3	Thyrox
Charge ASF	Hollywood Diet	Oxydrene	Tight
Cheat & Eat	Hoodia Gordonii	PediaLean	TrimSpa
Chitosan	Hot Rox	Pinnacle Masculine	Triple Lean
Citrimax	HydroBurn	ProLab Cuts II	Ultra Carb
Cortislim	Hydroxycut	Psyllium	Intercept
Cortisol	Hydrocitric Acid	Pyruvate	Ultra Diet
Country Mallow	Kaizen Caffeine	Redline	Pep
Cravex	Lava	Relacore	Xenadrine
Cutting Gel	Lean Matrix	Remedilean	XtremeLean
Dexatrim	Lean Out	Ripped Fuel	Zantrex
Diet Carb Block	Lean System	Shredded	Zotrin
Diet Fuel	LeanFire	Stacker	
Dymetadrine	Leptotril	Superdrine	
Xtreme			

SOURCE: Diet Pills. *Non Prescription Diet Pills.* Available at www.dietpills.com/category .aspx?categoryid=52. Accessed on February 18, 2007.

banned by the Food and Drug Administration (FDA) in 2003.[11] A federal judge in Utah later reversed the short-lived ban on ephedra. Within moments, e-mail inboxes were flooded with spam messages to "BUY BUY BUY" before ephedra was banned again. Since then, I've probably received hundreds of spam e-mails telling me how ephedra was "banned for being too effective." The truth is that the product was found to cause serious adverse effects such as heart palpitations, tremors, and insomnia. Regardless, at the time of the ban, between 12 and 17 million Americans had been using the product.

In spite of the lack of documented effectiveness and potential health risks, Americans spend approximately $1 billion a year on over-the-counter weight-loss products, and annual growth rates are forecasted at 11.5 percent or higher.[12]

Although this will undoubtedly change in the near future, there are currently only a couple of choices for prescription weight-loss medications. One choice that is no longer available, even though it was shown to be highly effective, is phen-fen. Phentermine and fenfluramine are two drugs that had been on the market since the 1970s but were not used in combination to fight obesity until the early 1990s.[13] Phentermine decreases appetite, while fenfluramine gives the feeling of increased satiety (fullness). A 1992 study indicated that this combination drug was more effective than exercise and diet alone for weight loss.[14] The same study documented very few side effects, which made the drug more appealing than its competitors. Not long after, millions of overweight Americans were using the drug combination in efforts to lose weight.

In 1996, physicians wrote more than 18 million prescriptions for a 30-day supply of phen-fen. Then in 1997, the phen-fen miracle unraveled as cases of heart valve malfunctions appeared to be linked to use of the drug. In 1997, the FDA asked the drug manufacturers to voluntarily withdraw both drugs from the market. By the time of the recall, about 6 million Americans and 77 million individuals worldwide had used one drug or the other. The phen-fen diet drug miracle was, in fact, too good to be true.[15]

Given the phen-fen fiasco, it is understandable that pharmaceutical companies have been leery about getting back into the obesity business. Currently, two antiobesity prescription pharmaceutical products—Xenical and Meridia—dominate the market, and neither has seen the success of phen-fen. A form of Xenical, marketed as Alli, was also approved in February 2007 for over-the-counter sales in the United States. The drug hit the shelves in the summer of 2007.[16]

Alli is the only FDA-approved weight-loss drug available to Americans without a prescription. It, and its prescription counterpart, which is sold at higher dosage, has been shown to support weight loss by helping individuals lose 50 percent more weight than by diet alone. That sounds good, although as we've shown above, for many individuals, 50 percent more weight loss than diet alone may still not be a whole lot of weight loss. Moreover, these drugs have some fairly nasty side effects, including oily spotting, flatulence with discharge, fecal urgency, fatty/oily stools, and abdominal pain and discomfort. Given the choice, I'd rather carry the extra pounds. But, clearly, many others would not as, according to the manufacturers of Alli, this drug alone is expected to generate more than $1.5 billion in annual sales.[17] As drug sales go, these are not blockbusters, but I guarantee we'll see a blockbuster obesity drug hit the market at some point. A drug that produces significant weight loss, even with a little extra flatulence, could easily be the next big thing.

The drug companies have recognized the potential windfall, and so are slowly wading back into the obesity market. One highly anticipated drug that will not hit the U.S. market anytime soon is rimonabant. It was developed by Sanofi Aventis and is already approved for use in several European countries.[18] The drug acts on the cannabinoid receptors in the brain to suppress hunger. These are the same receptors that are triggered after individuals smoke marijuana (i.e., cannabis). Some hippie-turned-chemist must have realized that blocking those receptors can produce an absence of hunger (think: munchies in reverse). And they say smoking pot doesn't get you anywhere.

Although analysts had predicted that the drug would be a multi-billion-dollar blockbuster drug when it hit the U.S. market, an FDA advisory panel recommended against approving the drug because of concerns that it increased the risk of neurological and psychological problems, including suicide. Even without this drug, sales for antiobesity agents in the United States are expected to triple by 2010 from $723 million in 2005 to $1.4 billion, but this number could be even larger depending on how effective other new drugs turn out to be in reducing weight without the nasty side effects of the current options.[19]

The Quick Fix

It's hard to walk past the tabloids in the grocery store checkout line without coming across a cover story documenting some celebrity's miraculous transformation following weight-loss surgery (think: Al Roker, or for you hipper readers, Randy Jackson from *American Idol*). Weight-loss surgery among celebrities should hardly come as a surprise. If you have lots of money, but little time to diet and exercise, what better way to lose weight fast? And who doesn't love the idea of a quick fix?

In fact, surgical treatments such as liposuction, gastric banding, and gastric bypass generally offer greater weight loss than what can be achieved by the available meds (and diet and exercise). Liposuction is the most commonly performed cosmetic surgery procedure in the United States.[20] It involves the surgical suctioning of fatty deposits from the body. Over 400,000 of these surgical procedures are performed annually. The most common areas for the procedure are the abdomen, buttocks, hips, thighs and knees, chin, upper arms, back, and calves.

In gastric banding, a band is placed around the upper portion of the stomach to control the passage of food through the stomach.[21] This limits the amount of food an individual can eat at one time. The band can be inflated or deflated by a physician, as necessary, to control the passing of food. Gastric bypass involves surgically bypassing part of the small intestine to prevent the absorption of food. Both surgeries can now be performed laparoscopically (i.e., without a large incision), reducing risks associated with open procedures.

However, these procedures are not for the faint of heart. For example, gastric bypass, although the most effective weight-loss technique available today, requires lifelong changes in the types and quantities of foods consumed. And, as with any major surgery, it includes risks of surgical and nonsurgical complications, and in rare instances, death. That is why an industry insider told me that when my time comes I should try banding first, and if that fails, then go with the bypass.

Bariatric procedures, including both bypass and banding, increased by more than 800 percent in the United States between 1998 and 2004.[22,23] Nearly 200,000 bariatric weight-loss procedures are now performed annually, and this number is likely to rise in the future. At a cost of up to $25,000 or more per procedure, it is no wonder that surgical treatments for obesity now represent a $3.5 billion annual business.[24] Therefore, it is not surprising that bariatric treatment centers and liposuction clinics are popping up throughout the nation as major profit centers for physicians and medical groups.

As with the pharmaceutical industry, the research and development budgets for obesity-fighting technologies are enormous. The company that develops the cure to obesity (unless it involves sustained diet and exercise) is sure to reap enormous profits, an opportunity that has not gone unnoticed by the pharmaceutical and medical device companies.

Bigger and Better

The weight-loss industry is far from the only one responding to the ObesEconomy. Take the apparel industry. In the past, an overweight woman had slim pickings at the mall. Oversized muumuus, baggy pants, eye-popping fluorescent colors, big floral prints, and plenty of polyester were common choices. But retailers have now taken notice of the high demand for fashionable plus-size clothing. They are creating lines of clothing that are designed to flatter plus-size bodies, and their advertising departments are increasingly targeting this population subset.

The reason for the change in marketing strategy is obvious. Plus-size clothing represents a $32 billion per year industry.[25] According to an analysis by the NPD Group, plus sizes are currently the fastest-growing segment in the apparel market.[26] In 2002, it was estimated that the plus-size category had grown 10 percent since the previous year. This should not be surprising given that, since 1985, the average American woman has grown from a size 8 to a size 14. In fact, 62 percent of women wear a size 14 or larger.

Clothing stores are increasingly incorporating a more extensive selection of plus-size clothing into their collections and are charging premium prices. Numerous retailers, including Talbots, are opening new stores solely for the plus-size market, and several designers are jumping on the plus-size clothing bandwagon. And that's not all: Sad as it is, the kids' plus-size clothing market was listed as one of the 13 hot businesses for 2005 by Entrepreneur.com.[27]

The costly investment in these garments has opened up the need for gadgets to protect the investment. Plus-size hangers are just one example. Some obese individuals also need assistance dressing themselves in their expensive threads. Button and zipper hooks that help with dressing, sock aids, and extra long shoe horns that reduce stress from bending and stretching are invaluable innovations for those who need them. They are increasingly being sold at stores catering to those with excess weight.

Overweight individuals often have fewer options for accessorizing their ensemble. Watch bands, bracelets, and necklaces can be too small. Of late, however, companies are popping up that offer entirely new lines of jewelry and accessories made solely for overweight consumers.

Furniture

Imagine how you would feel if you sat down in a chair only to have it collapse because it could not support your weight. Not only does this pose a significant risk of injury, but the potential for humiliation is high. For severely obese individuals, this represents a serious concern. The furniture market has responded with the emergence of reinforced furniture pieces. Fatcities.com is just one example of a web site that sells couches designed to accommodate individuals over 500 pounds. The couches have wider and deeper dimensions, as well as extra legs to support and balance the extra weight and special foam cushions that prevent sagging.

Several stores also provide lightweight portable chairs that can hold a lot of weight. These lightweight chairs can be carried around so that a comfortable chair (that fits) is readily available in malls, at friends' houses, in waiting rooms, at restaurants, and so on. Another company, liftchair .com, manufactures and sells lift chairs. These are recliners with lift seats that assist people who have trouble getting up on their own. The lift chairs are built with a capacity of about 700 pounds.

Even toddlers have not been ignored. The $250 Britax "Husky" car seat is about 10 pounds heavier and four inches wider than standard car seats.

The Great John Toilet Company manufactures and sells toilets that cater to the needs of larger people. This company provides toilets with longer and wider seats as well as an extra wide base for more stability. A second super-size toilet manufacturer, Big John Toilet Seat, announced that demand for the larger toilets doubled in the first half of 2005. Although not quite profitable yet, the company owners expect big payoffs in the future.[28]

Many hospitals have had to reinforce or replace their wall-mounted toilets that were not designed for individuals over 250 pounds. Hospitals have had these wall-mounted toilets snap right off the walls (an image that haunts me). Many have switched to floor-mounted toilets that are wider, longer, and deeper. One patient actually broke the toilet and then, during the fall, broke his tailbone.[29] Alternatively, facilities may purchase and install metal toilet supports that fit under wall-mounted toilets to provide support for up to 1,000 pounds.[30]

Medical Supplies

A 66-year-old severely obese woman was forced to crawl into an ambulance while having an asthma attack because the gurneys could not hold her.[31] This same individual refused regular physical exams because she couldn't get up onto the exam table. To avoid these types of incidents, hospitals and physicians' offices are adapting their practices and buying new equipment and supplies to better accommodate an increasingly obese patient population. In part to protect themselves from potential litigation from obese patients and the staff that attend to them, they are purchasing reinforced gurneys, extra large gowns, wheelchairs, larger blood pressure cuffs, wider exam rooms and operating tables, and hoists to assist health care workers with moving larger patients, in addition to reinforced toilets.

Hospitals and clinics are also replacing their beds and chairs to make them both stronger and wider and increasing the size of their doorways and bathrooms. Of course, these replacements come at a significant cost.[32] A single bed that includes a scale and can tip a patient to a standing position can run around $18,500. Oversized wheelchairs can cost about $2,500 (eight times an ordinary wheelchair), and operating tables to support severely obese patients cost over $30,000. There are now over 1,000 items specifically targeted to obese hospital inpatients, and suppliers of these products, while clearly filling a need, are making big money along the way.

Although hospitals are trying to keep up with growing waistlines, there are a few instances where they are coming up against a lack of technology to ensure appropriate diagnosis in the obese patient population. Currently, x-ray machines and other scanners can't penetrate the fat of some individuals, thus limiting their diagnostic capabilities. However, given the increasing demand for this technology, it is only a matter of time before newer machines are available without these limitations.

Getting Around

In Chapter 3, I mentioned seeing a large number of motorized assistive devices transporting mobility-impaired obese individuals around the county fair. These devices are also increasingly available at other locations, including grocery stores and casinos. Getting around on a motorized assistive device is much less exhausting and more practical for many obese individuals. As a result, it is no wonder that the demand for these products is increasing. One manufacturer of large electric scooters received over $2 million in revenue from "heavy customers." This represents about one fifth of the company's revenue.[33]

The car-manufacturing industry is also adapting to the ObesEconomy. Manufacturers such as Toyota are making larger seats and obese-friendly steering wheels to accommodate larger drivers and passengers.

Even test dummies have gained weight. For example, the old standard adult dummy weighed 170 pounds. The newest standard dummy, introduced in 2001, weighs in at 223 pounds.

And the ObesEconomy extends around the world. Australia's obesity crisis, for example, has forced health officials to revamp their fleet of ambulances to cope with a sharp rise in overweight patients. Car and air ambulances are being remodeled to carry heavier people.

Sporting Goods

Just because someone is overweight does not mean they do not enjoy active leisure. However, this experience can be diminished if they can't fit into the required gear. As a result, sporting good stores now offer specialty items like extra large personal flotation devices for swimming and boating, reinforced and larger bicycle seats, and specialized headgear.

Many golf shops offer golf tools that avoid the need for bending and picking up or placing the balls. Uncle Al owns one of these.

Sneakers have also been designed to handle the extra weight of obese individuals. One type of sneaker, manufactured by Z-Coil, has a large tungsten-steel coil mounted into the heel, hence the name. At $160 a pair, they are not cheap. But clearly the demand is there. In 2004, revenues from these shoes reached $10.8 million.[34]

A Vermont-based company, SuperSizedCycles.com, designs and sells bikes that are built to support the extra weight of heavy people. These bikes are built with extra reinforcements and padding, as well as different spacing for parts. They can usually carry up to 550 pounds. Some of the bikes also have electrical assistance, just in case the rider needs a little extra help to make it back home. These custom-built bicycles generally run from about $400 to $2,000.

Still Other Products and Services

Personal hygiene items are what launched Amplestuff.com. Nancy Summer, co-owner of Amplestuff, was frustrated that she could not reach every part of her body in the shower, so she started looking for products to assist her. In her search, she found the "sponge on a stick," which was later adapted by her colleague Bill Fabrey into the "ample-sponge." Since its start, Amplestuff has grown considerably and now offers over 1,000 different obesity-friendly products. These include high-capacity bathroom scales, larger towels and robes, bath benches, and baripeutic health and skin products, among others.

Plussizeyellowpages.com is the place to go to for information on obese-friendly services. In addition to providing information for the purchase of products, this web site directs individuals to several services such as dating services for larger people, weight acceptance organizations, and weight discrimination lawyers. ChunkEbusiness.com is a site dedicated to portraying larger people in a positive manner and selling weight-friendly gifts and artwork. Then there are the many dating sites, like BBPeopleMeet.com, bbwdatefinder.com, and largefriends.com, that specifically target overweight singles.

The private sector is not the only one responding to the obesity boom. The National Institutes of Health's research budget dedicated to obesity has swelled to over $590 million per year.[35] The U.S. Department of Health and Human Services (which includes the Centers for Disease Control and Prevention) and other government agencies are also increasing funding for obesity-related programs. This allows obesity researchers like me to earn a decent living without having to "sell out" to the drug or device industry (in truth, I routinely consult in these industries, so I guess I've already sold out). Several universities, including Virginia Tech, Columbia University, and the University of Pittsburgh, now boast research centers dedicated to the prevention and treatment of obesity. And most, if not all, of the funding comes from government grants; even the government is adapting to the ObesEconomy.

There's also a fairly new category of weight-loss catalysts being developed in the ObeseEconomy. Some of these products, in fact, have real potential to effectively reduce weight and improve the health of consumers. We explore these in the next section.

Invest in New Technology

Wait a minute. Didn't we explain in detail in Chapters 2 and 3 just why the rise in obesity rates is due in large part to our usage of new technology? Well, technology, it turns out, is not only the underlying cause of the rise in obesity rates, it will also be part of the solution. Our ObesEconomy is once again latching on to a market demand and supplying us with some really cool new technologies that even public health experts can get excited about. And I'm not just talking about new diet plans, weight-loss drugs, or medical devices.

Take the stand-up treadmill workstation, which attaches a regular treadmill to a computer workstation. This might allow even workaholics like me to burn off a few extra calories, although I'm not entirely convinced I have the coordination to pull it off. Okay, so maybe that one is not a winner. But what about *Dance Dance Revolution* and other active video games?

Dance Dance Revolution, or DDR, if you're cool, was first introduced in 1998 and has continued to grow in popularity. DDR is a home or arcade video game that includes a dance pad with arrow panels that are pressed using the player's feet in response to arrows that appear on a video screen. The arrows are synchronized to the beat of a chosen song, and players are scored based on their ability to time and position their steps. It would be impossible to be a DDR gamer without burning lots of calories. I first ran into DDR at Frankie's Fun House near my house in North Carolina. My wife and I stood in amazement as we watched a teenage boy, with sweat flying off his forehead, move his feet unbelievably fast to the beat of some hip song that I had never heard of. His friends actually seemed to think being good at this game was cool. This is one video game that I would gladly let my kids play. In fact, some schools are even using it in their gym classes.

DDR is hardly alone in the "Exertainment" niche. Other games are cropping up all the time. The latest Nintendo game system, the much-lauded Wii (pronounced "we") has received a slew of publicity for its innovative use of game controllers. Instead of sitting on a couch and mashing away at buttons, Wii players move their arms and wrists as if they were actually, say, swinging a tennis racket, throwing a bowling ball, or fighting in a boxing ring. As noted in a recent Time.com article, "the game may be virtual, but the physical exertion is real."[36]

A week after the Wii debuted in November 2006, the *Wall Street Journal* reported that the gaming console was leaving some users as sore as if they had just gone to the gym.[37]

Another game has individuals swinging golf clubs to let gamers virtually play some of the world's best courses. What a great stocking stuffer for Uncle Al!

And the benefits of active video games are not just theoretical. For example, in a report published by the Mayo Clinic, researchers found that children burned three times as many calories playing "active" video games versus playing traditional handheld video games.[38] (Of course, three times zero is still zero.)

But gaming isn't the only advancement. Technology has also made it easier for me to run, thanks to iPods, treadmills, and better running shoes.

The Internet, which undoubtedly is making us more sedentary, also offers health and fitness sites that provide plenty of tips and information. New interactive sites like www.traineo.com not only give people a place to plan, plot, and track their weight-loss and fitness goals, it also lets users tap the communal aspect of the Web by creating online support groups. Users can establish a group of four "motivators," people who will then receive regular e-mail updates on the Traineo users' exercise activities, and in turn, are expected to provide the user with weight-loss encouragement or advice. The result? More accountability and, potentially, more weight loss.

And that's just a handful of examples of the new technology now being developed. No doubt, these products will help some individuals lose weight.

In the Name of Progress

The fast-growing ObesEconomy highlights the adaptive nature of a market economy. As consumers have demanded new technologies and affordable, convenient, and tasty food, the market has adapted to provide those products. As a result, we have gained weight. But, once again, the market has come to the rescue by providing the products and services that are increasingly demanded by an overweight population with money to spend.

Given the enormous financial incentives for the private sector to develop new products and services to confront obesity, someday it may be a thing of the past.

But I'm not holding my breath that it will happen anytime soon. Till then, thank goodness for Goliath caskets, a maker of "right-sized" caskets. Every month, this Lynn, Indiana–based company ships four or five triple-wide caskets. These caskets are 44 to 54 inches wide, just about twice the size of the standard of 24 inches. Another oversized casket maker, Batesville Casket Company, has quoted 20 percent growth in the sales of their oversized caskets over the past five years, and they say they expect that growth will continue for the foreseeable future. I suspect they are right. But for those who want to buck this trend, we offer some helpful hints in the next chapter.

Chapter 12

How to Lose Weight Like an Economist

As I said in the introduction, this is definitely not a how-to-diet book. Lord knows there are enough of those floating around. Having said that, if you're an adult, I do not believe that the government has much of a role in helping you lose weight, and for reasons discussed in Chapter 10, I doubt your employer is going to be of much help either. Therefore, if you want to lose weight, you are likely going to have to go it alone. Of course, as we discussed in the previous chapter, if you have money to spend, you do have options. There are countless purveyors of weight-loss products and services who would *love* to assist you in your efforts to attain your optimal weight.

Now, I'm not about to open my own weight-loss clinics (although the thought has crossed my mind), but I've spent a lot of time thinking about successful weight-loss strategies over the past few years, both for myself and to incorporate into my research studies. I've generated a few ideas that are grounded in economic theory and that have shown some success in the real world, including my own weight-loss efforts.

I noted in Chapter 1 that I weighed 194 pounds when my son was born in 2000. Over the following 20 months, I lost about a pound per month. This may not seem like a lot of weight, but slow and steady weight loss is one of my keys to success. If you are losing weight quickly, you've likely made substantial changes to your diet and exercise patterns; changes that you'll probably find to be too costly to sustain. The government's public information campaign also recognizes this reality and encourages individuals to make "small steps to eat a more balanced diet and to stay physically active."

Since the pounds came off, I've managed to maintain a weight of about 174 pounds for the past five years, at least until recently. The past six months of working days and writing nights has made my workouts more costly (in terms of what I would be giving up), so I have put on a few pounds of late. Of course, it's worth it, right? Since this is the last chapter, I'm seeing a light at the end of the tunnel when I can get back to a more regular schedule. Ideally, I'd like to get down to 170 pounds, but that may require more sacrifices than I am willing to make. Regardless, since you've hung with the book this long, I'd like to share my proven approach to weight loss in hopes that some of you may benefit from this sage advice.

But before I get on my high horse, let me tell you a story. This is a story about great courage. It's about overcoming obstacles. It's taken straight from my favorite reality TV series, *The Biggest Loser*.

Deli owner Erik Chopin knew he was in trouble when he maxed out the 350-pound scale at his doctor's office. An athlete turned business owner/family man, Erik found that the demands of owning a business coupled with having young children made it difficult for him to keep up his once-rigorous exercise regime. (Sound familiar?) The trouble was that once he stopped exercising, the pounds began to accumulate.

"It's weird you gain this weight little by little. Each season comes, and the summer clothes from before didn't fit, and it happens every year," Erik said to a writer with the *Bucks County Courier Times*.[1]

So at 407 pounds, Erik was lucky enough to be selected as a contestant on *The Biggest Loser*. If you haven't seen the show, it goes like this: Obese contestants spend 11 weeks (if they last that long) on a

California ranch being whipped into shape by professional trainers. The contestants are divided into two teams (blue and red) and participate in challenges to try to earn prizes as well as immunity from elimination. The contestants exercise for at least three to four hours a day and practice eating a healthy diet. Each week, the teams are weighed in, and the team that collectively loses the least weight that week is forced to vote off one of its members. When there are only four finalists left, the contestants go home to diet and exercise on their own volition for four months. The person who loses the highest percentage of his/her weight wins $250,000 and the esteemed "Biggest Loser" title.

Just like any reality show, *The Biggest Loser* is riddled with drama. There's scheming, backstabbing, tantrums, tears, heroics, and jubilation. But, unlike most reality television (with the obvious exception of VH1's *Flavor of Love*), this show has some practical advice to give. In this case, it comes in the form of diet and exercise tips.

The success of contestants like Erik confirms a number of the messages that this book is trying to convey. Consistent with basic principles of economics, when you take someone out of our obesity-promoting environment, give them plenty of time to exercise and unlimited access to healthy foods, and provide them with large incentives for weight loss, the end result is that the pounds drop off. In other words, when you lower the costs of diet and exercise, and/or up the benefits of weight loss, people will lose weight—often lots of it.

All told, Erik, season three's *Biggest Loser*, dropped 214 pounds in eight months—that's 52 percent of his former body weight—making him the all-time *Biggest Loser*. But once the cameras were switched off, Erik found himself once again on his own—without a quarter-million-dollar prize or millions of TV viewers watching his every move. And there he was, back in his Long Island, New York, deli, surrounded by tempting mayo-laden salads, salami, pastrami, roast beef, cheeses, and baked goods.

So has he maintained his new lifestyle and lower weight? You may be surprised to find out that the answer is mostly yes. He regained 22 pounds—about 10 percent of the weight—but managed to keep the rest off (so far). Like Jared Fogle (a.k.a. the Subway guy), Erik has turned his weight loss into a lucrative career. He, too, is bringing home cash for showing off his skinny new physique. He now travels the lecture circuit, educating people about obesity and diabetes. As with Jared, regaining the weight would cost him a lucrative side business. It is this added incentive that has helped him keep (most of) the weight off.

Those of you who have ever tried to lose weight are keenly aware that weight loss is the easy part. In fact, many, if not most, of the diets on the market today will generate short-term weight loss. But, no matter what the diet or weight-loss method, weight *regain* within five years occurs for the vast majority of dieters.[2] This occurs because dieters are trying to maintain sustained changes in behavior in an (at best) unchanged environment. Unlike those on *The Biggest Loser*, the environment we live in does not allow us to exercise for three to four hours a day or to have unlimited access to healthy foods. In fact, if anything, the environment is providing us with just the opposite—it tempts us with low-cost, tasty, calorie-dense foods that help us to pack on the pounds and offers up modern conveniences that keep us sedentary as Gitmo detainees (or worse yet, lawyers).

And unlike Jared and Erik, the vast majority of us do not have large enough incentives to allow us to overcome these significant barriers. The reality is that given how difficult it is to maintain a normal weight in today's environment, for most of us, weight loss and the health benefits that go along with it, are not enough of an incentive. For proof, just ask Uncle Al—or any of the two thirds of Americans who are out of the "normal" weight range.

But are there strategies that we can invoke that might help us change the costs and benefits of behaviors related to obesity and allow us to sustain a lower weight? In my experience, the answer is yes, but it takes some creativity and a lot of work.

Economic Weight-Loss Techniques

It's too bad that real life doesn't mirror *The Biggest Loser*. If there were some big cash prize dangled in front of us, a camera following our every move, isolation from life's daily temptations and a personal trainer riding our butts, most of us would likely weigh less—a lot less. If you recall, I wrote earlier in the book that the desire to have credibility as an obesity researcher gave me some added incentive to lose weight, but

I certainly did not have personal trainers or three hours a day to exercise, nor did I have the big financial reward that accrued to Jared and Erik. I now have three kids, a demanding job, and a book to write. But I suspect most of you are equally busy and have other concerns that take a front seat to your diet and exercise regimen. That is part of the reason why we have so much trouble carving out time to exercise and prepare healthy meals.

Even with significant barriers, I've been successful at losing weight and keeping it off (at least until recently). Here are a few strategies that have worked for me that you may want to consider:

Set Long-Term Weight and Exercise Goals

I had always wanted to run a marathon. So when I started to get serious about losing weight, I decided that finishing a marathon would be the perfect goal for me to shoot for. It took me two and a half years to get in good enough shape to run one, and over four hours to finish the race, but finishing that first marathon still stands as one of my greatest achievements (second, of course, to landing the lovely Mrs. Finkelstein).

As we said earlier, losing weight is easy. It is keeping it off that is tough. Setting long-term goals will provide additional incentives to sustain those behavior changes. Moreover, I focused far more on sticking to my training schedule than I did on my weight. This was helpful, as I dropped only about one pound per month and some months no weight at all. This can be discouraging, but I found that focusing on completing the marathon helped keep me motivated. If you set and obtain appropriate goals—and they don't need to be marathons—you can't help but improve your health. The weight loss will follow.

Make Your Goals Public

As soon as I sign up for a marathon, I tell everyone I know about it. I do this not because I am egotistical (although I'm not denying that I am) but because it makes failure that much more costly and success that much sweeter. If I fail, I will have not only missed a personal goal, but everyone will know about it. If you don't like this strategy, bet a friend that you can lose 5 percent of your weight (5 percent is where significant health benefits materialize) and keep it off for a certain amount of time. If the wager is large enough, that will create an additional incentive to keep the weight off.

For me, the fear of public failure is partly what motivated me to get up at 5:45 AM many mornings to go out for a run before the kids woke up. In fact, through miles 21 to 23 of my first marathon, which are the toughest miles, I largely focused on how my friend—the former Sodexho employee I mentioned in Chapter 9 who, by the way, is very overweight (sorry K)—would have ridiculed me to no end had I not finished the race. That potential humiliation is what kept me moving forward during those tough miles. If you have friends like mine, you'll know exactly what I am talking about. My friends, by the way, were able to track my splits on the course web site, and I received many congratulatory phone calls before I even got back home from the race. These added accolades are partly what encouraged me to run several more marathons after I successfully completed my first.

One of the more successful weight-loss programs, Weight Watchers, uses a similar strategy to encourage individuals to lose weight. Members set weight-loss goals when they sign up for the program. At the start of every weekly meeting, members step on the scale. This weigh-in, quite unlike *The Biggest Loser*, is confidential. Nonetheless, it usually fuels the discussion for the rest of the meeting as participants either celebrate or lament their results—and discuss what they can do to make good on their goal for the following week's weigh-in.

"You think about that weigh-in every day over the course of the week," said Marsha Csaszar, who lost 35 pounds 25 years ago through the program. "When you think about your choices of dessert one night, you start to think about how that decision will affect the numbers on that scale and whether you will have good news or bad news to discuss with your group."

Joining Weight Watchers helped Marsha get the weight off. To keep it off, she signed up to be a group leader. Because Weight Watchers has a policy that leaders need to maintain a certain weight, she created an additional incentive to keep her weight off. In other words, she created an environment where gaining weight would have been especially costly. This strategy worked for her. Just like Jared and Erik (and me), she had to show that she could practice what she preached in order to make the big—well not very big in her and my case—bucks.

Along a similar line, I've heard there is a web site where you can submit scantily clad pre-weight-loss pictures of yourself along with your stated weight-loss goal. If you do not meet the goal by a certain date, you give the web site permission to post the pictures. What a great way to provide an additional incentive to shed those extra pounds.

Find an Exercise Buddy (or Several)

Although some people might be successful at maintaining weight loss without exercising, they are the rare exception. Research shows that successful maintainers of weight loss almost always watch their diet and exercise regularly. Having an exercise partner will make you more likely to stick to your exercise routine. This strategy works for a few reasons (all rooted in economic theory, of course). First, it adds an extra cost to any missed exercise sessions. Missing a workout means you are letting down your partner as well as yourself (just like Erik didn't want to let down his *Biggest Loser* teammates). Second, exercise, no matter what form it takes, is work. If it's not, you probably aren't doing it hard enough. One way to make it less painful (i.e., less costly) is to exercise with someone you enjoy. You should also choose activities that you think you can stick with for more than a few weeks.

As I noted in a previous chapter, basketball used to be my activity of choice, but I've taken to running because I can get it done faster, which is important given the increasing demands on my scarce free time. I have a few different running partners, and I much prefer running with them than running on my own. It helps pass the time, and I am far less likely to focus on the run. I also have a dog, and this, too, makes me more likely to go for a run or a walk, but for me, the human partner works better.

Measure and Document

Research shows that dieters who weigh themselves frequently tend to lose more weight.[3] This likely works because they are better able to identify whether their weight-loss strategies are working, and if not, to make the necessary changes. So frequent weigh-ins are helpful.

As I noted in Chapter 3, when I started my quest to lose weight, not only did I weigh myself regularly, but I went out and bought a pedometer (step counter) and tracked my weekly steps on an Excel spreadsheet.

I had a goal of taking 70,000 steps per week (or an average of 10,000 steps per day), as recommended by many health organizations. Ten thousand steps translates into about five miles. Keeping tabs on my steps helped me know whether I was making that weekly goal. I found the pedometer to be a great measurement tool, and I did my best each week to hit the 70,000-step total through walking or running. There were quite a few Saturdays where I had to log 20,000 steps in to meet my weekly quota, but you'd be surprised at how many times I was able to make that happen. This inexpensive (they can be purchased for less than $20) and easy measurement tool is a great way to let you keep tabs on how much you are walking. All you have to do is hook it onto your waistband or belt.

In fact, there is a new model, called the Omron HJ-112 Digital Premium Pedometer, that I've been using for a research study. It has a 40-day memory and can differentiate between normal steps and aerobic steps. Aerobic steps are those you get in bouts of at least 10 minutes of consecutive walking or running. These are arguably the healthier steps to be taking. This pedometer also has an attachment that allows you to download the data directly into a spreadsheet and generate pretty graphs of your activity should you choose to do so. It also converts the steps to calories burned and distance traveled. I suspect there are similar models on the market, but I've had great success with the Omron.

Pedometers are a great example of how technology can help us in our efforts to lose weight. Armed with this information, it is that much easier to monitor energy expenditures and to find strategies (such as parking farther from the entrance to work and shops) that allow for taking a few extra steps here and there. In my experience, these can really add up.

I am not the only one who found the pedometer to be an extremely helpful measurement tool. In one of my recent studies, funded by the way, by the Centers for Disease Control and Prevention, colleagues and I gave an Omron pedometer to 50 participants. Roughly half also received a small financial incentive for taking extra aerobic steps. Both groups walked far more during the study period than adults their age, and those who received the financial incentive walked the most. Nearly all participants reported that the pedometer was a valuable tool in allowing them to quantify their activity levels, and quite a few participants purchased the pedometer for themselves at the end of the study. All participants, by the way, were age 50 and older.

A Few More Secrets to Success

Obviously, I'm not the only one who has lost weight and kept it off. In fact, there exists a National Weight Control Registry (NWCR) that keeps tabs on those who successfully lost weight and their strategies for keeping it off.[4] NWCR is touted as the largest study of individuals who have been successful at long-term maintenance of weight loss. The 629 women and 155 men in the registry—Marsha Csaszar is one, by the way—lost an average of 66 pounds and maintained a required minimum weight loss of 30 pounds for five years. Just over half of the sample, like Marsha, lost weight through formal programs and the rest lost weight on their own. NWCR sends out questionnaires to its participants in order to study the keys to long-term weight-loss maintenance.

NWCR's most recent study looked at how the diet and exercise behaviors of successful weight losers have changed between 1995 and 2003.[5] The results were hardly surprising. The paper concluded: "Despite changes in the diet over time, the variables associated with long-term maintenance of weight loss were the same: continued consumption of a low-calorie diet with moderate fat intake, limited fast food, and high levels of physical activity."

An earlier paper from NWCR studied weight regain and came to a similarly predictable conclusion: "Weight regain is due at least in part to failure to maintain behavior changes."[6]

Break out the Nobel Prize for these authors. The studies reaffirm what we all know. The key to long-term weight loss and weight maintenance is this: Eat less. Exercise more. Keep it up.

For those of you who would like to lose some weight, I recommend only making the diet and exercise changes that you think you can stick to about 80 percent of the time, no matter how few they happen to be. These changes, if you stick with them long enough, will push you in the right direction. How much weight you'll lose will depend on the extent of the changes you are willing to make at least 80 percent of the time, and how your body responds to these changes. If you make drastic changes in your diet and exercise patterns, you may lose some weight, but odds are you'll gain it back. As I said earlier, slow and steady weight loss is one of my keys to success. That is best accomplished by making only those changes that can be sustained for the long haul at least 80 percent of the time.

One of the problems with many of the diet books and other weight-loss strategies on the market today is that they try to get everyone who signs up for the program to follow the same approach. Eat carbs, don't eat carbs, eat rice, eat cabbage....We are all different, and effective weight-loss strategies need to recognize these differences. There are many strategies people can choose to lose weight; the trick is to adopt those that you can stick with most of the time. I suspect a lifetime of eating cabbage is fairly unlikely.

Here are a few additional strategies that have worked for me and/or members of the NWCR. If you can stick with these about 80 percent of the time, they should work for you as well.

Eat Less

Cut Out Sugar-Sweetened Beverages. As I noted in Chapter 1, when I moved to North Carolina, in addition to my penchant for Golden Corral, which is awesome, I could not get enough sweet tea. Sweet tea can really only be made in the South, and I'm sure it has hundreds of calories per glass, but it tastes wonderful. My first year in North Carolina, I drank it every day. I also would have a Coke from time to time, but sweet tea was my drink of choice. When I kicked my diet into high gear, I cut out the sweet tea and switched to diet soda. In fact, other than maybe a couple of beers over the weekend and a tall glass of orange juice in the morning, I now drink mostly water and have one Diet Coke with lunch every day. I bet this one change has probably saved me about 1,000 calories per week or more and been the single biggest factor in my efforts to keep the weight off. I went without sweet tea for 30 years before moving to North Carolina, so it was not that hard to quit (though writing this is giving me a bit of a craving).

But maybe you are a Pepsi junkie and cutting out your fix would really make you cranky. Perhaps even switching to the diet stuff wouldn't quite cut it. Well then, forget this piece of advice. You are the king or queen of your castle.

Buy Fewer Products that Come in Boxes and Cans. This may end up raising your food bill, but these are the products that generally have the most added sugars and added fats, and therefore the most calories. Fresh foods are not that different than they were a few hundred years ago and are far healthier and less calorie dense. If you eat fresh food, including fresh fruits and vegetables, you'll take on fewer calories and a lot more vitamins and minerals. More than likely, you'll lose weight.

Eat Out Less. As I've mentioned more than once, when my wife was pregnant with our first child, we ate out often, including at Golden Corral's all-you-can-eat buffet. I also went to Taco Bell (another fave) with my boss nearly every Friday. As I mentioned in Chapter 2, restaurant meals pack in far more calories than those prepared at home, and buffets—well, forget about it. Although we still eat out or get take-out about once a week, we have not been to the Corral in years and never go to buffets. I now go out to lunch maybe once every few months and bring a bagged lunch to work on most days instead of eating in the cafeteria, where the food is also fairly high in calories. These changes are a hassle because someone has to do the preparation and cooking (in the spirit of full disclosure, it's usually my wife). But this, too, probably saves me a few hundred calories per week and is a change I've been able to sustain most of the time. Not buying lunches also saves us some money, but I think the lovely wife exacts a premium on the days that she prepares my lunch.

Snack Smarter. Although it's difficult, I try hard to stay away from the free foods that often get passed around at work. I also try hard to eat only when I'm hungry, and not just because there is food around. I bring fruit to work every day and eat that when I feel the urge to snack. There really is no magic bullet to this one, but if you can avoid the processed snacks, that too will help you keep the weight off. It has for me.

Exercise More

Create a Routine. Almost all participants in the NWCR have something in common—they exercise, on average, at least an hour a day on most days of the week. Marsha, for example, only on very rare occasions misses her daily walk. "The best predictor of the ones who are not going to regain are the ones who are doing the most physical activity," says Dr. Holly Wyatt, an obesity expert at the University of Colorado.[7]

We gave you a few pointers above about how to make exercise more enjoyable. The key, however, is to stick with the 80 percent rule. Pick an exercise routine that you can stick with. Even if that means going for a long walk only once per week instead of once per day, if you stick to it, over the long haul, you will be better off than if you hit the gym five days a week, which more often than not, will dwindle down to zero days a week in a few weeks or months. A once-a-week walk might not get you into the NWCR, but it is still far better than something that will not be sustained.

Walk While You Talk. The more you move around, the more calories you'll burn. I now try and hold meetings at work while taking a stroll around our campus. I'll even occasionally call in for conference calls on my cell phone while out on my employer's walking paths. Every few hours I also force myself to get up and move around a bit. Every calorie burned helps.

Park Far Away from Your Destination and Take the Stairs. This strategy is easy—and telling. If you are looking for a parking spot right in front of the entrance and/or taking the elevator and not the stairs, then that should give you a good clue about how serious you are about weight loss.

Take the Batteries out of Your Remote Controls. I threw this one in as a reality check about the trade-offs we could be making if we were really serious about losing weight. I'm skeptical that anyone will follow this advice, I certainly don't. But if you did, I bet you would watch less television, move more, sleep better, and lose weight. But, c'mon, what are we, Amish?

Conclusion

No, we certainly are not Amish. If we were, there would be no need to write this book. The Amish have chosen not to be a part of the ObesEconomy. As a result, their rates of obesity are much lower and their activity levels are much higher. In fact, a researcher somehow convinced a bunch of Amish to wear pedometers for a week. Amish men logged about 18,000 steps per day and Amish women logged about 14,000 steps.[8] In comparison, I logged under 11,000 steps per day when I was training for my first marathon, and that is probably better than 99 percent of the non-Amish population.

Even without having to wear the bonnet or don the suspenders, few of us could sustain an Amish lifestyle 80 percent of the time, no matter how successful it would be in helping us lose weight. That lifestyle is way too costly in terms of what we'd be giving up. But what percentage of us would be willing to pull the batteries out of our remotes, give up drinking sugar-sweetened beverages, or make other costly changes to keep our weight off? I'd be willing to wager all of my book royalties (which could equate to hundreds of dollars) that the percentage of readers who will make these changes is also pretty low. So where does that leave us? With Dad and Uncle Al of course.

I noted in the introduction that Dad just cannot understand why an intelligent, wealthy individual like Uncle Al is, as Dad eloquently puts it: "fat and getting fatter." The answer, as we now know, is that Uncle Al's weight gain has been largely in response to a changing environment that has made it more costly to maintain a healthy weight.

Technological advancements have simultaneously lowered the cost of food consumption, increased the cost of being physically active at work and at home, and, by creating some really cool sedentary leisure-time activities, increased the opportunity costs of being physically active. Technology has also reduced the personal costs resulting from obesity by bringing a host of new drugs and devices to market that, even if they can't make us thin (yet), do a pretty good job of staving off many of the adverse health effects that obesity promotes. Given this reality, Uncle Al—and about two thirds of American adults—has decided that, in today's ObesEconomy, the costs of maintaining a lower weight are just not worth the effort. And who can blame him?

Dad further claimed not to care about Uncle Al's excess weight, but I never did believe him. In fact, there are some pretty good arguments why Dad should care. Among other concerns, rising rates of obesity are taking a toll on the profitability of U.S. businesses, and they are raising Dad's health insurance premiums and his taxes.

So what should be the response of business and government? Businesses have a range of options to consider to insulate themselves from the costs of obesity and/or to encourage Uncle Al and others to make healthier choices. Of course, their ultimate focus will be to employ those strategies that help the company's bottom line. Yet, there is little evidence to suggest that is best accomplished through intensive worksite wellness programs that target diet, exercise, and weight.

Government policy makers have a role here, too, although the high costs of obesity to Medicare and Medicaid is not sufficient justification for broad-based antiobesity measures, which, even if successful in reducing weight, may end up raising Dad's taxes even more. When it comes to adults, policy makers should focus on revisiting and revising past policies that might have inadvertently made it more difficult for Uncle Al and others to engage in healthy behaviors.

The most critical role for policy makers is to confront the rising rates of childhood obesity. Unlike Uncle Al, kids have neither the foresight nor the resources to make good diet and exercise choices, and parents and policy makers have largely failed in their efforts to instill those values in today's youth.

But even with the best efforts of industry and government, utility-maximizing individuals like Uncle Al, Cousin Carl, and lots of others will likely continue to choose a diet and exercise regimen that leads to excess weight (just like it took a famine—not government warnings—to curb Mauritanians from their traditional practice of force-feeding girls). Although Dad and public health officials would prefer that Uncle Al lose weight, and do it the old-fashioned way, through diet and exercise, Uncle Al is unwilling to make those sacrifices, even with full knowledge of the adverse health effects of his excess weight.

There is, however, one small ray of hope for Dad and others interested in confronting rising rates of obesity. Advancements in technology have been behind the rise in obesity rates, yet they may also be what help to turn these rates around. These advancements may come in the form of active video games or workstations, or in the form of a pill or a procedure, or who knows what else. As we described in Chapter 11, the economy is incredibly adaptive, and since the demand is there, innovative suppliers will continue to identify new products and services that will make it easier for Uncle Al and others to get thin—not fat.

I, too, am looking forward to benefiting from some of these advancements. Maybe the next-generation active workstation will allow me to safely burn off enough calories during the workday so that I can go back to indulging in sweet tea and Golden Corral feasts. But until that day comes, I, for one, am sticking to running marathons. Uncle Al, however, has selected a different path, and whether Dad likes it or not, it is Uncle Al's choice.

Notes

Chapter 1: Craze or Crisis?

1. Harter, P. 2007. "Mauritanians question the 'fat' look." BBC News, April 26.

2. Centers for Disease Control and Prevention. "About BMI for children and teens."www.cdc.gov/nccdphp/dnpa/bmi/childrens_BMI/about_childrens_BMI.htm.

3. Tanner, L. 2007. "Expert panel says to call kids 'obese.'" ABC News Online, June 13. http://abcnews.go.com/Health/wireStory?id=3271834.

4. National Center for Health Statistics. "Prevalence of overweight among children and adolescents: United States, 2003–2004." Centers for Disease Control and Prevention, www.cdc.gov/nchs/products/pubs/pubd/hestats/overweight/overwght_child_03.htm.

5. Ibid.

6. Strauss, R. S., and H. A. Pollack. 2001. "Epidemic increase in childhood overweight, 1986–1998." *Journal of the American Medical Association* 286, no. 22: 2845–2848.

7. Musher-Eizenman, D. R., S. C. Holub, A. B. Miller, S. E. Goldstein, and L. Edwards-Leeper. 2004. "Body size stigmatization in preschool children: The role of control attributions." *Journal of Pediatric Psychology* 29, no. 8: 613–620.

8. Schwimmer, J. B., T. M. Burwinkle, and J. W. Varni. 2003. "Health-related quality of life of severely obese children and adolescents." *Journal of the American Medical Association* 289, no. 14: 1813–1819.

9. Must, A., and R. S. Strauss. 1999. "Risks and consequences of childhood and adolescent obesity." *International Journal of Obesity and Related Metabolic Disorders* 23, supplement 2: S2–S11.

10. Loke, K. Y. 2002. "Consequences of childhood and adolescent obesity." *Asia Pacific Journal of Clinical Nutrition* 11, no. 3: S702–S704; Braet, C., and M. van Winckel. 2000. "Long-term follow-up of a cognitive behavioral treatment program for obese children." *Behavior Therapy*, 31, no. 1: 55–74; Neumark-Sztainer, D., and P. J. Hannan. 2000. "Weight-related behaviors among adolescent girls and boys: results from a national survey." *Archives of Pediatric and Adolescent Medicine* 154, no. 6: 569–577; Striegel-Moore, R. H., G. B. Schreiber, A. Lo, et al. 2000. "Eating disorder symptoms in a cohort of 11- to 16-year-old black and white girls: The NHLBI growth and health study." *International Journal of Eating Disorders* 27, no. 1: 49–66; Must and Strauss, 1999.

11. Crandall, C. S. 1995. "Do parents discriminate against their heavyweight daughters?" *Personality and Social Psychology Bulletin* 21, no. 7: 724–735.

12. Ludwig, D. S., C. B. Ebbeling, D. Kerr, W. H. Dietz, and T. N. Robinson. 2005. "Overweight children and adolescents." *New England Journal of Medicine* 353: 1070–1071.

13. Ibid.

14. Consensus Panel. "Type 2 diabetes in children and adolescents." American Diabetes Association, http://care.diabetesjournals.org/cgi/reprint/23/3/381.pdf.

15. Cox, E., D. Mager, A. Behm, and S. Miller. 2006. "2002–2005 trends in the prevalence of antidiabetic drug therapy in children age 5 years to 19 years." Express Scripts.

16. Daniels, S. R. 2006. "The Consequences of Childhood Overweight and Obesity." *Future Child* 16, no. 1: 47–67; Loke, 2002; Deckelbaum, R. J., and C. L. Williams. 2001. "Childhood obesity: The health issue." *Obesity Research* 9, supplement 4: 239S–243S; Must and Strauss, 1999.

17. Kaplowitz, P. B., E. J. Slora, R. C. Wasserman, S. E. Pedlow, and M. E. Herman-Giddens. 2001. "Earlier onset of puberty in girls: Relation to increased body mass index and race." *Pediatrics* 108, no. 2: 347–353, http://pediatrics.aappublications.org/cgi/content/abstract/108/2/347.

18. Costa, D. L., and R. H. Steckel. 1995. "Long-term trends in health, welfare, and economic growth in the United States." National Bureau of Economic Research Historical Working Paper, H0076.

19. National Center for Health Statistics. "Health, United States, 2006." Centers for Disease Control and Prevention, www.cdc.gov/nchs/data/hus/hus06.pdf#073.

20. Data from National Health and Nutrition Examination Survey (NHANES) II, NHANES III, and NHANES 99-02.

21. Mokdad, A. H., J. Marks, D. F. Stroup, and J. L. Gerberding. 2004. "Actual causes of death in the United States, 2000." *Journal of the American Medical Association* 291, no. 10, March 10.

22. National Diabetes Information Clearinghouse. "Total prevalence of diabetes among people aged 20 years or older, United States, 2005." National Institute of Diabetes and Digestive and Kidney Diseases, http://diabetes.niddk.nih.gov/dm/pubs/statistics/#9.

23. Diabetes Mellitus Interagency Coordinating Committee, National Institute of Diabetes and Digestive and Kidney Diseases. 2001. "Diabetes prevention program meeting summary."

24. Field, A., E. Coakley, A. Must, et al. 2001. "Impact of overweight on the risk of developing common chronic diseases during a 10-year period." *Archives of Internal Medicine* 161, no. 13: 1581–1586.

25. "Obesity—complications." The Mayo Clinic, www.mayoclinic.com/health/obesity/DS00314/DSECTION=6.

26. Steinfeld, J. D., and A. W. Cohen. 1993. "Obstetrical problems in the obese patient." In A. J. Stunkard and T. A. Wadden (eds.), *Obesity Theory and Therapy*, 2nd ed. (pp. 327–334). New York: Raven Press.

27. Edwards, L. E, W. L. Hellerstedt, I. R. Alton, M. Story, and J. H. Himes. 1996. "Pregnancy complications and birth outcomes in obese and normal-weight women: Effects of gestational weight change." *Obstetrics and Gynecology* 87: 389–394.

28. Galtier-Dereure, F., F. Montpeyroux, P. Boulot, J. Bringer, and C. Jaffiol. 1995. "Weight excess before pregnancy: Complications and cost." *International Journal of Obesity and Related Metabolic Disorders* 19, no. 7 (July): 443–448.

29. Hood, D., and D. Dewan. 1993. "Anesthetic and obstetric outcome in morbidly obese parturients." *Anesthesiology* 79, no. 6 (December): 1210–1218.

30. Johnson, S., B. Kolberg, M. Varner, and L. Railsback. 1987. "Maternal obesity and pregnancy." *Surgery, Gynecology, & Obstetrics,* 164, no. 5 (May): 431–437.

31. Crane, S., M. Wojtowycz, T. Dye, R. Aubry, and R. Artal. 1997. "Association between pre-pregnancy obesity and the risk of cesarean delivery." *Obstetrics and Gynecology* 89: 213–216.

32. Ekblad, U., and S. Grenman. 1992. "Maternal weight, weight gain during pregnancy and pregnancy outcome." *International Journal of Gynaecology and Obstetrics* 39, no. 4 (December): 277–283.

33. Isaacs, J., E. Magann, R. Martin, S. Chauhan, and J. Morrison. 1994. "Obstetric challenges of massive obesity complicating pregnancy." *Journal of Perinatology* 14, no. 1 (January–February): 10–14.

34. Gross, T., R. Sokol, and K. Kin. 1980. "Obesity in pregnancy: Risks and outcome." *Obstetrics and Gynecology* 56, no. 4 (October): 446–450.

35. Castro, L., and R. Avina. 2002. "Maternal obesity and pregnancy outcomes." *Current Opinions in Obstetrics and Gynecology* 14, no. 6 (December): 60–66.

36. Bongain, A., V. Isnard, and J. Y. Gillet. 1998. "Obesity in obstetrics and gynaecology." *European Journal of Obstetrics, Gynecology, and Reproductive Biology* 77: 217–228.

37. Morin, K. 1998. "Perinatal outcomes of obese women: A review of the literature." *Journal of Obstetric, Gynecologic, and Neonatal Nursing* 27, no. 4 (July/August): 431–440.

38. Waller, D. K., J. L. Mills, J. L. Simpson, et al. 1994. "Are obese women at higher risk for producing malformed infants?" *American Journal of Obstetrics and Gynecology* 170, no. 2 (February): 541–548.

39. See note 35.

40. Galtier-Dereure, F., C. Boegner, and J. Bringer. 2000. "Obesity and pregnancy: Complications and cost." *American Journal of Clinical Nutrition* 71, supplement: 1242S–1248S.

41. Watkins, M. L., S. A. Rasmussen, M. A. Honein, L. D. Botto, and C. A. Moore. 2003. "Maternal obesity and risk for birth defects." *Pediatrics* 111, no. 5 (May): 1152–1158.

42. See note 19.

43. Puhl, R., and K. D. Brownell. 2001. "Obesity, bias and discrimination." *Obesity Research* 9, no. 12: 788–805; Carr, D., and M. A. Friedman. 2005. "Is obesity stigmatizing? Body weight, perceived discrimination, and psychological well-being in the United States." *Journal of Health and Social Behavior* 46, no. 3: 244–259.

44. Fontaine, K. R., D. T. Redden, C. Wang, A. O. Westfall, and D. B. Allison. 2003. "Years of life lost due to obesity." *Journal of the American Medical Association* 289: 187–193.

45. Peeters, A., J. J. Barendregt, F. Willekens, et al., for the Netherlands Epidemiology and Demography Compression of Morbidity Research Group. 2003. "Obesity in adulthood and its consequences for life expectancy: A life-table analysis." *Annals of Internal Medicine* 138: 24–32.

46. A BMI of 40 or above is defined as morbid obesity, which is approximately 100 pounds over the ideal weight.

47. See note 44.

48. Based on the census count of almost 6.5 billion people in the 2005 midyear count.

49. Wild, S., G. Roglic, A. Green, et al. 2004. "Global prevalence of diabetes." *Diabetes Care* 27: 1047–1053.

50. Ibid.

51. Kleinfield, N. R. 2006. "Modern ways open India's doors to diabetes." *New York Times,* September 13, www.nytimes.com/2006/09/13/world/asia/13diabetes .html?ex=1175486400&en=ae6c07778597dc05&ei=5070.

52. Goel, M. S., E. P. McCarthy, R. S. Phillips, and C. C. Wee. 2004. "Obesity among U.S. immigrant subgroups by duration of residence." *Journal of the American Medical Association* 292, no. 23: 2860–2867, http://jama.ama-assn .org/cgi/content/abstract/292/23/2860.

Chapter 2: I'll Take a Deep-Fried Coca-Cola

1. Associated Press. "High-calorie diet fattens prisoners at Guantanamo Bay." *USA Today,* www.usatoday.com/news/world/2006-10-03-guantanamo-weight_x.htm.

2. Hill, J. O., H. R. Wyatt, G. W. Reed, and J. C. Peters. 2003. "Obesity and the environment: Where do we go from here?" *Science* 299, no. 5608: 853–855.

3. Centers for Disease Control and Prevention. 2004. "Trends in intake of energy and macronutrients—United States, 1971–2000." *Morbidity and Mortality Weekly Report* 53, no. 4: 80–82, www.cdc.gov/mmwr/preview/mmwrhtml/mm5304a3.htm.

4. Author calculation from Council of Economic Advisors. 2005. *Economic Report of the President, 2005.* Washington, DC: U.S. Government Printing Office, http://a257.g.akamaitech.net/7/257/2422/17feb20051700/www.gpoaccess .gov/eop/2005/2005_erp.pdf.

5. Author calculation from "Consumer Price Index—all urban consumers." United States Bureau of Labor Statistics, http://data.bls.gov/PDQ/outside .jsp?survey=cu.

6. Economic Research Service. "Data sets—food availability." United States Department of Agriculture, www.ers.usda.gov/data/foodconsumption/Food AvailQueriable.aspx#midForm.

7. Putnum, J. J., J. E. Allshouse, and L.S. Kantor. 2002. "U.S. per capita food supply trends: more calories, refined carbohydrates, and fats." *Food Review* 25, no. 3: 2–15.

8. Block, G. 2004. "Foods contributing to energy intake in the US: Data from NHANES III and NHANES 1999–2000." *Journal of Food Composition and Analysis* 17, no. 3–4: 439–447.

9. Cutler, D. M., E. L. Glaeser, and J. M. Shapiro. 2003. "Why have Americans become more obese?" National Bureau of Economic Research Working Paper, 9446.

10. Schlosser, E. 2002. *Fast Food Nation.* New York: Houghton Mifflin.

11. Ibid., pp. 113–114.

12. See note 6.

13. See note 9.

14. Wikipedia. "Microwave Oven." http://en.wikipedia.org/wiki/Microwave_oven.

15. See note 9.

16. Jeffery, R. W., and J. Utter. 2003. "The changing environment and population obesity in the United States." *Obesity Research* 11, supplement: 12S–22S.

17. Fields, S. 2004. "The fat of the land: Do agricultural subsidies foster poor health?" *Environmental Health Perspectives* 112, no. 14: A820–A823.

18. Bray, G. A., S. J. Nielsen, and B. M. Popkin. 2004. "Consumption of high-fructose corn syrup in beverages may play a role in the epidemic of obesity." *American Journal of Clinical Nutrition* 79, no. 4: 537–543.

19. See note 6.

20. Drewnowski, A. 2003. "Fat and sugar: An economic analysis." *Journal of Nutrition* 133, no. 3: 838S–840S. [Energy density reported in kJ/g, author conversion to Calories/lb (i.e., kcals/lb)]

21. Ibid.; energy cost reported in $/MJ, author conversion to $/100 calories (i.e., $/100 kcals).

22. Ibid.

23. Ibid.

24. Cade, J., H. Upmeier, C. Calvert, and D. Greenwood. 1999. "Costs of a healthy diet: Analysis from the UK Women's Cohort Study." *Public Health Nutrition* 2, no. 4: 505–512.

25. "Labor force statistics from the current population survey." United States Bureau of Labor Statistics, http://data.bls.gov/PDQ/outside.jsp?survey=ln; "Charting the U.S. labor market in 2005." United States Bureau of Labor Statistics, www.bls.gov/cps/labor2005/home.htm; "Labor force participation rate of women by age of youngest child, 1975–2005." United States Bureau of Labor Statistics, www.bls.gov/opub/ted/2006/dec/wk1/art01.htm, www.bls.gov/opub/ted/2006/dec/wk1/art01.txt.

26. Lin, B. H., E. Frazao, and J. Guthrie. 1999. "Away-from-home foods increasingly important to quality of American diet." *Agriculture Information Bulletin,* no. AIB749.

27. Diliberti, N., P. L. Bordi, M. T. Conklin, L. S. Roe, and B. J. Rolls. 2004. "Increased portion size leads to increased energy intake in a restaurant meal." *Obesity Research* 12, no. 3: 562–568.

28. [No author listed]. 2005. "Ruby Tuesday: Portion cuts led to 5% sales dip." *Nation's Restaurant News,* January 24, http://findarticles.com/p/articles/mi_m3190/is_4_39/ai_n9480901.

29. Martin, A. 2007. "Will diners still swallow this?" *New York Times,* March 25.

30. Horsley, S. 2006. "Wendy's 'Biggie' portion gone in name only." *All Things Considered,* NPR, June 20.

31. Young, L. R., and M. Nestle. 2002. "The contribution of expanding portion sizes to the US obesity epidemic." *American Journal of Public Health* 92, no. 2: 246–249.

32. Committee on Prevention of Obesity in Children and Youth, Institute of Medicine. 2005. *Preventing Childhood Obesity: Health in the Balance.* Washington, DC: National Academies Press.

33. Ibid.

34. Schazenach, D. W. 2005. "Do school lunches contribute to childhood obesity?" Harris School Working Paper Series, University of Chicago, http://harrisschool.uchicago.edu/centers/chppp/papers/schanzenbach-do_school.pdf.

35. Anderson, P. M., K. F. Butcher, and P. B. Levine. 2003. "Economic perspectives on childhood obesity." *Journal of Economic Perspectives* 3Q: 30–48.

36. Centers for Disease Control and Prevention's School Health Policies and Programs Study (SHPPS), 2000.

37. Wansink, B. 2006. *Mindless Eating: Why We Eat More Than We Think.* New York: Bantam Books.

Chapter 3: Why We're Moving Less

1. Based on the rough estimate: 100 calories burned per mile for a 160-pound person.

2. Sturm, R. 2004. "The economics of physical activity: Societal trends and rationales for interventions." *American Journal of Preventive Medicine* 27, no. 3S: 126–135.

3. Centers for Disease Control and Prevention. 2005. "Trends in leisure-time physical inactivity by age, sex, and race/ethnicity—United States, 1994–2004." *Morbidity and Mortality Weekly Report* 54, no. 39: 991–994, www.cdc.gov/mmwr/preview/mmwrhtml/mm5439a5.htm.

4. METs compendium as reported in: Ainsworth, B. E., W. L. Haskell, M. C. Whitt, et al. 2000. "Compendium of physical activities: An update of activity codes and MET intensities." *Medicine and Science in Sports and Exercise* 32, supplement 9: S498–S504.

5. Lanningham-Foster, L., L. J. Nysse, and J. A. Levine. 2003. "Labor saved, calories lost: The energetic impact of domestic labor-saving devices." *Obesity Research* 11, no. 10: 1178–1181.

6. Cutler, D. M., E. L. Glaeser, and J. M. Shapiro. 2003. "Why have Americans become more obese?" National Bureau of Economic Research Working Paper, 9446.

7. See note 2.

8. Jeffery, R. W., and J. Utter. 2003. "The changing environment and population obesity in the United States." *Obesity Research* 11, supplement: 12S–22S.

9. U.S. Census Bureau. "Quarterly retail e-commerce sales 4th quarter 2006." U.S. Department of Commerce, www.census.gov/mrts/www/data/html/06Q4.html.

10. Shape Up America, www.shapeup.org.

11. Dimitri, C., A. Effland, and N. Conklin. 2005. "The 20th century transformation of U.S. agriculture and farm policy." United States Department of Agriculture Electronic Information Bulletin, no. 3, www.ers.usda.gov/publications/EIB3/EIB3.htm.

12. Ibid.

13. Lakdawalla, D., and T. Philipson. 2002. "The growth of obesity and technological change: A theoretical and empirical examination." Working Paper 8946. Cambridge, MA: National Bureau of Economic Research.

14. Lakdawalla, D., and T. Philipson. 2007. "Labor supply and weight." *Journal of Human Resources* 42, no. 1: 85–116.

15. Federal Highway Administration. "Planning, Chapter 1: National summary." U.S. Department of Transportation, http://www.fhwa.dot.gov/ctpp/jtw/jtw1.htm.

16. See note 2.

17. See note 2.

18. Frank, L. D., and P. O. Engelke. 2001. "The built environment and human activity patterns: Exploring the impacts of urban form on public health." *Journal of Planning Literature* 16, no. 2: 202–218.

19. Shape Fit. "Physical activity fact sheet." www.shapefit.com/physical-activity-fact-sheet.html.

20. Sturm, R. 2005. "Childhood obesity—what we can learn from existing data on societal trends, part 1." *Preventing Chronic Disease* 2, no. 1: A12, www.cdc.gov/pcd/issues/2005/jan/94_0038.htm.

21. Koplan, J. P., C. T. Liverman, and V. I. Kraak (eds.). 2005. *Preventing Childhood Obesity: Health in the Balance.* Washington, DC: National Academies Press (full text available at www.nap.edu).

22. Andersen, R. E., et al. 1998. "Relationship of physical activity and television watching with body weight and level of fitness among children." *Journal of the American Medical Association* 279: 938–942.

23. See note 20.

24. See note 21.

25. See note 21.

Chapter 4: So Where Else Can We Lay the Blame?

1. Segal, N. L., and D. B. Allison. 2002. "Twins and virtual twins: Bases of relative body weight revisited." *International Journal of Obesity and Related Metabolic Disorders* 26, no. 4: 437–441.

2. Stunkard, A. J., J. R. Harris, N. L. Pederson, and G. E. McClearn. 1990. "The body-mass index of twins who have been reared apart." *New England Journal of Medicine.* 322, no. 21 (May 24): 1483–1487.

3. Allison, D. B., M. C. Neale, M. I. Kezis, et al. 1996. "Assortative mating for relative weight: Genetic implications." *Behavior Genetics* 26, no. 2: 103–111.

4. Allison, D. B., A. Pietrobelli, M. S. Faith, et al. 2003. "Genetic influences on obesity." In R. Eckel (ed.), *Obesity: Mechanisms & Clinical Management* (pp. 1–74). New York: Elsevier.

5. World Health Organization. 2005. "The SuRF Report 2. Surveillance of chronic disease risk factors." www.who.int/ncd_surveillance/infobase/web/surf2/start.html.

6. Rush, E. C., L. D. Plank, and W. A. Coward. 1999. "Energy expenditure of young Polynesian and European women in New Zealand and relations to body composition." *American Journal of Clinical Nutrition* 69, no. 1: 43–48.

7. Whitaker, R. C., J. A. Wright, M. S. Pepe, K. D. Seidel, and W. H. Dietz. 1997. "Predicting obesity in young adulthood from childhood and parental obesity." *New England Journal of Medicine* 337, no. 13: 869–873.

8. Frayling, T. M., N. J. Timpson, M. N. Weedon, et al. 2007. "A common variant in the FTO gene is associated with body mass index and predisposes to childhood and adult obesity." *Science* 316, no. 5826: 889–894.

9. Oliveria, S. A., R. C. Ellison, L. L. Moore, et al. 1992. "Parent-child relationships in nutrient intake: the Framingham Children's Study." *American Journal of Clinical Nutrition* 56, no. 3: 593–598.

10. DiLorenzo, T. M., R. C. Stuckey-Ropp, J. S. Vander Wal, and H. J. Gotham. 1998. "Determinants of exercise among children. II. A longitudinal analysis." *Preventive Medicine* 27, no. 3: 470–477.

11. Trost, S. G., L. M. Kerr, D. S. Ward, and R. R. Pate. 2001. "Physical activity and determinants of physical activity in obese and non-obese children." *International Journal of Obesity and Related Metabolic Disorders,* 25, no. 6: 822–829.

12. Sacerdote, B. 2004. "What happens when we randomly assign children to families?" Working Paper 10894. Cambridge, MA: National Bureau of Economic Research.

13. Vogler, G. P., T. I. A. Sorensen, A. J. Stunkard, M. R. Srinivasan, and D. C. Rao. 1995. "Influences of genes and shared family environment on adult body mass index assessed in an adoption study by a comprehensive path model." *International Journal of Obesity* 19, no. 1: 40–45.

14. Valencia, M. E., P. H. Bennet, E. Ravussin, et al. 1999. "The Pima Indians in Sonora, Mexico." *Nutrition Reviews* 57, no. 5: S55–S58; Marchand, L. H., and the National Diabetes Information Clearinghouse. "Obesity associated with high rates of diabetes in the Pima Indians." National Institute of Diabetes and Digestive and Kidney Diseases, http://diabetes.niddk.nih.gov/dm/pubs/pima/

obesity/obesity.htm; Scientific American Frontiers. "Fighting the thrifty gene." Public Broadcasting Service, www.pbs.org/saf/1110/features/fighting.htm.

15. Neel, J. V. 1962. "Diabetes mellitus: A 'Thrifty' genotype rendered detrimental by 'Progress'?" *American Journal of Human Genetics* 14: 353–362; Hill, J. O., H. R. Wyatt, and E. L. Melanson. 2000. "Genetic and environmental contributions to obesity." *Medical Clinics of North America* 84, no. 2: 333–346; Connor, S. 2003. "Scientists link obesity to 'thrifty gene' of our ancestors." *The Independent* (London), February 7.

16. Scientific American Frontiers. "Fighting the thrifty gene." Public Broadcasting Service. www.pbs.org/saf/1110/features/fighting.htm.

17. Council of Economic Advisers. 2004. *Economic Report of the President, 2004.* Washington, DC: U.S. Government Printing Office.

18. Bluestone, B., S. Rose. 1997. "Overworked and underemployed: Unraveling an economic enigma." *American Prospect* 8, no. 31: 58–69.

19. Keith, S. W., D. T. Redden, P. T. Katzmarzyk, et al. 2006. "Putative contributors to the secular increase in obesity: Exploring the roads less traveled." *International Journal of Obesity* 30, no. 11: 1585–1594.

20. Kimm, S. Y., E. Obarzanek, B. A. Barton, et al. 1996. "Race, socioeconomic status, and obesity in 9- to 10-year-old girls: The NHLBI Growth and Health Study." *Annals of Epidemiology* 6, no. 4: 266–275.

21. Armstrong, J., and J. J. Reilly. 2002. "Breastfeeding and lowering the risk of childhood obesity." *Lancet* 359, no. 9322: 1249–1250.

22. Michels, K. B., W. C. Willett, B. I. Graubard, et al. 2007. "A longitudinal study of infant feeding and obesity throughout life course." *International Journal of Obesity,* April 24, www.nature.com/ijo/journal/vaop/ncurrent/abs/0803622a.htm.

23. Barber-Madden, R., M. A. Petschek, and J. Pakter. 1987. "Breastfeeding and the working mother: Barriers and intervention strategies." *Journal of Public Health Policy* 8, no. 4: 531–541.

24. National Center for Health Statistics. 2005. "National immunization survey: Table 1: Breastfeeding rates by socio-demographic factors, 2005." Centers for Disease Control and Prevention.

25. National Association of Chain Drug Stores. "Industry facts-at-a-glance." www .nacds.org/wmspage.cfm?parm1=507.

26. Author's calculations based on data from the 2004 Medical Expenditure Panel Survey (MEPS).

27. Critser, G. "American prescription drug use." Web site of Daniel J. Murphy, DC, www.danmurphydc.com/Critser.pdf.

28. Senior Care Pharmacists, www.seniorcarepharmacist.com.

29. Espey, E., J. Steinhart, T. Ogburn, and C. Qualls. 2000. "Depo-Provera associated with weight gain in Navajo women." *Contraception* 62, no. 2: 55–58.

30. Sharma, A. M., T. Pischon, S. Hardt, I. Kunz, and F. C. Luft. 2001. "Hypothesis: Beta-adrenergic receptor blockers and weight gain. A systematic analysis." *Hypertension* 37, no. 2: 250–254.

31. Riley, G. "The relationship between weight gain and medications for depression and seizures." Net Nutritionist, www.netnutritionist.com/fa12.htm.

32. Mosby's Drug Consult. "Top 200 Most Prescribed Drugs in 2003." www .mosbysdrugconsult.com/DrugConsult/Top_200.

33. Aronne, L. J. 2002. "Drug-induced weight gain: Non-CNS medications." In L. J. Aronne (ed.), *A Practical Guide to Drug-Induced Weight Gain* (pp. 77–91). Minneapolis, MN: McGraw-Hill.

34. Wrong Diagnosis? "Medications or substances causing weight gain." www .wrongdiagnosis.com/symptoms/weight_gain/side-effects.htm.

35. Blackburn, G. L. 2003. "Medications that may cause weight gain and their potential alternatives." Keep It Off, www.keepitoff.com/physician/ medications_that_cause_weight_gain.pdf.

36. See note 31.

37. Allison, D. B., J. L. Mentore, M. Heo, et al. 1999. "Antipsychotic-induced weight gain: A comprehensive research synthesis." *American Journal of Psychiatry* 156, no. 11: 1686–1696.

38. Lamberti, J. S., T. Bellnier, and S. B. Schwarzkopf. 1992. "Weight gain among schizophrenic patients treated with clozapine." *American Journal of Psychiatry* 149, no. 5: 689–690.

39. Gupta, S., T. Droney, S. Al-Samarrai, P. Keller, and B. Frank. 1999. "Olanzapine: Weight gain and therapeutic efficacy." *Journal of Clinical Psychopharmacology* 19, no. 3: 273–274.

40. Blackburn, G. L. 2003. "Medications that may cause weight gain and their potential alternatives." Keep It Off, www.keepitoff.com/physician/ medications_that_cause_weight_gain.pdf.

41. Ibid.

42. Ibid.

43. Ibid.

44. Klesges, R. C., and S. A. Shumaker. 1992. "Understanding the relations between smoking and body weight and their importance to smoking cessation and relapse." *Health Psychology* 11, supplement: 1–3.

45. U.S. Department of Health and Human Services. 1990. *The Health Benefits of Smoking Cessation: A Report of the Surgeon General.* Collingdale, PA: DIANE Publishing, http://books.google.com/books?id=7vzpW2kaMs4C&pg=PA8& lpg=PA8&dq=surgeon+general+%22the+health+consequences+of+smokin g+cessation%22&source=web&ots=hZAybU5qVJ&sig=PpIOKCaxo7oA_ Shw_eqPagr0LgM#PPA7,M1.

46. Chou, S. Y., M. Grossman, and H. Saffer. 2004. "An economic analysis of adult obesity: Results from the behavioral risk factor surveillance system." *Journal of Health Economics* 23, no. 3: 565–587.

47. Gregg, E. W., Y. J. Cheng, B. L. Cadwell, et al. 2005. "Secular trends in cardio-vascular disease risk factors according to body mass index in US adults." *Journal of the American Medical Association* 293; 1868–1874.

48. von Kries, R., A. M. Toschke, H. Wurmser, T. Sauerwald, and B. Koletzko. 2002. "Reduced risk for overweight and obesity in 5- and 6-year-old children by duration of sleep—a cross-sectional study." *International Journal of Obesity and Related Metabolic Disorders* 26, no. 5: 710–716.

49. Gangwisch, J. E., D. Malaspina, B. Boden-Albala, and S. B. Heymsfield. 2005. "Inadequate sleep as a risk factor for obesity: Analysis of the NHANES I." *Sleep* 28, no. 10: 1289–1296.

50. Spiegel, K., R. Leproult, and E. Van Cauter. 1999. "Impact of sleep debt on metabolic and endocrine function." *Lancet* 354, no. 9188: 1435–1439.

51. Spiegel, K., R. Leproult, M. L'hermite-Baleriaux, et al. 2004. "Leptin levels are dependent on sleep duration: Relationships with sympathovagal balance, carbohydrate regulation, cortisol, and thyrotropin." *Journal of Clinical Endocrinology and Metabolism*, 89, no. 11: 5762–5771.

52. Taheri, S., L. Lin, D. Austin, T. Young, and E. Mignot. 2004. "Short sleep duration is associated with reduced leptin, elevated ghrelin, and increased body mass index." *Public Library of Science Medicine* 1, no. 3: e62.

53. Lovgren, S. 2005. "U.S. racking up huge 'sleep debt.' *National Geographic News*, February 24, news.nationalgeographic.com/news/2005/02/0224_050224_sleep.html.

54. Ibid.

55. MSNBC. 2006. "Are Americans getting enough shuteye?" MSNBC, July 31. www.msnbc.msn.com/id/11590296/.

56. Hale, L. 2005. "Who has time to sleep?" *Journal of Public Health* 27, no. 2: 205–211.

57. Danielson, D. K. 2007. "Is your BlackBerry ruining your sex life?" *Forbes*, January 11, www.forbes.com/leadership/2007/01/11/leadership-blackberry-treo-cx_pink_0111blackberry.html.

58. See note 19.

59. See note 19.

60. Mader, T. L. 2003. "Environmental stress in confined beef cattle." *Journal of Animal Science* 81, E. supplement 2: E110–E119.

61. Energy Information Administration, www.eia.doe.gov.

62. See note 19.

63. See note 19.

64. Mead, M. N. 2004. "Origins of obesity—chemical exposures." *Environmental Health Perspectives,* May 24, www.findarticles.com/p/articles/mi_m0CYP/is_6_112/ ai_117423252.

65. See note 19.

66. Noren, K., and D. Meironyte. 2000. "Certain organochlorine and organobromine contaminants in Swedish human milk in perspective of past 20–30 years." *Chemosphere* 40, no. 9: 1111–1123.

67. Henig, R. 2006. "Fat factors." *New York Times Magazine,* August 13.

Chapter 5: Beware: Moral Hazard

1. Johansson, P., and M. Palme. 2005. "Moral hazard and sickness insurance." *Journal of Public Economics* 89, no. 9–10: 1879–1890.

2. Horowitz, J. K., and E. Lichtenberg. 1993. "Insurance, moral hazard, and chemical use in agriculture." *American Journal of Agricultural Economics* 75, no. 4: 926–935.

3. Gropp, R., and J. Vesala. 2004. "Deposit insurance, moral hazard and market monitoring." *Review of Finance* 8, no. 4: 571–602.

4. Khwaja, A. W. 2006. "A life cycle analysis of the effects of Medicare on individual health incentives and health outcomes." Working Paper. Durham, NC: Fuqua School of Business, Duke University, , www.aeaweb.org/annual_mtg_papers/2007/0106_1015_0604.pdf.

5. Klick, J., and T. Stratmann. 2004. "Diabetes treatments and moral hazard." Law and Economics Working Paper no. 05-21. Tallahassee, FL: Florida State University College of Law, http://ssrn.com/abstract=766825.

6. Rice, T., and K. R. Morrison. 1994. "Patient cost sharing for medical services: A review of the literature and the implications for health care reform." *Medical Care Review* 51, no. 3: 235–287.

7. Cheng, S. H., and T. L. Chiang. 1997. "The effect of universal health insurance on health care utilization in Taiwan. Results from a natural experiment." *Journal of the American Medical Association* 278, no. 2: 89–93.

8. Selby, J. V., B. H. Fireman, and B. E. Swain. 1996. "Effect of a copayment on use of the emergency department in a health maintenance organization." *New England Journal of Medicine* 334, no. 10: 635–641.

9. Lurie, N., N. B. Ward, M. F. Shapiro, and R. H. Brook. 1984. "Termination from Medi-Cal—does it affect health?" *New England Journal of Medicine* 311, no. 7: 480–484.

10. Lurie, N., N. B. Ward, M. F. Shapiro, C. Gallego, R. Vaghaiwalla, and R. H. Brook. 1986. "Termination of Medi-Cal benefits: a follow-up study one year later." *New England Journal of Medicine* 314, no. 19: 1266–1268.

11. Brook, R. H., E. B. Keeler, K. N. Lohr, J. P. Newhouse, et al. 2006. "The health insurance experiment: A classic RAND study speaks to the current health care reform debate." RAND Health Research Highlights, www.rand .org/pubs/research_briefs/2006/RAND_RB9174.pdf.

12. Gregg, E. W., Y. J. Cheng, B. L. Caldwell, et al. 2005. "Secular trends in cardiovascular disease risk factors according to body mass index in US adults." *Journal of the American Medical Association* 293, no. 15: 1868–1874.

13. Ibid.

14. Avenell, A., T. J. Brown, M. A. McGee, et al. 2004. "What are the long-term benefits of weight reducing diets in adults? A systematic review of randomized controlled trials." *Journal of Human Nutrition and Dietetics* 17, no. 4: 317–335.

15. Mosby's Drug Consult. "Top 200 Most Prescribed Drugs in 2003." www .mosbysdrugconsult.com/DrugConsult/Top_200/.

16. Aucott, L., A. Poobalan, W. C. Smith, et al. 2005. "Effects of weight loss in over-weight/obese individuals and long-term hypertension outcomes: A systematic review." *Hypertension* 45, no. 6: 1035–1041.

17. Lindholm, L. H., H. Ibsen, B. Dahlof, et al. 2002. "Cardiovascular morbidity and mortality in patients with diabetes in the Losartan Intervention For Endpoint reduction in hypertension study (LIFE): A randomised trial against atenolol." *Lancet* 359, no. 9311: 1004–1010.

18. Poobalan, A., L. Aucott, W. C. Smith, et al. 2004. "Effects of weight loss in overweight/obese individuals and long-term lipid outcomes—a systematic review." *Obesity Reviews* 5, no. 1: 43–50.

19. Taylor, A. J., S. M. Kent, P. J. Flaherty, et al. 2002. "Arterial biology for the investigation of the treatment effects of reducing cholesterol: A randomized trial comparing the effects of atorvastatin and pravastatin on carotid intima medial thickness." *Circulation* 106, no. 16: 2055–2060.

Chapter 6: So We're Fat—Who Cares?

1. Stenson, J. 2007. "Is your job making you fat? Employment may be especially gainful for desk workers." MSNBC.com, February 6, www.msnbc.msn.com/ id/16927021/.

2. Evans, W. D., J. M. Renaud, E. Finkelstein, D. B. Kamerow, and D. S. Brown. 2006. "Changing perceptions of the childhood obesity epidemic." *American Journal of Health Behavior* 30, no. 2 (March/April): 167–176.

3. The Pew Research Center for the People and the Press. 2004. "Survey experiment shows polls face growing resistance, but still representative." Washington, DC: Pew Research Center for the People and the Press, http://people-press .org/reports/pdf/211.pdf. Accessed on April 24, 2006.

4. Blumberg, S. J., J. V. Lake, and M. L. Cynamon. 2006. "Telephone coverage and health survey estimates: Evaluating the need for concern about wireless substitution." *American Journal of Public Health* 96, no. 5: 926–931.

5. Curtin R., S. Presser, and E. Singer. 2005. "Changes in telephone survey nonresponse over the past quarter century." *Public Opinion Quarterly* 69, no. 1: 87–98.

6. Cowburn, G., and L. Stockley. 2005. "Consumer understanding and use of nutrition labeling: A systematic review." *Public Health Nutrition* 8, no.1: 21–28.

7. Finkelstein, E. A., I. C. Fiebelkorn, and G. Wang. 2003. "National medical spending attributable to overweight and obesity: How much, and who's paying?" *Health Affairs* W3: 219–226.

8. Ibid.

9. Finkelstein, E. A., I. C. Fiebelkorn, and G. Wang. 2004. "State-level estimates of annual medical expenditures attributable to obesity." *Obesity Research* 12, no. 1: 18–24.

10. Finkelstein, E. A, I. C. Fiebelkorn, and G. Wang. 2005. "The costs of obesity among full-time employees." *American Journal of Health Promotion* 20, no. 1: 45–51.

11. Musich, S., D. Napier, and D. W. Edington. 2001. "The association of health risks with workers' compensation costs." *Journal of Occupational & Environmental Medicine* 43, no. 6: 534–541.

12. Bhattacharya, J., and M. K. Bundorf. 2005. "The incidence of the healthcare costs of obesity." Working Paper 11303, Cambridge, MA: National Bureau of Economic Research.

13. [No author listed]. 2004. "Report: Obesity-related disability claims, costs are up." *Business and Legal Reports*, February 24. http://hr.blr.com/news.aspx?id=9356.

14. Burton, W. N., D. J. Conti, C. Y. Chen, A. B. Schultz, and D. W. Edington. 1999. "The role of health risk factors and disease on worker productivity." *Journal of Occupational & Environmental Medicine* 41, no. 10: 863–877.

15. Cournot, M., J. C. Marquie, D. Ansiau, et al. 2006. "Relation between body mass index and cognitive function in healthy middle-aged men and women." *Neurology* 67, no. 7: 1208–1214.

16. "Link between obesity and memory? Researchers examine hormone that turns off hunger." *Science Daily,* June 14, 2006. www.sciencedaily.com/releases/2006/06/060614090511.htm.

17. Gortmaker, S. L., A. Must, J. M. Perrin, A. M. Sobol, and W. Dietz. 1993. "Social and economic consequences of overweight in adolescence and young adulthood." *New England Journal of Medicine* 329, no. 14: 1008–1012.

18. Cawley, J. 2004. "The impact of obesity on wages." *Journal of Human Resources* 39, no. 2: 451–474.

19. Finkelstein, E. A., C. J. Ruhm, and K. M. Kosa. 2005. "Economic causes and consequences of obesity." *Annual Review of Public Health* 26: 239–257.

20. Bhattacharya, J., and M. K. Bundorf. 2005. "The incidence of the healthcare costs of obesity." Working Paper 11303, Cambridge, MA: National Bureau of Economic Research.

21. Pagan, J. A., and A. Davila. 1997. "Obesity, occupational attainment, and earnings." *Social Science Quarterly* 78, no. 3: 756–770.

22. Haskins, K., and H. E. Ransford. 1999. "The relationship between weight and career payoffs among women." *Sociological Forum* 14, no. 2: 295–318.

23. Averett, S., and S. Korenman. 1996. "The economic reality of the beauty myth." *Journal of Human Resources* 31, no. 2: 304–330.

24. Cawley, J., and S. Danziger. 2004. "Obesity as a barrier to the transition from welfare to work." Working Paper 10508, Cambridge, MA: National Bureau of Economic Research.

25. Ellin, A. 2005. "The military issues order to shape up." *New York Times,* September 29.

26. Associated Press. 2006. "Obesity takes heavy toll on military." FoxNews .com, July 6, www.foxnews.com/story/0,2933,161523,00.html; Associated Press. 2005. "Are U.S. troops too fat to fight? Officials increasingly worried about troops being too fat to fight." MSNBC.com, July 5.www.msnbc .msn.com/id/8423112/.

27. Ibid.

28. www.obesity.org/subs/pressroom/military_press.shtml.

29. See note 25.

30. See note 26.

31. See note 26.

Chapter 7: The Role of Government

1. Office of Management and Budget. 2003. "Circular A4: Regulatory analysis." www.whitehouse.gov/omb/circulars/a004/a-4.pdf.

2. National Restaurant Association. 2007. "State smoking restrictions."www .restaurant.org/government/state/smoking_200701_nrachart.pdf.

3. Herel, S. 2005. "S.F. board votes to ban smoking in city's parks." *San Francisco Chronicle,* January 26. http://sfgate.com/cgi-bin/article.cgi?file=/c/a/2005/ 01/26/MNG12B0HH71.DTL.

4. Although the lighthouse is a common example of a public good, recent empirical evidence actually calls this into question. For an interesting discussion of

this issue, see Foldvary, F. E. 2003. "The lighthouse as a private-sector collective good." www.independent.org/publications/working_papers/article.asp?id=757.

5. National Park Service, www.nps.gov.

6. HealthierUS.gov. "Steps to a HealthierUS Initiative." www.healthierus.gov/STEPS.

7. www.obesity.org/subs/fastfacts/Obesity_Research.shtml.

8. Institute of Medicine Food and Nutrition Board. 1998. "Assessing readiness in military women: The relationship of body, composition, nutrition, and health."www.iom.edu/CMS/3788/4615/6822.aspx.

9. Ellin, A. "The military issues order to shape up."*New York Times,* September 9, 2005.

10. Ibid.

11. Akerlof, G. A. 1970. "The market for 'lemons': Quality uncertainty and the market mechanism."*Quarterly Journal of Economics* 84, no. 3: 488–500.

12. U.S. Food and Drug Administration Center for Food Safety and Applied Nutrition. 2004. "Calories count—report of the Working Group on Obesity (executive summary)."www.cfsan.fda.gov/~dms/owg-toc.html#execsum.

13. British Broadcasting Corporation. 2005. "McDonald's puts fat facts on food." BBC News online, October 25. http://news.bbc.co.uk/2/hi/business/4376758.stm.

14. MSNBC News Service. 2006. "New York City passes trans fat ban." MSNBC .com, December 5. www.msnbc.msn.com/id/16051436/.

15. Ibid.

16. OurChart50.xls, from http://usfoodpolicy.blogspot.com/2006/12/how-good-is-online-restaurant-nutrition.html [Direct link: mysite.verizon.net/vzeehy04/web/OurChart50.xls]; QSRmagazine.com. "The QSR 50: The game in '05." *QSR Magazine,*www.qsrmagazine.com/reports/qsr50/.

17. Becker, G. 2006. "Comment on the New York ban on trans fat."www .becker-posner-blog.com/archives/2006/12/comment_on_the_4.html.

18. Ibid.

Chapter 8: Weighing the Public Policy Issues (for Adults)

1. http://news.bbc.co.uk/2/hi/health/6897221.stm.

2. Cohen, D. 2007. "A desired epidemic: Obesity and the food industry." Special to washingtonpost.com's Think Tank Town, February 20.

3. Ad Council. "Obesity prevention."www.adcouncil.org/default.aspx?id=54.

4. White, D. 2007. "Hold the fries and the district menu labeling."*Washington Post,* May 6.

5. Associated Press. 2006. "Obesity bigger threat than terrorism?" March 26. www.cbsnews.com/stories/2006/03/01/health/main1361849.shtml.

6. Editorial. 2007. "Ending an addiction: Time to move away from farm subsidies." *Sacramento Bee,* April 24.

7. Wilkins, J. 2007. "Food stamp focus to shift." *Albany Times Union,* March 14.

8. Townsend, M. S., J. Peerson, B. Love, C. Achterberg, and S. P. Murphy. 2001. "Food insecurity is positively related to overweight in women." *Journal of Nutrition* 131, no. 6: 1738–1745.

9. Fox, M. K., and N. Cole. 2004. "Nutrition and health characteristics of low-income populations, vol. 1: Food stamp program participants and nonpartici-pants." United States Department of Agriculture, Economic Research Service, E-FAN-04-014-1.

10. Ver Ploeg, M. L., and L. Mancino. 2007. "The vanishing weight gap: Trends in obesity among adult food stamp participants (US) (1976–2002)." *Economics & Human Biology* 5, no. 1: 20–36.

11. United States Department of Agriculture, Food and Nutrition Service. 2007. "Implications of restricting the use of food stamp benefits—summary." www.fns.usda.gov/oane/MENU/Published/FSP/FILES/ProgramOperations/FSPFoodRestrictions.pdf.

12. Evans, D., E. Finkelstein, D. Kamerow, and J. Renaud. 2005. "Public percep-tions of childhood obesity." *American Journal of Preventive Medicine* 28, no. 1: 26–32.

13. ConsumersUnion.org. 2005. "New report shows food industry advertising overwhelms government's '5 a Day' campaign to fight obesity and promote healthy eating." September 13. www.consumersunion.org/pub/core_health_care/002657.html.

14. Teisl, M. F., N. E. Bockstael, and A. Levy. 2001. "Measuring the welfare effects of nutrition information." *American Journal of Agricultural Economics* 83, no. 1: 133–149.

15. Finkelstein, E. A., I. C. Fiebelkorn, and G. Wang. 2004. "State-level estimates of annual medical expenditures attributed to obesity." *Obesity Research* 12, no. 1: 18–24.

16. Sallis, J., and K. Glanz. 2006. "The role of built environments in physical activity, eating, and obesity in childhood." www.futureofchildren.org, Spring, www.futureofchildren.org/usr_doc/05_5562_sallis-glanz.pdf.

17. Ibid.

18. Ewing, R., T. Schmid, R. Killingsworth, A. Zlot, and S. Raudenbush. 2003. "Relationship between urban sprawl and physical activity, obesity, and morbidity." *American Journal of Health Promotion* 18, no. 1: 47–57.

19. Frank, L. D., M. A. Andresen, and T. L. Schmid. 2004. "Obesity relationships with community design, physical activity, and time spent in cars." *American Journal of Preventive Medicine* 27, no. 2: 87–96.

20. Vandegrift, D., and T. Yoked. 2004. "Obesity rates, income, and suburban sprawl: An analysis of US states." *Health Place* 10, no. 3: 221–229.

21. Geauga County Government. "2000 Community Census Statistics." www.co.geauga.oh.us/communities/census.htm.

22. Stello, S. 2007. "Stacking up the calories: Survey by Davis health advocacy group shows menu choices are confusing." April 18. www.davisenterprise.com/articles/2007/04/18/news/257new0.txt.

23. Ibid.

24. Squires, S. 2007. "District may add data to the menu." washingtonpost.com, March 6, www.washingtonpost.com/wp-dyn/content/article/2007/03/02/AR2007030201531_pf.html.

25. Silverman, F. 2007. "They're all bad for you, but should they be illegal?" *New York Times,* April 1.

26. Weiss, S. C. 2006. "Menu labeling comments presented by National Restaurant Association at hearing of New York City Department of Health and Mental Hygiene." restaurant.org, October 30. www.restaurant.org/pressroom/pressrelease.cfm?ID=1331.

27. Kral, T. V. E., L. S. Roe, and B. J. Rolls. 2002. "Does nutrition information about the energy density of meals affect food intake in normal-weight women?" *Appetite* 39, no. 2: 137–145.

28. Stubenitsky, K., J. I. Aaron, S. L. Catt, and D. J. Mela. 2000. "The influence of recipe modification and nutritional information on restaurant food acceptance and macronutrient intakes." *Public Health Nutrition* 3, no. 2: 201–209.

29. U.S. Food and Drug Administration. 2004. "Calories count." www.cfsan.fda.gov/~dms/owg-toc.html.

30. Park, M.Y. 2002. "Ailing man sues fast-food firms." foxnews.com, July 24. www.foxnews.com/story/0,2933,58652,00.html.

31. Burnett, D. 2007. "Fast-food lawsuits and the cheeseburger bill: Critiquing Congress's response to the obesity epidemic." *Virginia Journal of Social Policy & the Law* 14, no. 3: 357–417.

32. Ibid.

33. Olson, W. 1995. "Civil suits: Loser-pays makes lawsuits fairer in Europe. It could work here, too." www.reason.com/news/show/29696.html. Accessed on May 9, 2007.

34. CNN. 2003. "Lawsuit dropped as Oreo looks to drop the fat." cnn.com, May 14. www.cnn.com/2003/LAW/05/14/oreo.suit/.

35. Gunther, M. 2006. "Guacamole and green tea." cnnomney.com, December 20. http://money.cnn.com/2006/12/20/news/companies/pluggedin_gunther_labels.fortune/index.htm.

36. Fox News. 2005. "McDonald's to pay $8.5M in trans fat lawsuit." foxnews .com, February 12. www.foxnews.com/story/0,2933,147200,00.html.

37. Lawyersandsettlements.com. 2005. "Settlements and verdicts."www.lawyer sandsettlements.com/case/mcdonalds_vegetarian.

38. Donovan, G. 2002. "Hindus sue Pizza Hut over beef in cheese." *National Catholic Reporter,* May 31, http://findarticles.com/p/articles/mi_m1141/is_30_38/ ai_87353899.

39. Markon, J. 2005. "Dairy industry sued over weight-loss claims." washington post.com, June 29. www.washingtonpost.com/wp-dyn/content/article/ 2005/06/28/AR2005062800834.html.

40. Gruber, J., and M. Frakes. 2006. "Does falling smoking lead to rising obesity?" *Journal of Health Economics* 25, no. 2: 183–197.

41. Brownell, K. 1994. "Get slim with higher taxes." *New York Times,* December 15.

42. Battle, E. K., and K. D. Brownell. 1997. "Confronting a rising tide of eating disorders and obesity: Treatment vs. prevention and policy." *Addictive Behaviors* 21, no. 6: 755–765.

43. Jacobson, M. H., and K. D. Brownell. 2000. "Small taxes on soft drinks and snack foods to promote health." *American Journal of Public Health* 90, no. 6: 854–857.

44. Ibid.

45. West Virginia Code 11-19-2.

46. Nebraska House Bill 1164.

47. Gelbach, J. B., J. Klick, and T. Stratmann. 2007. "Cheap donuts and expensive broccoli: The effect of relative prices on obesity." Working Paper, Tallahassee, FL: Florida State University College of Law.

48. Oliver, J. E., and T. Lee. 2005. "Public opinion and the politics of obesity in America." *Journal of Health Politics, Policy and Law* 30, no. 5: 923–954.

49. Brownell, K. 2005. "The chronicling of obesity: Growing awareness of its social, economic, and political contexts." *Journal of Health Politics, Policy and Law* 30, no. 5: 955–964.

Chapter 9: Weighing the Public Policy Issues (for Kids)

1. Associated Press. 2006. "Obesity bigger threat than terrorism?" March 26. www.cbsnews.com/stories/2006/03/01/health/main1361849.shtml.

2. Belkin, L. 2006. "The school lunch test." *New York Times Magazine,* August 20.

3. Huhman, M., L. D. Potter, F. L. Wong, et al. 2005. "Effects of a mass media campaign to increase physical activity among children: Year-1 results of the VERB campaign." *Pediatrics* 116, no. 2 (August): e277–e284.

4. Oliver, J., and T. Lee. 2002. "Public opinion and the politics of America's obesity epidemic." Working Paper RWP02-017, Cambridge, MA: Harvard University, Kennedy School of Government.

5. Evans, D., E. Finkelstein, D. Kamerow, and J. Renaud. 2005. "Public perceptions of childhood obesity." *American Journal of Preventive Medicine* 28, no. 1: 26–32.

6. "Mother defends triple overweight son." maltastar.com, www.maltastar.com/pages/msFullArt.asp?an=10179.

7. Powell, B., P. T. Powell von Hippel, D. B. Downey, and N. J. Rowland. 2007. "Changes in Children's body mass index during the school year and during summer vacation." *American Journal of Public Health* 97, no. 4.

8. Wechsler, H., N. D. Brener, S. Kuester, and C. Miller. 2001. "Food service and foods and beverages available at school: Results from the School Health Policies and Programs Study, 2000." *Journal of School Health* 71: 313–324.

9. Institute of Medicine. 2007. "Nutrition standards for foods in schools: Leading the way toward healthier youth." April 25, www.iom.edu/CMS/3788/30181/42502.aspx.

10. CSPI. 2007. "Institute of Medicine school food recommendations should be law of the land, says CSPI." http://cspinet.org/new/200704251.html.

11. Cullen, K. W., J. Eagan, T. Baranowski, E. Owens, and C. de Moor. 2000. "The effect of a la carte/snack bar school foods on children's lunch fruit and vegetable intake." *Journal of the American Dietetic Association* 100: 1482–1486.

12. Kubik, M. Y., L. A. Lytle, P. J. Hannan, C. L. Perry, and M. Story. 2003. "The association of the school food environment with dietary behaviors of young adolescents." *American Journal of Public Health* 93, no. 7: 1168–1173.

13. Whitmore, D. 2004. "Do school lunches contribute to childhood obesity?" University of Chicago, October 5.

14. Wechsler, H., N. D. Brener, S. Kuester, and C. Miller. 2001. "Food service and foods and beverages available at school: Results from the school health policies and programs study." *Journal of School Health* 71: 313–324.

15. Harnack, L., J. Stang, and M. Story. 1999. "Soft drink consumption among U.S. children and adolescents: Nutritional consequences." *Journal of the American Diet Association* 99: 436–441.

16. Ludwig, D. S., K. E. Peterson, and S. L. Gortmaker. 2001. "Relation between consumption of sugar-sweetened drinks and childhood obesity: A prospective, observational analysis." *Lancet* 357: 505–508.

17. Spiegel, J. 2007. "Nutrition; Law's side effect: Putting school budgets on a diet, too." *New York Times,* January 7. http://select.nytimes.com/search/restricted/article?res=F60D16FF3F540C748CDDA80894DF404482.

18. Lappé, A. 2006. "Doing lunch." *The Nation*, August 27, www.thenation.com/doc/20060911/lappe.

19. Bower, A. 2006. "Retooling school lunch." *Time,* June 11. www.time.com/time/magazine/article/0,9171,1200781,00.html.

20. See note 18.

21. See note 18.

22. Squires, S. 2007. "USDA seeks more healthful school meals." washingtonpost.com, April 7. www.washingtonpost.com/wp-dyn/content/article/2007/04/06/AR2007040601874.html.

23. French, S. A., M. Story, R. W. Jeffery, et al. 2003. "Pricing strategy to promote fruit and vegetable purchase in high school cafeterias." *Journal of the American Dietetic Association* 97: 1008–1010.

24. Associated Press. 2007. "Arkansas' obesity report cards get failing grade." February 7. www.msnbc.msn.com/id/16994609/.

25. Etelson, D., D. Brand, P. Patrick, and A. Shirali. 2003. "Childhood obesity: Do parents recognize this health risk?" *Obesity Research* 11: 1362–1368, www.obesityresearch.org/cgi/content/abstract/11/11/1362#otherarticles.

26. The National Association for Sport and Physical Education (NASPE) and the American Heart Association (AHA). 2006. "The shape of the nation." May 2.

27. Cawley, J., C. D. Meyerhoefer, and D. Newhouse. 2005. "The impact of state physical education requirements on youth physical activity and overweight." NBER Working Paper No. 11411.

28. Fardy, P., A. Azzollini, and A. Herman. 2004. "Health-based physical education in urban high schools: The PATH program." *Journal of Teaching in Physical Education* 23: 359–371.

29. Satcher, D. 2005. "Healthy and ready to learn: Research shows that nutrition and physical activity affect student academic achievement." *Educational Leadership* 63: 26–30.

30. Smith, S. 2007. "America's kids are fatter than ever. What's to blame?" *Boston Globe,* April 23.

31. Story, M., and S. French. 2004. "Food advertising and marketing directed at children and adolescents in the US." *International Journal of Behavioral Nutrition and Physical Activity* 1, no. 3.

32. The Kaiser Family Foundation. 2007. "Food for thought: Television food advertising to children in the United States." March. www.kff.org/entmedia/upload/7618.pdf.

33. Borzekowski, D. L., and T. N. Robinson. 2001. "The 30-second effect: An experiment revealing the impact of television commercials on food preferences of preschoolers." *Journal of the American Dietetic Association* 101: 42–46.

34. Martin, A. 2007. "Kellogg to phase out some food ads to children." *New York Times,* June 14.

35. The Kaiser Family Foundation. 2007. "Food for thought: Television food advertising to children in the United States." March. www.kff.org/entmedia/upload/7618.pdf.

36. American Academy of Pediatrics. 1995. "Children, adolescents, and advertising. Committee on Communications, American Academy of Pediatrics" [PubMed Abstract]. *Pediatrics* 95: 295–297.

37. Souza, A. 2007. "Class focuses on nutrition, not just cooking." *Merced Sun-Star,* April 20.

Chapter 10: The Employer's Dilemma

1. Linnan, L., M. Bowling, G. M. Lindsay, et al. 2006. "Results of the 2004 National Worksite Health Promotion Survey." *American Journal of Public Health* 67, no. 6.

2. Bureau of Labor Statistics. 2006. "Job openings and labor turnover." www.bls .gov/news.release/jolts.toc.htm. Accessed on July 7.

3. Bureau of Labor Statistics. 2006. "Employee tenure." www.bls.gov/news .release/tenure.toc.htm. Accessed on July 7.

4. Buchwald, H., Y. Avidor, E. Braunwald, et al. 2004. "Bariatric surgery: A systematic review and meta-analysis." *Journal of the American Medical Association* 292, no. 14: 1724–1737.

5. Ibid.

6. Cimochowski, G. E., M. D. Harostock, and P. J. Foldes. 1997. "Minimal operative mortality in patients undergoing coronary artery bypass with significant left ventricular dysfunction by maximization of metabolic and mechanical support." *Journal of Thoracic and Cardiovascular Surgery* 113, no. 4: 655–666.

7. Finkelstein, E. A., and D. S. Brown. 2005. "A cost-benefit simulation model of coverage for bariatric surgery among full-time employees." *American Journal of Managed Care* 11, no. 10: 641–646.

8. Finkelstein, E. A., and D. S. Brown. 2006. "Why does the private sector under-invest in obesity prevention and treatment?" *North Carolina Medical Journal* 67, no. 4: 310–312.

9. Greenhouse, S., and M. Barbaro. 2005. "Wal-Mart memo suggests ways to cut employee benefit costs." *New York Times,* October 26. www.nytimes.com/2005/10/26/business/26walmart.ready.html?ei=5070&en=ed1299 cbdae2f79b&ex=1175486400&pagewanted=all.

10. Cutland, L. 2005. "Policy shift may cut patient pool for weight loss surgery." *San Jose Business Journal,* December 2. http://sanjose.bizjournals.com/sanjose/stories/2005/12/05/story8.html.

11. Snowbeck, C. 2005. "Health insurers backing off obesity surgeries." *Pittsburgh Post-Gazette,* July 1. www.post-gazette.com/pg/05182/531444.stm.

12. Snow-Clarke, S. 2004. "Insurers cut coverage of bariatric surgery." *Tampa Bay Business Journal,* February 13, www.bizjournals.com/tampabay/stories/2004/02/16/story6.html.

13. Pelletier, K. R. 2005. "A review and analysis of the clinical and cost-effectiveness studies of comprehensive health promotion and disease management programs at the worksite: Update VI 2000–2004." *Journal of Occupational and Environmental Medicine* 47, no. 10: 1051–1059.

14. Ibid.

15. Ibid.

16. Thorpe, K. E., C. S. Florence, D. H. Howard, and P. Joski. 2004. "The impact of obesity on rising medical spending." *Health Affairs* W4: 480–486.

17. French, S. A., R. W. Jeffery, M. Story, et al. 2001. "Pricing and promotion effects on low-fat vending snack purchases: The CHIPS Study." *American Journal of Public Health* 91, no. 1: 112–117.

18. French, S. A., R. W. Jeffery, M. Story, P. Hannan, and M. P. Snyder. 1997. "A pricing strategy to promote low-fat snack choices through vending machines." *American Journal of Public Health* 87, no. 5: 849–851.

19. Hannan, P., S. A. French, M. Story, and J. A. Fulkerson. 2002. "A pricing strategy to promote purchase of lower fat foods in a high school cafeteria: Acceptability and sensitivity analysis." *American Journal of Health Promotion* 17, no. 1: 1–6.

20. Jeffery, R. W., P. D. Thompson, and R. R. Wing. 1978. "Effects on weight reduction of strong monetary contracts for calorie restriction or weight loss." *Behaviour Research and Therapy* 16, no. 5: 363–369.

21. Jeffery, R. W., W. M. Gerber, B. S. Rosenthal, and R. A. Lindquist. 1983. "Monetary contracts in weight control: Effectiveness of group and individual contacts of varying size." *Journal of Consulting and Clinical Psychology* 51, no. 2: 242–248.

22. Jeffery, R. W., W. M. Bjornson-Benson, C. L. Kurth, and S. L. Johnson. 1984. "Effectiveness of monetary contracts with two repayment schedules of weight reduction in men and women from self-referred and population samples." *Behavior Therapy* 15, no. 3: 273–279.

23. Jeffery, R. W., W. L. Hellerstedt, and T. L. Schmid. 1990. "Correspondence programs for smoking cessation and weight control: A comparison of two strategies in the Minnesota Heart Health Program." *Health Psychology* 9, no. 5: 585–598.

24. Finkelstein, E. A., L. A. Linnan, D. F. Tate, and B. Birken. 2007. "A pilot study testing the effect of different levels of financial incentives on weight loss among overweight employees." *Journal of Occupational and Environmental Medicine* 49, no. 9: 981–989.

25. Sampalis, J. S., F. Sampalis, and N. Christou. 2006. "Impact of bariatric surgery on cardiovascular and musculoskeletal morbidity." *Surgery for Obesity and Related Diseases* 2, no. 6: 587–591.

26. See note 7.

27. Edington, D. W. 2006. "Who are the intended beneficiaries (targets) of employee health promotion and wellness programs?" *North Carolina Medical Journal* 67, no. 6: 425–427.

Chapter 11: The ObesEconomy

1. Crawford, K. 2007. "Fat America: A big opportunity." Available at http://money.cnn.com/2006/06/02/technology/business2_fatamerica0605/index.htm. Accessed on June 26.

2. Tsai, A. G., and T. A. Wadden. 2005. "Systematic review: An evaluation of major commercial weight loss programs in the United States." *Annals of Internal Medicine* 142, no. 1: 56–66.

3. NewsTarget. 2007. "U.S. weight loss market worth $46.3 billion in 2004—forecasts to reach $61 billion by 2008." Available at www.newstarget.com/006133.html. Accessed on June 26.

4. Weight Watchers. 2007. "Weight Watchers annual report, 2006." Available at http://library.corporate-ir.net/library/13/130/130178/items/241113/WTW2006AR.pdf.

5. The Duke Rice Diet Clinic. 2007. "Residential clinic costs." Available at www.ricedietprogram.com/r_enroll_accomodate.html. Accessed on February 18.

6. *Entrepreneur* Staff Writer. 2004. "13 Hot Businesses for 2005." Entrepreneur.com. November 12. Available at www.entrepreneur.com/startingabusiness/businessideas/article73778.html.

7. First Research. 2007. Fitness centers industry profile excerpt. Available at www.firstresearch.com/Industry-Research/Fitness-Centers.html. Accessed on February 18.

8. Curves. 2007. "About Curves." Available at www.curves.com/about_curves/. Accessed on February 18.

9. Weisbaum, I. 2007. "Diet-pill pushers get pushed back." Available at www.msnbc.msn.com/id/16491115]. Accessed on January 31.

10. Federal Trade Comission. 2006. "The facts about weight loss products and programs." Available at www.cfsan.fda.gov/~dms/wgtloss.html. Accessed on December 11.

11. CNN. 2007. "Government announces ban on ephedra." Available at www.cnn.com/2003/HEALTH/12/30/ephedra/. Accessed on February 18, 2007.

12. See note 3.

13. "History of phentermine." Available at www.phentermine.com/phentermine_ history.htm. Accessed on June 26, 2007.

14. Ibid.

15. Ibid.

16. GlaxoSmithKline. 2007. "FDA approves Alli (orlistat 60 mg capsules) over the counter." Available at www.medicalnewstoday.com/medicalnews.php?newsid =62807]. Accessed on February 18.

17. Associated Press. 2007. "Diet pill isn't a magic bullet, Drugmaker Says." MSNBC Online, May 22. Available at www.msnbc.msn.com/id/18805163/.

18. Capell, K. 2007. "Will Sanofi's wonder drug save the day?" Available at http://uk.biz.yahoo.com/23112006/244/sanofi-s-wonder-drug-save-day .html. Accessed on February 18.

19. Farrigan, C., and K. Pang. 2002. "Obesity market overview." *Nature Reviews* 1: 257–258.

20. MedicineNet. 2007. Definition of liposuction. Available at www.medterms .com/script/main/art.asp?articlekey=7855. Accessed on February 18.

21. MedicineNet. 2007. Definition of gastric banding. Available at www.medterms .com/script/main/art.asp?articlekey=20954. Accessed on February 18, 2007.

22. Ecinosa, W. E. D. M. Bernard, C. A. Steiner, et al. 2005. "Use and costs of bariatric surgery and prescription weight-loss medications." *Health Affairs* 24, no. 4: 1039–1046.

23. Zhao, Y., W. Ecinosa. 2007. "Bariatric surgery utilization and outcomes in 1998 and 2004." Available at www.hcup-us.ahrq.gov/reports/statbriefs/sb23.pdf. Accessed on February 18.

24. See note 3.

25. Spaeder, K. 2007. "The plus-sized market is ripe for business opportunity if you offer high-quality products." Available at www.entrepreneur.com/ startingabusiness/businessideas/article170738.html. Accessed on February 6.

26. Cohen, Marshall. 2007. "Are plus sizes on the rise?" The NPD Group. Available at www.npdfashionworld.com. Accessed on January 31.

27. See note 6.

28. Crawford, K. 2006. "The big opportunity." *Business 2.0 Magazine Online*, June 5. Available at http://money.cnn.com/magazines/business2/business2_archive/ 2006/06/01/8378500/index.htm.

29. Perez-Pena, R., and G. Glickson. 2007. "As obesity rises, health care indignities multiply." Available at http://query.nytimes.com/gst/fullpage.html?res= 9A03E2D8123AF93AA15752C1A9659C8B63&sec=health&spon=&page wanted=print. Accessed on February 18.

30. ContractorMag. 2007. "Great John vs. Big John." Available at www .contractormag.com/articles/newsarticle.cfm?newsid=494. Accessed on June 22.

31. Rundle, R. 2007. "U.S.' s obesity woes put a strain on hospitals in unexpected ways." Available at www.karlloren.com/diet/p6.htm. Accessed on February 12.

32. See note 29.

33. Cambanis, T. 2007. "Kibbutz finds a US market: Obese consumers driving demand for Israeli scooters." Available at www.boston.com/news/world/articles/2006/12/26/kibbutz_finds_a_us_market/. Accessed on February 18.

34. Goodman, L. 2007. "Growth industry." Available at www.self.com/magazine/articles/2006/05/15/1204growth_1_of_7. Accessed on June 26.

35. National Institutes of Health. 2007. "Estimates of funding for various diseases, conditions, research areas." Available at www.nih.gov/news/fundingresearchareas.htm. Accessed on February 18.

36. Schmidt, T. S. 2007. "Is the Wii really good for your health?" Time.com, February 1. Available at www.time.com/time/business/article/0,8599,1584697,00.html.

37. Ibid.

38. Lanningham-Foster, L. T. B. Jensen, R. C. Foster, et al. 2006. "Energy expenditure of sedentary screen time compared with active screen time for children." *Pediatrics*, 118, no. 6 (December): e1831–e1835.

Chapter 12: How to Lose Weight Like an Economist

1. Ciavaglia, J. 2007. "Losers don't come much bigger than him." *Bucks County Courier Times*, April 10. www.phillyburbs.com/pb-dyn/news/94-04102007-1328016.html.

2. Barclay, L. 2007. "Certain factors associated with weight regain after weight loss." *Medscape Medical News*, www.medscape.com/viewarticle/558092. Accessed on June 26.

3. Swan, N. "The effects of lifestyle modification and drugs on obesity." www.abc.net.au/rn/talks/8.30/helthrpt/stories/s1514207.htm.

4. The National Weight Control Registry, www.nwcr.ws/.

5. Phelan, S., H. R. Wyatt, J. O. Hill, and R. R. Wing. 2006. "Are the eating and exercise habits of successful weight losers changing?" *Obesity* 14, no. 4: 710–716.

6. McGuire, M. T. R. R. Wing, M. L. Klem, W. Lang, and J. O. Hill. 1999. "What predicts weight regain in a group of successful weight losers?" *Journal of Consulting and Clinical Psychology* 67, no. 2: 177–185.

7. Rawe, J. 2007. "Fat chance." *Time*, June 11. www.time.com/time/specials/2007/article/0,28804,1626795_1627112_1626456,00.html.

8. "Medicine & science in sports & exercise." Conducted by David R. Bassett Jr. and associates of the University of Tennessee, January 2004.

About the Authors

Dr. Eric Finkelstein, PhD, MHA (Chapel Hill, NC) has published over 30 peer-reviewed articles and one textbook on the economics of obesity and other health behaviors. His research has appeared in top health and medical journals and been the subject of countless news stories. His publications have been featured on the front page of USA Today and have been covered in The Economist, Time, Forbes, the Washington Post, and many other newspaper, radio, and television outlets.

Laurie Zuckerman (Chapel Hill, NC) left a corporate public relations job to make writing her full-time career. She contributes columns and feature articles to a number of business journals and lifestyle magazines and writes for businesses ranging from Fortune 500s to start-ups with a focus on health care, high tech, and business.

Index